KEY CONCEPTS IN BUSINESS PRA(

Palgrave Key Concepts

Palgrave Key Concepts provide an accessible and comprehensive range of subject glossaries at undergraduate level. They are the ideal companion to a standard textbook, making them invaluable reading for students throughout their course of study and especially useful as a revision aid.

The key concepts are arranged alphabetically so you can quickly find terms or entries of immediate interest. All major theories, concepts, terms and theorists are incorporated and cross-referenced. Additional reading or website research opportunities are included. With hundreds of key terms defined, **Palgrave Key Concepts** represent a comprehensive must-have reference for undergraduates.

Published

Key Concepts in Accounting and Finance
Key Concepts in Business Practice
Key Concepts in Human Resource Management
Key Concepts in International Business
Key Concepts in Management
Key Concepts in Marketing
Key Concepts in Operations Management
Key Concepts in Politics
Key Concepts in Strategic Management
Linguistic Terms and Concepts
Literary Terms and Criticism (*third edition*)

Further titles are in preparation

www.palgravekeyconcepts.com

Palgrave Key Concepts
Series Standing Order ISBN 1-4039-3210-7
(*outside North America only*)

You can receive future titles in this series as they are published by placing a standing order. Please contact your bookseller or, in case of difficulty, write to us at the address below with your name and address, the title of the series and the ISBN quoted above.

Customer Services Department, Macmillan Distribution Ltd,
Houndmills, Basingstoke, Hampshire RG21 6XS, England

Key Concepts in Business Practice

Jonathan Sutherland and Diane Canwell

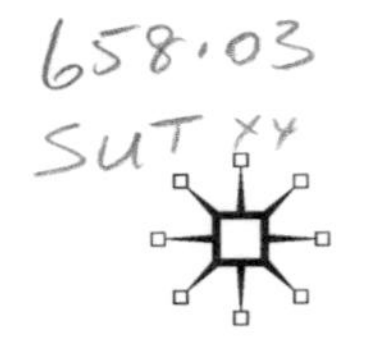

First published 2004 by
PALGRAVE MACMILLAN
Houndmills, Basingstoke, Hampshire RG21 6XS and
175 Fifth Avenue, New York, N.Y. 10010
Companies and representatives throughout the world

PALGRAVE MACMILLAN is the global academic imprint of the Palgrave Macmillan division of St. Martin's Press, LLC and of Palgrave Macmillan Ltd. Macmillan® is a registered trademark in the United States, United Kingdom and other countries. Palgrave is a registered trademark in the European Union and other countries.

ISBN 1–4039–1531–8 paperback

This book is printed on paper suitable for recycling and made from fully managed and sustained forest sources.

A catalogue record for this book is available from the British Library.

A catalog record for this book is available from the Library of Congress.

10 9 8 7 6 5 4 3 2 1
13 12 11 10 09 08 07 06 05 04

Printed and bound in Great Britain by
Creative Print & Design (Wales), Ebbw Vale

Contents

Introduction

The term 'business practice' in itself is an enormously wide area of study and encompasses aspects of all business-related disciplines. In effect, business practice refers to the administration, the planning, the coordination, monitoring and control of all aspects of a business operation. Theoretically, of course, business practice seeks to take the best of all business experience and to apply it to a single organization.

Recognizing the enormous increase in internet-based commerce, transactions and interaction between businesses and their customers, this glossary contains a number of web-orientated terminologies, many of which will be somewhat alien to more traditional forms of business. Business practice, like many other aspects of business studies in general, begins with the formation and management of organizations in their simplest forms. As the organizations become more complex, not necessarily in size but in the activities in which they are involved, the process of business practice can become a bewildering and consuming process.

Over recent years business practice has not been immune to radical change, not only in the legislation and regulations which underpin the responsibilities of business owners and managers, but also in technology and the automation of systems. Equally, business practice has been transformed by increased expectations from customers who not only expect products and services to be of merchantable quality, at a fair and equitable price, but who also expect the businesses with whom they deal to be socially and ethically responsible.

Business practice is not a discipline which can be considered apart – it is integral to every operation, every decision and every idea that the organization may adopt.

The structure of the glossary

Every attempt has been made to include all of the key concepts in this discipline, taking into account currently used terminology and jargon common throughout business practice in organizations around the world. There are notable differences in legislation and procedure when we compare different forms of business organization, some definitions of accounting terminology and developments in internet-based transactions and the other subdivisions of the discipline in the United Kingdom, Europe, the United States and Japan. Increasingly in Europe, for example, there is a harmonization process in train which is gradually seeking to standardize regulations and procedures.

The key concepts have been arranged alphabetically in order to ensure that the reader can quickly find the term or entry of immediate interest. It is normally the case that a brief description of the term is presented, followed by a more expansive explanation.

The majority of the key concepts have the following in common:

- They may have a reference within the text to another key concept identified by a word or phrase that is in **bold** type – this should enable readers to investigate a directly implicated key concept should they require clarification of the definition at that point.
- They may have a series of related key concepts which are featured at the end of the definition – this allows readers to continue their research and investigate subsidiary or allied key concepts.
- They may feature book or journal references – a vital feature for the reader to undertake follow-up research for more expansive explanations, often written by the originator or by a leading writer in that particular field of study.
- They may include website references – it is notoriously difficult to ensure that websites are still running at the time of going to print, let alone several months beyond that time, but in the majority of cases long-established websites or governmental websites that are unlikely to be closed or to have a major address change have been selected.

Glossary terms – a guide

Whilst the majority of the key concepts have an international flavour, readers are cautioned to ensure that they have accessed the legislation, in particular, which refers to their native country or to the country in which they are working.

It is also often the case that there are terms which have no currency in a particular country as they may be allied to specific legislation of another country. Readers are cautioned to check whether the description includes a specific reference to such law, and not to assume in all cases that the key concept is a generic one and that it can be applied universally to business practice.

In all cases, references to other books, journals and websites are based on the latest available information. It has not always been possible to ensure that the key text or printed reference is in print, but most well-stocked college or university libraries should have access to the original materials. In the majority of cases, when generic business books have been referenced, these are, in the view of the writers, the best and most easily available additional reading texts.

Absenteeism

Strictly speaking, 'absenteeism' refers to chronic absence from work. In effect, this is deliberate absence. A business can calculate the level of absenteeism within its workforce (excluding absence caused by ill-health, and genuine absences) by using the following formula:

$$\text{Absentee rate} = \frac{\text{number of staff absent}}{\text{staff total}} \times 100.$$

Absenteeism can drastically affect the production and profitability of a business and, obviously, the business may need to reschedule projects, miss deadlines and ensure that any vital duties carried out by the absent individual are covered. There are, of course, a number of reasons why absenteeism could creep into the habits of an employee, such as:

- *The nature of the job* – physical conditions may be poor, working hours inconvenient, and the job may be stressful or boring, or the employees may not have good inter-personal relations, or they may feel alienation. These problems could be overcome by offering more flexible ways of working, or perhaps considering **job enrichment** or **job rotation** systems.
- *Characteristics of the individual* – it has been suggested that both age and gender can have an impact on absenteeism. Certainly, studies that look at absenteeism in relation to length of service suggest that longer-serving employees are less prone. Other factors may include health, family responsibilities or travelling difficulties. Again, these problems could be overcome by a more flexible approach to staffing and by closer supervision.
- *Motivating factors* – whilst bonuses or non-financial incentives can have an impact on absenteeism, the statutory availability of sick pay has the reverse effect. Ultimately, in terms of motivation, reducing absenteeism relies on managers' ability to persuade employees to come to work and, perhaps, the readiness of the business itself to institute **disciplinary procedures** in the correct places.

Most businesses will tend to develop an attendance policy which addresses the following issues:

- the question of what is an allowable absence;
- whether days will be paid if missed immediately before and after a holiday;
- the attitudes towards excused and unexcused absences;
- the setting up of a system which alerts managers to patterns of absences or lateness.

Frayne, Collette A., *Reducing Employee Absenteeism through Self-Management Training.* Westport, CT: Greenwood Press, 1991.

Tylczak, Lynn and Hicks, Tony, *Attacking Absenteeism.* New York: Crisp Publications, 1990.

Absorbed overhead

Absorbed overheads are overhead costs which are added to the **direct costs** of products or services. An absorption rate, such as a fixed amount per direct labour hour, is included in the costs of specific products or services. There is sometimes a difference between the overhead costs incurred and the overhead costs absorbed. In these cases, when the overhead costs are not fully absorbed, they are said to be under-absorbed. Conversely, if the overhead costs are less than the amount being absorbed, then they are said to be over-absorbed.

Bell, Jan and Ansari, Shahid, *Manufacturing Overhead Allocation: Traditional versus Activity-Based.* New York: McGraw-Hill, 1997.

ACAS

See **Advisory Conciliation and Arbitration Service (ACAS) (UK).**

A

Access control list

An access control list (ACL) is in effect a table which tells a computer operating system which **access rights** each user may have on a particular system. It will therefore define the files, directories or objects to which each individual may have access. For practical purposes each object, file or directory has a security attribute which identifies its importance on the access control list. Commonly, the ability to write to files or execute files implies full access to that particular part of the system. In Windows NT/2000 each system object has an access control list. Each of these has one or more access control entries, which consist of the name of a user or the names of a number of users. The system administrator or the individual who created the object in question normally creates the access control list for that object.

Schneier, Bruce, *Applied Cryptography: Protocols, Algorithms and Source Code in C*. New York: John Wiley, 1995.

Stallings, William, *Cryptography and Network Security: Principles and Practice*. New York: Prentice-Hall, 2002.

Access rights

Access rights are designed to be flexible, giving each user tailored access rights to ensure that they have access to what they need and no access to what they do not need. Although access rights can be complex, it is usual for most users to have a normal access right to the system. Provided that individuals are assigned to a particular project, using particular software or programs, then they will have access to those elements of the system. Alternatively, the system administrator would have full access rights with the ability to add or delete projects, and to manage users, business information and other elements contained within the system. For complex projects which require a number of users to have access rights to information or programs, a project manager will normally be assigned to confirm or deny access rights to various users. The project manager will be able to change the users' access rights in cooperation with the system administrator.

Accountability/responsibility matrix

The accountability and responsibility matrix is a concept designed by David Brin (see Figure 1). Brin contends that individuals see the top two boxes of the matrix as being good and the bottom two boxes as being bad. Businesses or society require boxes 1 and 3 since these create accountability. Businesses and society are averse to boxes 2 and 4 since they pit employees against one another.

Brin, David, *The Transparent Society: Will Technology Force Us to Choose Between Privacy and Freedom?* New York: Perseus Books Group, 1999.

Accounts payable

'Accounts payable' is a finance-related term which refers to money owed by a business to its suppliers. Businesses keep an open account detailing the money owed to creditors for products and services purchased by the business. Financial analysts and accountants are concerned with the relationship between accounts payable and the

Accountability matrix

1 Tools that help me see what others are up to	2 Tools that prevent others from seeing what I am up to
3 Tools that help others see what I am up to	4 Tools that prevent me from seeing what others are up to

Brin argues:

- Where it says 'others' insert some person or group, such as 'government' or 'corporations' or whoever you perceive as a dangerous power centre.
- People are likely to call 'good' any device, law or technical advance that enhances the effectiveness of 1 or 2. In contrast, whatever comes along that increases the effectiveness of 3 or 4 may raise your discomfort, if not ire.
- If our aim is to live in a society that is fair and free, the tools needed by our commons will be those favouring 1 and 3.
- The most dangerous trends, laws, and technologies are those promoting 2 and 4, pitting citizens against one another in an arms race of masks, secrets and indignation.

Figure 1 Brin's accountability and responsibility matrix

purchases to give an indication as to the efficiency of day-to-day financial management within the business.

Schaeffer, Mary S., *Essentials of Accounts Payable*. New York: John Wiley, 2002.

Accounts receivable

'Accounts receivable' is a tally of the money owed to a business by its customers. It is the measure of outstanding debt payable to the business for products and services which have been sold by the business to its customers, but where the payment has not yet been collected. Accounts receivable is a key aspect in analysing the liquidity of the business. In other words, its ability to meet current financial obligations, without the requirement of securing additional funding to cover those obligations. An assessment is made as to the likelihood of payment from accounts receivable and a schedule of probable payment dates can be assessed, particularly when the business needs to ensure that it will have sufficient funds to cover its financial obligations.

Schaeffer, Mary S., *Essentials of Credit, Collections and Accounts Receivable*. New York: John Wiley, 2002.

Acquisition

The most common use of the term 'acquisition' is in describing the process of one business purchasing another business, or indeed individuals purchasing an existing business. Acquisitions may also refer to takeovers in which a business attempts to gain control over another business. In circumstances when the takeover is acceptable, this is known as a friendly takeover and when the takeover is opposed it is known as a hostile takeover.

'Acquisition' can also refer to the process of obtaining a loan or another form of finance.

'Acquisition' can equally be applied to the purchase of a property by a business.

See also **Acquisition cost** and **Acquisition evaluation**.

Weston, J. Fred and Weaver, Samuel C., *Mergers and Acquisitions*. New York: McGraw-Hill, 2001.

Acquisition cost

Acquisition cost in the marketing sense is the average investment of money (advertising and loss-leading products) for a particular business to acquire a new customer. Businesses will calculate the life-time value of a customer, and then use this figure to calculate what an acceptable level of customer acquisition cost is for them.

Acquisition evaluation

An **acquisition** can normally be typified by six distinct phases. Four of these deal with the actual acquisition itself and the last two consider the post-acquisition phase. The first stage is to create a pre-acquisition team, which carries out a review of the industry and examines the business's existing strategic goals, identifying benefits and costs related to any proposed acquisition. The next phase is to evaluate whether the target business fits with the strategic criteria of the purchasing organization. Risk analyses are carried out, as well as a search for **synergy**. It may also be appropriate for the business to examine the organizational, financial and legal structure of the target. The third stage is to examine any restructuring or changes in the assets which may be required in order to integrate the target business. Once these stages have been undertaken the acquisition itself, specifically the transaction which needs to be carried out to obtain the business, can go ahead, subject to the full approval of the board or owners of the business that is being acquired and provided there are no issues which arise in respect of acquiring the business on a legal basis. In some cases government involvement may be necessary, particularly if the acquisition impacts upon the balance of the market (the acquisition may mean that a monopoly situation will arise).

Once the acquisition has been undertaken there is a period of integration, when issues raised in the pre-acquisition period are dealt with, including modifications and the implementation of any required integration. The final period of evaluation considers what lessons could be learned for future acquisitions in respect of integration, structuring and management.

Thompson, Jr, Samuel C., *Business Planning for Mergers and Acquisitions*. Durham, NC: Carolina Academic Press, 2001.

Action planning

Action planning is an integral part of both goal-setting and problem solving, yet in many business contexts it is a neglected area. Action planning can assist a business to plan for the future, ensuring that future situations as they change can be controlled. At its most basic, action planning is, in effect, the conversion of goals or objectives into a series of steps, in order to ascertain what has to be done, by whom and by when. This is variously known as either an action planning process or an event track. The process of formulating the event track follows a set series of procedures:

1. decide on a goal or objective;
2. identify the sequence of actions required to achieve this;
3. refine the initial plan by identifying where it may go wrong;
4. having identified what may go wrong, formulate plans or actions to deal with these problems.

The action plan should describe how the business gets from where it is now to where it wishes to be, describing in detail how the business proposes to do this. There needs to be a secondary process running alongside the action plan, which checks to see whether the action plan is working.

Effective action planning requires the participation of all relevant **stakeholders**, who must be aware of their role in the process. A full action plan event track is likely to incorporate the following aspects:

1. Development of a rough action plan, which combines individual work from the participants, listing their proposed activities to reach the goal. Once this has been completed all of the activities are

discussed and, perhaps using a voting technique, the most appropriate ones are chosen. These then need to be arranged in the correct sequence.

2 The action plan now needs to be refined. Above all, the action plan needs to be robust; each event needs to be detailed in terms of *what*, *when* and *who*.
3 Assumptions – checks are needed regarding any assumptions made in the creation of the action plan. These may include skills, time, finance and materials. There may also be assumptions regarding coordination. Above all, the participants need to consider how unexpected problems may be dealt with if they arise.
4 Contingency plan – no matter how complex the creation of the action plan may have been, it is imperative that a contingency plan is created, which may need to be instituted in the event of the action planning going off track. This means that a monitoring process needs to be put in place, together with a clear idea of how to solve potential problems that may require immediate action in order to ensure that the goal is finally reached.

Kaplan, Robert S. and Norton, David P., *The Balanced Scorecard: Translating Strategy into Action*. Boston, MA: Harvard Business School Press, 1996.

Active listening

The purpose of active listening is to improve mutual understanding. This involves a radically different approach to the process of listening and responding. The assumption is that when individuals talk to one another they do not necessarily listen. There may be other issues which distract them. There is a particular problem in situations where two individuals are in conflict with one another, as they are more concerned with formulating a response than with what is actually being said.

The concept of active listening requires the listener to carefully absorb what the speaker has said and then to repeat it back to the first speaker in the listener's own words. In this way the original speaker can be apprised of whether the listener actually understood and whether there is any conflict in the intent of what was said. It is a question of interpretation and this is often the root cause of misunderstandings between individuals during a conversation. By repeating what has been said, the two individuals can hope to move towards a consensus through confirming understanding. The process also avoids the two individuals contradicting one another by claiming that the other said something which they did not say. Providing the two individuals are attuned to one another in this way, they are likely to explain in detail precisely what they mean, and conflict can be avoided.

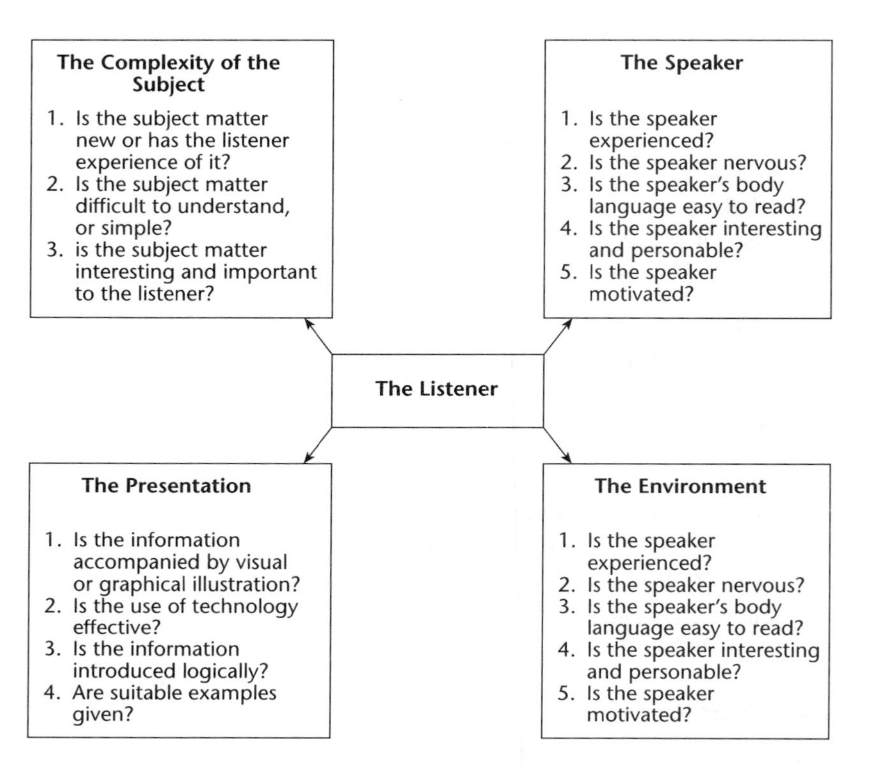

Figure 2 Factors affecting active listening

Figure 2 illustrates what external factors can affect an individual's ability to actively listen. In order to actively listen, the listener should attempt to:

- focus attention on the subject by stopping all non-relevant activities beforehand so as to be oriented with the speaker or the topic;
- review mentally what they already know about the subject and organize in advance relevant material to develop it further;
- avoid distractions by sitting appropriately close to the speaker and avoiding a window or talkative colleague;
- set aside any prejudices or opinions and be prepared to listen to what the speaker has to say;
- focus on the speaker;
- let the presentation run its course before agreeing or disagreeing;
- actively respond to questions and directions.

Westra, Matthew, *Active Communication*. London: Wadsworth Publishing, 1995.

Activity-based costing (ABC)

Essentially, activity-based costing is an accounting method, or information system, which seeks to link costs with activities that generate those costs. The key aspect is the identification and measurement of cost drivers. Each complex activity is broken down into specific activities, which could include how long it might take to set machinery up to begin producing a product, any associated delays whilst production is under way, movement of materials to and from the machine during production, and all other activities associated with that production period.

Activity-based costing can be applied to all types of activities, including, for example, the delivery of products to customers, which may include time taken to load the vehicle, the distance between delivery points, the number of stops made and any known or predicted hold-ups during the delivery process. All of these individual activities represent the accumulated costs for the whole process. Each activity can then be assessed in terms of its cost in order to identify ways in which the costs can be driven down.

Activity-based management (ABM) is the process of controlling and improving factors identified during activity-based costing. Typically, an organization may consider how to deal with specific activities which defy attempts to drive down costs. **Outsourcing**, for example, may be a solution. ABM also considers the impact on costs if operations are expanded or reduced, and attempts to discover whether the costs will be constant regardless of the level of operation, or whether they are related directly to the level of operation.

Cokins, Gary, *Activity-Based Cost Management: An Executive's Guide*. Chichester: John Wiley, 2001.

Activity-based management (ABM)

Activity-based management is the application of **Activity-based costing (ABC)** results for process and profit improvement. ABM aims to generate a number of improvement initiatives and provide the business with a clearer view of the profitability of its products or services. The associations can be best described as in Figure 3.

Whilst ABC is calculated by the finance department, ABM needs to be a more widespread concern as it can identify the main resource consumption drivers. In most cases, teams are deployed to undertake ABM activities.

See also **Activity-based costing (ABC)**.

Pryor, Tom, *Using Activity-Based Management for Continuous Improvement*. Arlington, TX: ICMS, 2000.

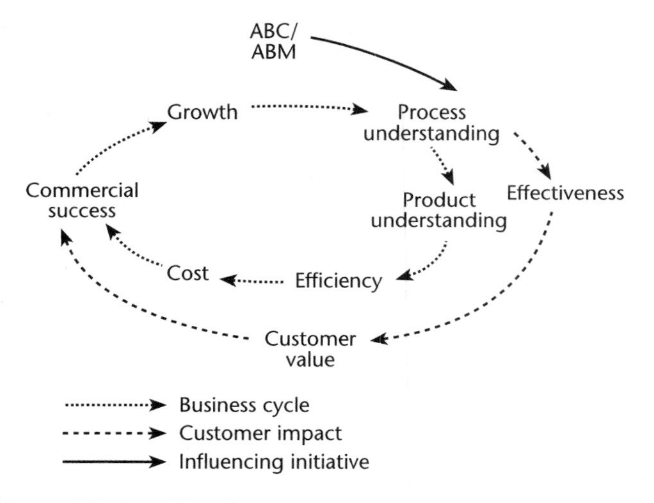

Figure 3 Activity-based costing

Advanced planning and scheduling software

Essentially, advanced planning and scheduling (APS) is a software system which creates detailed schedules for orders. Unlike material requirements planning (MRP) and **enterprise resource planning (ERP)**, which produce basic plans largely based on fixed **lead times**, APS combines both manufacturing and scheduling to create very detailed schedules.

Gunther, H. and Beek, P., *Advanced Planning and Scheduling Solutions in Process Industry.* Berlin and Heidelberg: Springer-Verlag, 2003.

A

Advertising networks

Advertising networks are the internet's equivalent of an advertising agency. There are a number of organizations, such as Engage and DoubleClick, which create profiles of web-users, based on their browsing and on-line shopping habits. Rather like a conventional agency working in conventional media, the advertising network can then suggest specific advertisements on specific web pages which match the profile of the target market.

Advisory Conciliation and Arbitration Service (ACAS) (UK)

ACAS can trace its history back to 1896. Some 80 years later in 1976, after several changes of name, the organization was finally put on a statutory footing. ACAS operates as a mediator during problems or disputes between employers and employees. Its primary role is to encourage good working relationships between employers and employees and to help set up structures and systems, as well as taking a practical role in dispute settlement. ACAS has been inextricably involved in most of the major industrial or labour disputes in Britain, particularly since the 1970s.

ACAS not only deals with broader industrial disputes, but also focuses on individual complaints which have been referred to employment tribunals. On average they settle around 75% of cases which have been referred to an employment tribunal, obviating the need for the tribunal to consider the case. In summation, ACAS is involved in four main areas of activity:

- the providing of impartial information and help (on average ACAS takes 750,000 calls a year on its helpline);
- prevention and resolution of problems between employers and employees (ACAS is successful in over 90% of all cases);
- settlement of complaints about employees' rights (around 70% of potential employment tribunal cases referred to ACAS are resolved by ACAS);
- fostering effective working relationships through seminars and workshops. Small businesses in particular are targeted, as well as those without clearly identified human resource management departments.

www.acas.org.uk

Affiliate programme

An affiliate programme is a form of advertising on the internet which aims to reward an affiliate (who is a self-selected advertiser) for pushing web traffic to a business.

Affiliate programmes are sophisticated multi-level marketing schemes where existing customers attempt to attract other customers by endorsing the business and carrying banner advertising and links. Some systems allow for multi-tiered affiliation, which rewards affiliates for the traffic generated by other affiliates that an affiliate has recruited.

Some larger web-based businesses, such as Amazon, have their own affiliate programmes, but there are more generic systems such as Beefree, Linkshare or CommissionJunction. Affiliates have the potential to earn significant money by signing up for an affiliate programme to use excess advertising inventory (unsold banners).

Gray, Daniel, *The Complete Guide to Associate and Affiliate Programs on the Net: Turning Clicks into Cash*. New York: McGraw-Hill, 1999.

Affiliates

The first major affiliate programme to be launched on the internet was designed and run by Amazon, which now has more than 400,000 participating sites. Affiliates are owners of websites who can divert or direct particular web traffic from their own website to a merchant, such as www.amazon.com, via electronic links.

In business terms, affiliate programmes can be beneficial to both the affiliate (sometimes known as an associate) and the merchant company. The relationship is rather like digital franchising, as the affiliates receive a percentage of the sales which they generate at the merchant's site. The merchant receives the endorsement of the third-party website and in effect has multiplied its sales force across the internet.

Affinity/KJ diagram (Jiro Kawakita)

A KJ diagram is a special form of **brainstorming** which is used to gather ideas and opinions. The purpose of the exercise is to group ideas that are naturally related to one another by identifying a single concept which groups those ideas together. The individuals involved in the brainstorming exercise are asked to focus primarily on their creative thinking. Once all of the ideas have been noted, usually on index cards or on post-it notes, the group is then encouraged to link these various ideas under common themes.

Affirmative action (US)

The term 'affirmative action' is most closely associated with various legislative moves in the United States regarding the elimination of discrimination against employees or applicants for employment.

The concept goes somewhat further than requiring an employer not to discriminate on the grounds of race, creed, colour or national origin, as it requires the employer to take positive steps to ensure that those chosen for employment, and those who are in employment, are treated without regard to their race and other considerations. In effect, the associated legislation calls for equality in employment.

In US terms, the fundamental rights of an individual are enshrined in the 13th, 14th and 15th Amendments of the US Constitution. However, in 1961 President John F. Kennedy issued Executive Order 10925, which established the President's Committee on Equal Employment

Opportunity. This, in turn, led to the Civil Rights Act of 1964. Amongst other things the Act stated:

> No person in the United States shall, on the ground of race, color or national origin, be excluded from participation in, be denied the benefits of, or be subjected to discrimination under any program or activity receiving Federal financial assistance.

Indeed, this approach, beginning with Federal employees or those working for organizations employed by Federal governments, is often the way that the US seeks to impose fundamental changes in perceptions. Following the Civil Rights Act of 1964, President Johnson issued Executive Order 11246, which prohibited discrimination and introduced the concept of affirmative action 'through a positive, continuing program in each department and agency'. Shortly after this the Executive Order was amended to include discrimination on the basis of gender.

Affirmative action, therefore, not only enshrines anti-discrimination policy during recruitment and employment, but also promotes active measures to encourage and aid those who have hitherto been discriminated against.

Curry, George E. (ed.), *The Affirmative Action Debate*. Reading, MA: Addison-Wesley, 1996.

After-sales service

After-sales service has become a feature of full product and customer support often used as a prime discriminator between competing businesses. Typically, after-sales service, which was formerly associated wholly with the carrying out of repairs and maintenance, and giving advice to customers who had purchased products and services, is now seen as an integral part of the overall marketing strategy.

After-sales service has become a major expectation of customers and is now considered to be an important component of closing a sale. The availability of after-sales service has latterly been associated with the offering of extended warranties beyond the normal guarantee period of the product. These insurance services, sold at a premium, underwrite and compensate for loss leaders offered by the business in order to attract customers. Strictly speaking, these do not fall into the standard understanding of after-sales service as the implication is that customers are being persuaded to purchase after-sales service, rather than the service being seen as an integral part of sales and marketing, customer retention and satisfaction.

Aggregate planning

Aggregate planning, or an aggregate plan, is a means by which an organization can convert its business or marketing plan into a workable production plan. There is a considerable difference between the generalizations contained within a business plan, which tends to focus on costs, revenue and profit, and a production plan, which needs to break down units by production and quantify inputs and outputs. A production plan is essential for a complex organization which is producing a variety of different products. There will be differences, particularly in costs, associated with each type of product. Typically, the production plan will need to incorporate the costs associated with holding stock, the costs associated with changes in capacity and any **opportunity costs**.

Aggregate planning is intermediate-range planning of general levels of employment and output to balance supply and demand. In this respect, the term 'aggregate' implies that the planning is carried out for groups of products (or product types) rather than individual products.

A planner would take into account the projected demand, capacity and costs of various options in devising an aggregate plan. Typically, the variables considered would be the output rate, employment level, overtime/under-time and subcontracting. The primary focus of aggregate planning is to achieve output objectives at the lowest possible cost.

It is rarely possible to structure a plan that guarantees optimal conditions; therefore planners often resort to trial-and-error methods to achieve an acceptable plan. Aggregate planners might try the following strategies:

- Maintain a level workforce and meet demand variations in some other manner.
- Maintain a steady rate of output, and use some combination of inventories and subcontracting to meet demand variations; however, varying employment levels are costly, disruptive and result in low employee morale.
- Match demand period by period with some combination of workforce variations, subcontracting and inventories.
- Use a combination of decision variables.

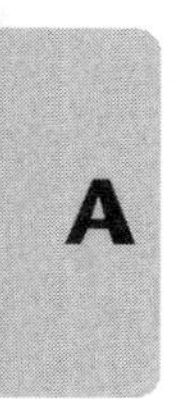

In order to plan effectively, estimates of the following issues must be available to planners:

- demand for each period;
- capacity for each period;
- costs (regular time, overtime, subcontracting, backorders, etc.).

However, in order to translate an aggregate plan into meaningful terms for production, it must be disaggregated (broken down into specific product requirements). This will assist in the determination of requirements in respect of labour, materials and inventories.

Brandimarte, Paolo and Villa, A., *Modeling Manufacturing Systems: From Aggregate Planning to Real-time Control*. Berlin and Heidelberg: Springer-Verlag, 1999.

Aggregation

Aggregation is the process of identifying the total value of a variable or measure by adding up or summing that variable or measure. The term is especially used in macroeconomics as the most common items which are aggregated are demand, supply and expenditures on gross domestic product, which result in aggregate demand, aggregate supply and aggregate expenditures.

Businesses can use aggregation to make calculations of the aggregate values of demand, supply and expenditure across the broad range of their activities (especially if they have multiple manufacturing and production facilities).

Aktiengesellschaft (Germany)

Literally translated, this German form of business is a 'stock corporation'. AGs, as they are known, tend to be publicly traded companies. They have two boards of directors; the first is known as the *Vorstand*, which comprises the senior management of the business. They also have an *Aufsichsrat*, which, again literally translated, means 'supervisory board'. These directors in effect represent the shareholders and oversee the functioning of the management of the business. Under German law, an individual cannot be a member of both of the boards. An AG has a minimum share capital and must have at least five shareholders.

All-channel sales

'All-channel sales' refer to the total amount of activity which a business undertakes in order to get its products or services to the market. Different businesses have a variety of all-channel sales mixes, which may be limited in number or may incorporate virtually every type of business-to-market sales channel. Typically, all-channel sales will include sales made by the sales force, distributors, retailers, resellers, tele-marketing programmes and tele-sales. Other businesses may also include catalogue sales and other direct mail activities, sales through the internet and other forms of direct selling, such as email.

Alternative work arrangements

Increasingly, management has looked for ways in which productivity, lower levels of sick and family leave, improved morale, recruitment and retention can be achieved. One such way is to introduce alternative work arrangements. The system, when applied to situations where the employers still require their workforce to attend work at a specific location, helps reduce traffic and parking pressures, as well as extending hours of cover and service to customers or clients.

Typically, there has been a shift from standard working hours, with fixed arrival and departure times, to a more flexible approach. Alternatively, employees can work longer shifts for up to four days a week under compressed working week systems. Clearly there is also an opportunity here, within the scope of alternative working arrangements, to offer employees the opportunity to work at home, perhaps engaged in telecommuting or tele-work.

The normal procedure in setting up a system of alternative working arrangements requires the cooperation of both the employees and their immediate manager. Normally decisions will be based on the job function for which each individual is responsible, taking into account staffing needs, budgetary considerations and the availability of space in the office. Work schedules still need to be maintained and there needs to be a degree of supervision in all cases of alternative working arrangements. The introduction of alternative working arrangements needs to be advantageous both to the business and to the employees in question and should be viewed in consideration of any associated advantages and disadvantages to both parties.

Estess, Patricia Schif, *Work Concepts for the Future: Managing Alternative Work Arrangements*. New York: Crisp Publications, 1996.

A

American Arbitration Association (AAA)

The function of the American Arbitration Association is somewhat more complex than that of **ACAS**, as it has to encompass specific variations in arbitration rules and procedures in the various US states.

The AAA is recognized as being one of the leaders in a number of arbitration areas, which include employer–employee relations, grievance issues and contractual issues.

www.adr.org

Angel investor

Angel investors are most closely associated with new start-up businesses. Angel investors can be differentiated from venture capital funds as they directly inject the cash into the start-up business, rather than operating under a specific fund. For the most part angel investors tend not to invest huge amounts in any one business, but provide what is known as seed money to a wide variety of different businesses in order to spread their risks. The seed money, as the name implies, is sufficient funding to allow the new business to begin to grow developing systems, technologies, products and services which may not otherwise be able to reach the market. Angel investors are seen as a viable and more immediate alternative to conventional bank loans, as the cash is usually available quickly and there may not be the degree of conditions attached to the investment. Angel investors in the US, for example, provide $20bn each year in seed money. Angel investors are never assured of a significant return on their investment and may well invest in the business for the longer haul rather than providing a short-term loan.

Van Osnabrugge, Mark, and Robinson, Robert J., *Angel Investing: Matching Startup Funds with Startup Companies – A Guide for Entrepreneurs, Individual Investors and Venture Capitalists.* New York: Jossey-Bass, 2000.

Applet

Literally, an applet is a small, or little, **application**. In the original version of Windows the drawing and writing programs were known as applets. More commonly, in internet terms, an applet is a small program which is sent along with a web page to the user; a typical example is Java, an object-orientated programming language. Java applets can make immediate calculations, carry out simple tasks and perform interactive animations without the user having to interact again with the server.

Application

In information technology terms an application is the use of a product, system or technology. 'Application' is also used as a shortened form of 'application program'.

An application program is designed to carry out a particular function for the user, such as word processing or compiling and using a database. In internet terms applications also include image editing or communication programs.

Applications themselves use the computer's operating system and other supporting applications in order to function.

Application hosting

A service in which a vendor houses shared or dedicated servers and applications for a business at the provider's controlled facilities. The vendor is responsible for the day-to-day operations and maintenance of the application. Normally application hosting is based on a service arrangement with vendors, who have provided the hardware, software and networking infrastructure which enable another business to run applications externally. They do this by connecting electronically using a browser. The vendor may offer the services directly, or, more commonly, through an arrangement between the vendor and an **application service provider (ASP)**. In effect, application hosting is an IT **outsourcing** solution.

Application program interface

An application program interface (API) is the way in which a computer operating system requires a programmer to write a particular application. The programmer uses the operating system or another application and must follow the general rules required by those programs in order to successfully write a functioning application.

Application service provider (ASP)

Application service providers are businesses which deliver application functionality and associated services across a network, to numerous customers, using a rental, or usage-based, transaction pricing model.

Key advantages are:

- The monthly rental helps the business to spread the costs.
- There is no need to buy expensive hardware, specialist support staff or system development, as maintenance and upgrades are handled by the ASP.
- Remote access is possible assuming an internet connection.
- The ASP should routinely back-up data, as well as updating technology by investing in its equipment and software.

The disadvantages are:

- Unless a good performance internet connection is guaranteed, then speed may be a problem.
- Security may be an issue, as sensitive data is stored outside the business.

- ASP communication or equipment breakdowns will adversely affect the business (usually a 99.9% uptime is guaranteed).

www.cnet.com/internet/zero-1497812-7-1556562.html

APS

See **advanced planning and scheduling software.**

Arbitration

Arbitration is the non-judicial intervention by a third party, with the intention of intervening and settling a dispute. An impartial and objective third party is given the power to determine the outcome of the dispute, unlike conciliation or mediation, where the disputing parties retain control. Although arbitration is only binding by mutual agreement and not by law, the two disputing parties agree to accept the findings of the arbitrator. The arbitration board is usually comprised of an independent chairperson, with an equal number of individuals appointed by the two disputing parties.

In Britain the **Advisory Conciliation and Arbitration Service (ACAS)** is active in assisting dispute resolutions between employers and trade unions. There are other forms of arbitration, including pendulum and voluntary arbitration. Pendulum arbitration requires the arbitrator to make an award wholly in favour of either the employer's final offer or the union's final claim. The arbitrator therefore has to make a straight choice between what may be two diametrically opposed views. Pendulum arbitration tends to take place in situations where there is an existing non-strike agreement. Pendulum arbitration is also known as 'final offer arbitration'.

Voluntary arbitration normally takes place when other forms of negotiation have failed and is therefore used as the final resort. The procedure is triggered either by both parties realizing that without arbitration there would be no agreement, or, in some cases, when one party has decided that negotiations will proceed no further without the intervention of an arbitrator. It is common practice for both of the disputing parties to agree any terms of reference for the arbitrator.

Goldberg, Stephen B., Sander, Frank E. A. and Rogers, Nancy H., *Dispute Resolution: Negotiation, Mediation and Other Processes*. New York: Aspen Publishers, 1999.

Argenti's failure model

John Argenti, a business consultant, suggested that businesses tend to fail because they are not looking where they are going. In other words, they do not effectively monitor their own performance and neither do they identify changes in the business environment. Argenti argued that it is not change itself which causes a business to fail; it is the management that has made the mistake and, in the majority of cases, those mistakes were inbuilt in the business from the very beginning. As a business develops over a period of years, imbalances and gaps appear in the business's management structure. These defects lead to poor decision making, normally exemplified by cash flow problems or high staff turnover. Argenti argues that autocratic leaders are often one of the main reasons why a business may fail. Initially the autocrat will be making decisions which appear, and indeed are, appropriate to the business and its short-term prospects. The presence of an autocratic leader means that the rest of the directors are inherently passive, therefore when the autocrat makes a mistake, they do not have the forcefulness to point out the problems to the autocrat.

The normal response to a business beginning to fail is to throw money at the problem. This simply exacerbates the cash flow problems. In many cases these businesses do not recognize the warning signs, as they will approach each problem as simply being a short-term issue and will, therefore, remain optimistic. Once the business has entered the borrowing spiral, it will become more indebted without addressing the underlying causes of the problems.

Articles of association

A business's articles of association are submitted along with its **memorandum of association** to the registrar of companies when it applies for incorporation. The articles govern the dealings between the business and its shareholders. In the past there were often potential dispute issues arising out of these articles, as shareholders had little recourse when the business breached an agreement made under the articles. Under the terms of the Financial Services Act (1986) businesses are now required to pay compensation for misleading shareholders within their articles of association.

The Companies Act (1985) also allows shareholders to obtain damages or other compensation if their rights have been ignored by the business.

Collectively, the memorandum and articles define the purpose of a business and the rights and obligations of its members. In most cases separate shareholder agreements are used in order to regulate management participation and policies towards dividends. In effect a contractual agreement is drawn up and used, particularly by smaller businesses, to restrict share dealings in order to prevent external parties from gaining control of the business.

A business may seek to alter its articles of association by special resolution, provided they are valid 'as if originally contained in [the articles] and are subject in like manner to alteration by special resolution'. It is also possible for the shareholders to alter the articles and they do not need to have a meeting or pass a resolution, provided there is unanimous consent. There are some limitations to changing the articles in as much as shareholders cannot be forced to accept more shares, neither can they be required to contribute a greater investment in the business's capital in excess of what was originally required.

There is a further stipulation in as much as the power to change the articles must be exercised 'bona fide for the benefit of the company as a whole'. This means that majority shareholders are prevented from making changes to the articles, in their own self-interest, which would prejudice a minority shareholder.

Assertiveness

Assertiveness is usually taken to mean the expression of thoughts, feelings or beliefs in a direct, honest and above all appropriate manner. There is often confusion between the words 'assertive' and 'aggressive'. 'Assertiveness' means influencing, listening and negotiating in order to achieve willing cooperation. 'Aggressiveness', on the other hand, implies the desire to always get one's own way, regardless of the views, opinions or standpoint of others.

Assertiveness tends to ignore the fact that other individuals may have problems and responsibilities which, from their standpoint, do not allow them to accept, cooperate or negotiate. True assertiveness suggests that the assertive individual is not burdened by these considerations.

Assertiveness training has been a popular trend in recent years, teaching individuals the following main points:

- using the word 'I' instead of 'he', 'she' or 'everyone';
- getting straight to the point;
- not allowing others to sidetrack you;
- being prepared to compromise;
- using non-verbal communication, such as suitable facial expressions, eye contact and a firm, but pleasant voice;
- remaining calm and attentive in order to make the other individual more prepared to compromise;
- practising **active listening**;
- requiring time to think;

- only apologizing if there is good reason to do so;
- learning to say 'no';
- always paraphrasing the other individual's point of view so that they will appreciate that you have understood what they have said.

Burley-Allen, Madelyn, *Managing Assertively: How to Improve your People Skills – A Self-Teaching Guide*. New York: John Wiley, 1995.

Asset management

Asset management is an investment service which is offered by a number of financial institutions. In effect the service combines elements of banking and brokerage. More generally the term can be applied to a business's actions in respect of managing and maintaining their assets through periodic review, assessment and reassessment, **acquisition** and divestment.

Authentication

The most common forms of authentication in information technology are the typing in of user names and passwords to access information on a computer system or email account. In effect, authentication allows the computer system to know whether it is dealing with the correct recipient. It also allows the system to understand and log where and from whom particular information was derived.

Authorization

Authorization, in information technology terms, is precisely the same as receiving a signed authorization on paper from a senior manager to carry out a particular task or make a specific purchase. Computerized authorizations normally take the form of a password, which may simply be a series of numbers or letters, which can be inputted into a computer system in order to access **applications** or information.

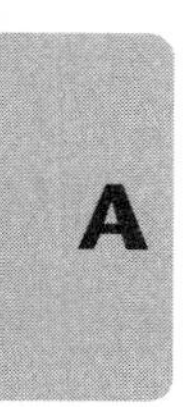

Authorization is particularly crucial in allowing employees in remote locations to access closed areas of a business's website when it is impractical to give either a verbal or a conventionally signed authorization.

Automated purchasing system

An automated purchasing system is a piece of networked software which links a business to a specific vendor. The business and the vendor will already have an ongoing purchasing and supply arrangement. The business will have already approved the products and services on offer, as well as the pricing structure. In this way, the business's employees can connect to the vendor via a web browser in order to make routine purchases and carry out regular tasks and other activities, such as the purchase of tickets whilst making travel arrangements.

In the case of large and complex multi-site organizations, it is advantageous for purchases to be made using an automated purchasing system. All purchases are routed through the automated system, which not only streamlines the buying process, but also allows the business to negotiate favourable prices and delivery schedules with the vendors. By combining all of the business's purchasing power, considerable savings can be made.

Automated response (auto response)

Automated response is a software application related to **email** which enables the users to send automated emails when they are unable to respond to incoming emails. The facility is often used as an out-of-office reply and can include some form of personalization, incorporating the recipient's name in the message.

Autonomy

Autonomy is a measure of an individual's independence within his or her job role. Autonomy implies that within the context of their work, individuals have a degree of control over what they do, the order in which they do it and the processes involved in carrying it out. Autonomy also suggests that aside from not requiring close supervision or management in order to carry out the function, the individuals may have a larger influence over their own working environment. Truly autonomous workers, therefore, are those who are enabled by offering alternative work arrangements or a form of remote working, such as telecommuting, tele-work, or homeworking.

Backflush costing

Backflush costing is most closely associated with a **just-in-time** production system. It applies the costs to the output of a process. As costs do not mirror the flow of products through the production process itself, they are attached to the output produced. This is done on the assumption that those backflush costs are a more realistic measure of the actual costs incurred. In other words, the backflush costs are applied to the finished stock and the cost of sales.

Bad debt

Bad debts are debts which are unlikely to be repaid to a business, possibly because the customer has become insolvent. In many cases businesses will set aside a sum of money to cover bad debts. This fund is referred to as the bad debt reserve. In the UK it is more commonly known as 'provision for bad debt' or 'doubtful debt'. Businesses will seek to write-off their bad debts by setting aside funds for this purpose.

Balanced scorecard

A balanced scorecard is an integrated means of measuring organizational performance. Aside from looking at the organization's ability to innovate, manage finances and deal with customers, it also addresses internal operations, including human resource management.

Very few organizations are able to align their strategies effectively and so most are not able to operate at maximum efficiency. Using the concept of a balanced scorecard, the business can seek to understand, all the way down to individuals within an organization, the exact nature of the key performance indicators that need to be controlled, and thus facilitate the understanding of relationships within the organization. Whilst the deployment of a balanced scorecard system can help in this understanding, its true value is in enabling a business to implement and track key initiatives. This means providing across the length and breadth of the business a greater vision and utilization of resources.

Kaplan, Robert S., Lowes, Arthur and Norton, David P., *Balanced Scorecard: Translating Strategy into Action*. Boston, MA: Harvard Business School Press, 1996.
Kaplan, Robert S. and Norton, David P., *Strategy-focused Organization: How Balanced Scorecard Companies Thrive in the New Business Environment*. Boston, MA: Harvard Business School Press, 2000.

Bandwidth

Bandwidth is a measure over a given time period, which is usually a second, illustrating how much information can be carried over a given communication link. In digital systems bandwidth is expressed as bits of data per second, or bps. A standard 56K modem would normally have a bandwidth of 57,600 bps. Analog systems express bandwidth in terms of the difference between the highest frequency signal and the lowest frequency signal, frequency being measured as the number of cycles of change per second.

Banner advertising

A banner ad is an advertisement in the form of a banner design inside a graphics frame, usually at the header or footer of a web page. Visitors to the web page are encouraged to click on the banner ad to take them directly to an associated or reciprocal link. Many websites have banner ads in order to generate income from the organization placing the banner ad on the website. A fee is usually payable per click on the banner ad. In other cases, reciprocal banner ads are placed on a website in exchange for a banner ad on another organization's website.

Zeff, Robbin, *Advertising on the Internet* (2nd edn). Chichester: John Wiley, 1999.

Basic hours

'Basic hours' is a human resource management term used to describe the normal contracted attendance hours of a worker, excluding any time the employees may attend their work during overtime.

Behavioural theory

The concept of behavioural theory is derived from the field of psychology and is often referred to as behaviourism. In essence there are two forms of behaviourism, the first of which, known as classical conditioning, suggests that individuals behave on the basis of reflex learning. They are conditioned by repetition to continue to behave in a particular way in similar circumstances. A slightly more sophisticated version is known as operant conditioning and states that when individuals exhibit a particular behaviour and understand the consequences of what they have done, this is reinforced, making it more likely that they will do it again.

In management terms, particular behaviours can indeed be reinforced in order to ensure that the correct response in certain circumstances is largely guaranteed. Equally, if individuals are not given encouragement and praise for particular behaviour, then it is likely that this form of behaviour will cease. As far as this form of psychology theory is concerned, management involves behaviour modification, using praise and discipline and, perhaps, rewards, in order to reinforce desired behaviour. It is suggested that praise is a far more potent form of reinforcement than criticism or punishment and that positive feedback is of prime importance in order to ensure behaviour modification.

Behaviourally anchored rating scales (BARS)

This system utilizes critical incidents to evaluate performance, which focus performance appraisal on employee behaviours that can be changed. Thus, a BARS system describes examples of 'good' or 'bad' behaviour. These examples are 'anchored', or measured, against a scale of performance levels. What constitutes the various levels of performance is clearly defined in the evaluation figure. Spelling out the behaviour associated with each level of performance helps minimize some of the problems noted in earlier evaluations.

The construction of BARS begins with the identification of important job dimensions, which are the most important performance factors in an employee's description. Short statements are developed that describe both desirable and undesirable behaviours [anchors]. Then they are 'retranslated' or assigned to one of the job dimensions. This task is usually a group project and the assignment is for 60–70 per cent of the group to agree the dimensions. The group, consisting of individuals familiar with the job, then assigns each 'anchor' a number, which represents how 'good' or 'bad' the behaviour is. When numbered, these anchors are fitted to a scale, as in Figure 4.

Behaviourally anchored rating scales require extensive time and effort to develop and maintain, and separate BARS forms are necessary to accommodate different types of jobs in an organization.

Aiken, Lewis R., *Rating Scales and Checklists: Evaluating Attitudes, Behavior, and Personality*. Chichester: John Wiley, 1996.

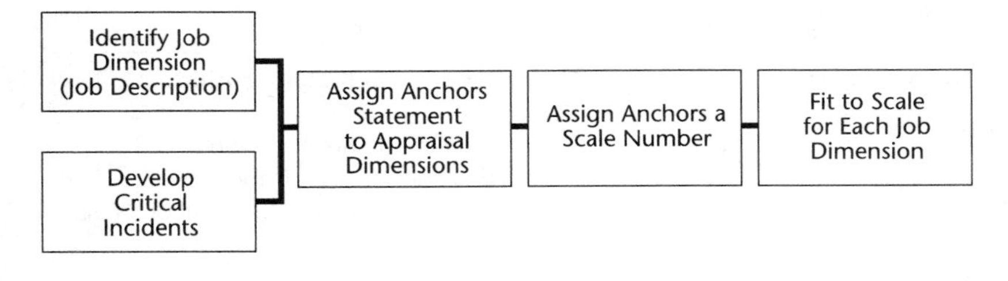

Figure 4 A flow diagram of the BARS construction process

Belbin, Dr Meredith

Belbin suggested that the most effective teams include 5–7 individuals who have a specific blend of team roles. He identified nine team-role types (see Table 1), which implies that an individual has the capacity to perform more than one role in the team.

Table 1 Building an effective team

Team role type	Characteristics and contribution
Completer/finisher	An individual who attempts to finish tasks on time while seeking out any errors or omissions. Tends to take a conscientious approach to work. They prefer to carry out the work themselves rather than delegate.
Coordinator	A promoter of joint decision-making with the ability to clarify goals. Keen to delegate but is often seen as manipulative and willing to pass on work to others.
Implementer	A disciplined and reliable individual who has the ability to transform ideas into practical solutions. Is often seen as slow to adopt new ways of working due to their inflexibility.
Monitor/evaluator	Has the ability to take a wider view and assess all available options. Not considered to be a great motivator and often appears to lack essential drive.

⇒

B

Table 1 Building an effective team (*continued*)

Team role type	Characteristics and contribution
Plant	Essentially a problem solver who is both imaginative and creative. Is more preoccupied with communication than the detail of a task.
Resource investigator	Highly communicative and usually able to identify and deploy useful resources and contacts. Since their contribution is based on their enthusiasm for progress, they can be over optimistic and lose interest if little progress is being made.
Shaper	Able to deal with pressure and to overcome obstacles. They tend to be rather abrasive individuals who can often offend.
Specialist	Has access to specialist information and is often single-minded. They tend to be able only to contribute to certain aspects of a task and are quite technically focused.
Team worker	Cooperative and diplomatic listeners who wish to avoid conflict. They tend to be indecisive and lack the ability to contribute under pressure.

Belbin also created four categories to identify the different types of teams:

- *Stable extroverts*, who excel in roles which place a focus on liaison and cooperation. These are ideal human resource managers.
- *Anxious extroverts*, who tend to work at a higher pace than others and exert pressure on other people. They are typified by a sales manager.
- *Stable introverts*, who work well with a small, stable team, where relationships are a high priority. They are ideal local government officials.

- *Anxious introverts*, who rely on self-direction and persistence and are often committed to the longer term. The majority of creative individuals fall into this category.

Belbin, R. Meredith, *Team Roles at Work*. Oxford: Butterworth-Heinemann, 1995.
Belbin, R. Meredith, *Management Teams: Why They Succeed or Fail*. Oxford: Butterworth-Heinemann, 1996.
Belbin, R. Meredith, *Beyond the Team*. Oxford: Butterworth-Heinemann, 2000.

www.belbin.com/meredith.html

Benchmarking

A benchmark is a predetermined set of standards against which future performance or activities are measured. Usually, benchmarking involves the discovery of the best practice for the activity, either within or outside the business, in an effort to identify the ideal processes and prosecution of an activity.

The purpose of benchmarking is to ensure that future performance and activities conform with the benchmarked ideal in order to improve overall performance. Increased efficiency is key to the benchmarking process as, in human resource management terms, improved efficiency, reliability of data and effectiveness of activities will lead to a more competitive edge and ultimately greater profitability.

Damelio, Robert, *The Basics of Benchmarking*. Shelton, CT: Productivity, 1995.

Benefits administration

Increasingly, employers have introduced flexible benefit systems and require cost-effective administrative systems in order to manage them. An employer will offer a range of benefits from which the employees can choose, assuming that they are eligible for those particular benefits. Since each benefits package is tailored to an individual employee, the potential difficulties in managing these complex systems are beginning to be offset by complex human resource software **applications**. Complex benefit structures were in the past impractical, particularly because the administrative burden of managing a matrix of differing benefits to each individual employee, or subgroup of employees, was not cost-effective. It is now possible, using software or on-line packages, to monitor, select and amend benefits packages.

Bias

A term associated with market research which refers to errors in a sample survey. Bias may relate to the use of an unrepresentative sample upon which a series of assumptions may later be made. Commonly, bias is also associated with the conduct of market researchers in the field who, deliberately or inadvertently, impose a bias on the research findings. Typically, bias may creep into a survey when researchers become overzealous in their attempts to collect data which support their preconceived ideas of results. It is possible that the respondents pick up on this desire to collect the appropriate responses and as a result provide the researchers with responses that they feel that the researchers are seeking rather than a true response to the questioning.

Bias can, in most cases, be eliminated or reduced by the introduction of clear and efficient supervision and monitoring of the data collection. Periodic spot checks, observation and cross-checking of results can reveal the degree to which bias has influenced the data that has been collected by the researchers. Some forms of data collection are more prone to bias than others: market research carried out without the benefit of close supervision tends to be more biased than systems set up with integral supervision, such as telephone market research.

Biometrics

Biometrics is the latest trend in **authentication**. It has been incorporated into several science-fiction and action adventure films in the past, but is now being developed for conventional use. Rather than requiring an alpha-numeric code to authenticate an individual, biometrics promises to use fingerprints, retina scans and voice patterns in order to allow authorized individuals access to buildings, areas within the workplace and computer systems. In practice, using biometrics may require an employee to place a thumbprint on a pad beside a work station in order to log on and acquire the requisite authentication.

Bonuses

There are a wide variety of different bonus schemes which are in operation in various businesses. Bonuses usually relate to additional payments, made on a monthly or an annual basis, as a reward for good work, as compensation for dangerous work or as a share of the profits.

Other businesses will offer bonuses in relation to referrals. This is an integral part of human resource management's approach to difficulties in finding new employees for hard-to-fill jobs, specifically those with special skill requirements. Many businesses will offer a referral bonus payment to existing employees for referring qualified candidates who are subsequently employed by the business. Clearly there are strict regulations in respect of the suitability of the candidate and the length of service that the referred candidate actually completes (usually part of the payment is held back until the referred candidate has been working for the business for six months).

There are difficulties in using this system in particular, as there may be conflicts of interest. Some human resource departments come under intense pressure from existing employees to shortlist candidates that they have referred. In many cases there is also a system set up to ensure that improper promises or assurances of employment to prospective candidates are not made by existing employees.

Keenan, William, *Commissions, Bonuses and Beyond: The Sales and Marketing Management Guide to Sales Compensation Planning*. New York: McGraw-Hill Education, 1994.

Boston Growth Matrix

The Boston Consulting Group (BCG) was founded in 1963 by Bruce D. Henderson as the Management and Consulting Division of the Boston Safe Deposit and Trust Company (The Boston Company).

The theory underlying the Boston Matrix is the **product life cycle** concept which states that business opportunities move through life-cycle phases of introduction, growth, maturity and decline. Boston classification (or BCG matrix) is a classification developed by the Boston Consulting Group to analyse products and businesses by market share and market growth. In this, cash cow refers to a product or business with high market share and low market growth, dog refers to one with a low market share and low growth, problem child (question mark, or wild cat) has low market share and high growth, and a star has high growth and high market share (see Figure 5).

These phases are typically represented by an anti-clockwise movement around the Boston Matrix quadrants in the following order:

- From a market entry position as a question-mark product. Products are usually launched into high growth markets, but suffer from a low market share.
- To a star position as sales and market share are increased. If the investment necessary to build sales and market share is successfully made, then the product's position will move towards the star position of high growth/high market share.
- To a cash cow position as the market growth rate slows and market leadership is achieved. As the impact of the product life cycle takes effect and the market growth rate slows the product will move from

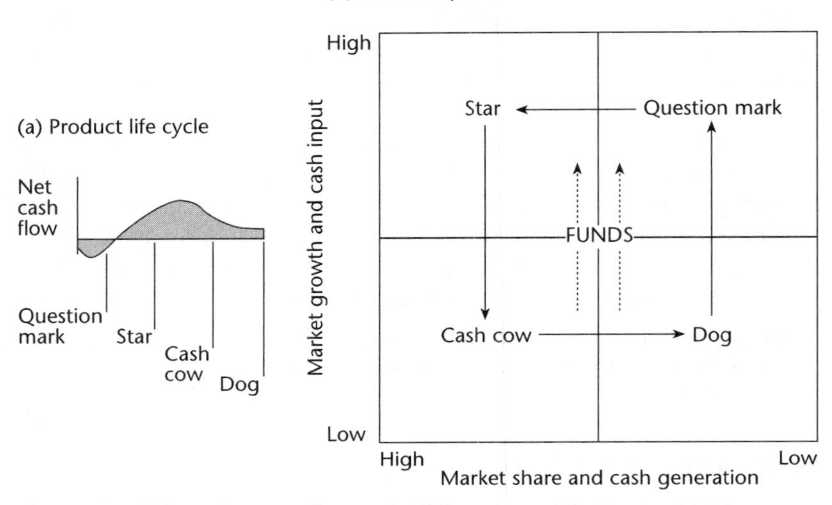

Figure 5 Linkage between the product life cycle and the Boston Matrix

the star position of high growth to the cash cow position of low growth/high share.

- Finally to a dog position as investment is minimized as the product ages and loses market share (see Figure 6).

At each position within the matrix there are a number of opportunities open to the business. For example, at the cash cow stage the options are either to invest to maintain market share, or to minimize investment in the product, maximize the cash returns and grow market dominance with other products.

www.bcg.com

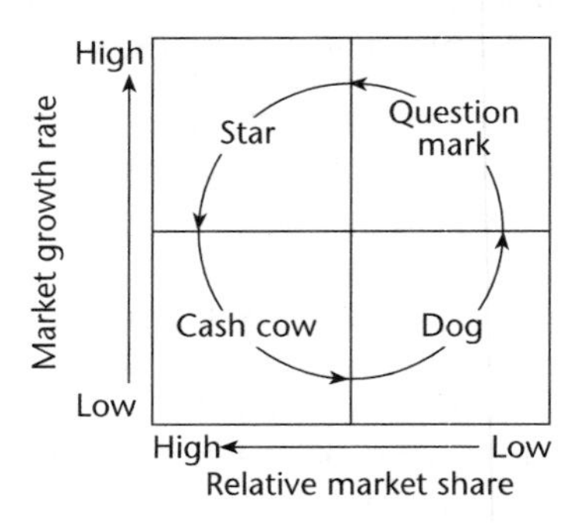

Figure 6 The anti-clockwise movement around the Boston Matrix

Bottleneck

'Bottleneck' is a term associated with the management of the production process. A bottleneck is effectively a system which cannot, for a variety of reasons, reach the levels of capacity which are demanded. A bottleneck can, therefore, seriously limit the total amount of production on a given production line because production is limited to the total capacity which the bottleneck is able to achieve.

Clearly, organizations seek to avoid blocking a bottleneck process because the bottleneck is already unable to reach the desired capacity levels and this would simply restrict even more their ability to produce.

Bottom–up planning

Bottom-up planning is a form of consultative management. The planning system encourages employee participation in both problem solving and decision making. In effect it is a form of empowerment, which aims to encourage flexibility and creativity across the organization. Bottom–up planning is also closely associated with organizations which have a flat structure. In other words, the hierarchy of the organization has few tiers of management, allowing employees far greater access to key decision-makers within the organization on a day-to-day basis. Bottom–up planning is the opposite of what is known as a **top–down planning** approach.

Brainstorming

Brainstorming sessions are carried out as a group activity. Members of the group are encouraged to put forward their first ideas about a problem and how it might be solved, in order to generate as many ideas as possible, even if they are not always usable alternatives. Brainstorming involves members from various parts of the organization and it is seen as a way of encouraging creativity and innovation. Sometimes the members of the group are required to literally shout out their first thoughts about a subject.

Breakeven analysis and the breakeven point

In order to identify an organization's breakeven point, it is necessary to consider the relationships between the various costs and sales in an integrated manner. The breakeven point is defined as being the point at which the level of sales is not great enough for the business to make a profit and yet not low enough for the business to make a loss. In other words, earnings from sales are just sufficient for the business to cover its total costs. This occurs when total revenue from sales exactly equals the total cost of production.

Breakeven point occurs when total cost = total revenue

From this it can be assumed that if the total revenue from sales is greater than the total costs, then the organization concerned makes a profit. Conversely, if the opposite is true, and the total revenue is less than the total costs, then the organization will make a loss. It is essential that organizations take this very important factor into account. The organization will find that it is essential to determine how many units of output it must produce and sell before it can reach its breakeven point. The total cost of the unit of production is made up of two factors, the fixed and variable costs, where:

Total cost = fixed costs + variable costs

And the total revenue is given by the number of products sold, multiplied by the selling price:

Total revenue = price × quantity

The drawing up and labelling of a breakeven chart (see Figure 7) makes the calculation of the breakeven point easier. The breakeven chart requires a considerable amount of labelling in order to be able to identify exactly what the chart is describing about the breakeven point.

As can be seen in the diagram in Figure 7, the breakeven chart will include:

B

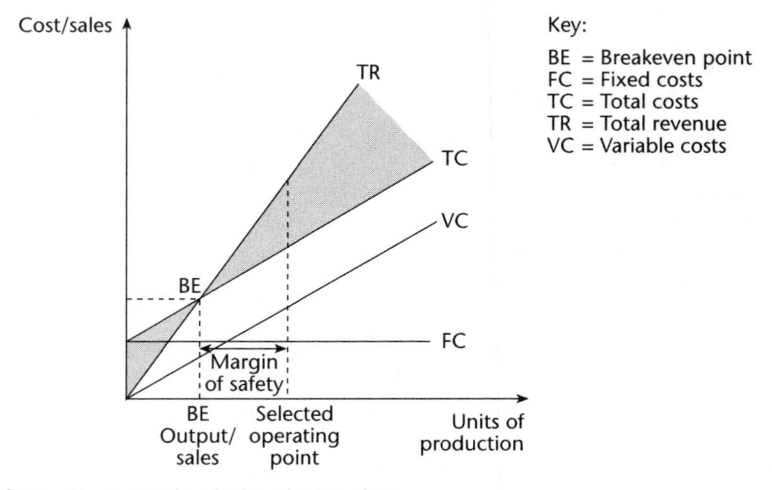

Figure 7 Example of a breakeven chart

- Units of production – which is considered to be the most completed product and not, importantly, the components which make up that product.
- Fixed costs (FC) – which are the costs that do not alter in relation to changes in demand or output. They have to be paid regardless of the business's trading level.
- Variable costs (VC) – such as raw materials, components, labour and energy, which change in direct proportion to changes in output. Breakeven charts require the assumption that some costs vary in direct proportion to changes in output. In fact, it is unlikely that any costs are totally variable as raw materials, for example, are likely to cost less per unit if the organization buys in bulk. In this instance, it cannot be assumed that the cost of raw materials will double if output doubles.
- Total costs (TC) – these are simply the sum of all fixed and variable costs.
- Sales and costs – sales are the income generated from the selling of the units of production to customers. Costs, on the other hand, are expenses incurred by the organization in the purchase of raw materials, other fixed costs and variable costs.
- Breakeven point (BE) – this is the point at which sales levels are high enough for the organization not to make a loss but not high enough for it to make a profit. In other words, this is the point where total sales equal total costs.
- Profit – in terms of the breakeven chart, and the breakeven point, this is achieved when the revenue (TR) from sales exceeds total costs.
- Loss – in terms of the breakeven chart, and the breakeven point, this occurs when revenue from sales has not met the total costs.
- Selected operating point – this is the planned production and sales level which is assumed to be the same as that in given data.
- Margin of safety – this is the amount by which the selected operating point exceeds the breakeven point. This indicates the amount by which sales could fall from the planned level before the organization ceases to make a profit.

The simplest way to calculate the breakeven point is either to find the intersection of total revenue and total cost on the breakeven chart, or to use the following formula:

$$\text{Breakeven point} = \frac{\text{fixed costs}}{\text{contribution per unit (selling price} - \text{variable cost)}}$$

Budgetary control

Budgetary control is related to the establishment and management of budgets by responsible budget holders. Budgetary control tries to ensure that objectives of any given policy or project are achieved within the confines of any set budget. Budgetary control also includes the analysis of how any relevant finance has been used and whether there has been any variation from the original plans. Budgetary control can be applied to virtually every form of financial commitment and it is imperative that the budget holders understand the inter-relationships between budgeting and budgetary control. There are strong links between each form of budget, as can be seen in the diagram in Figure 8.

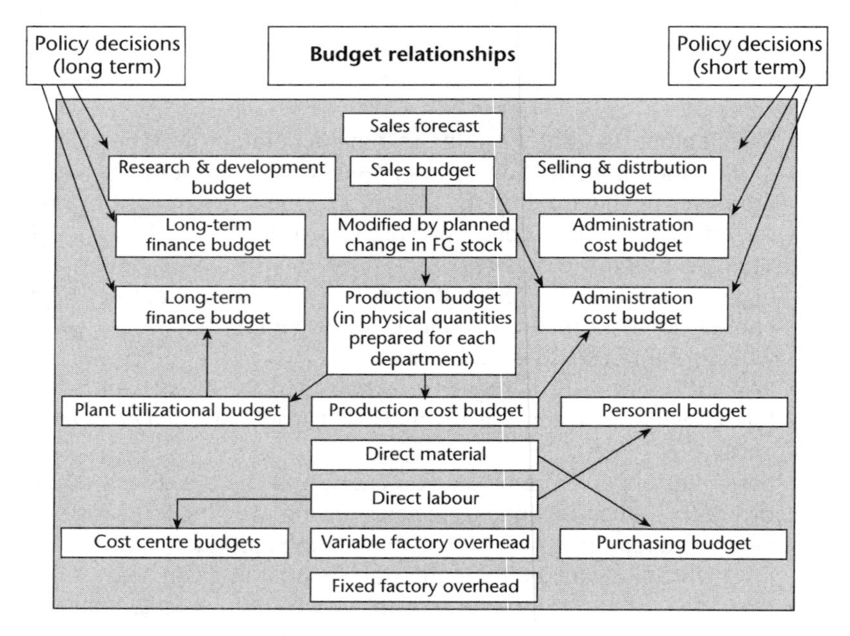

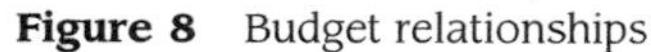
Figure 8 Budget relationships

In this particular example we can see that all of the budgets are derived from the sales forecast and that the budgets for all other activities derive from that sales forecast. In this respect, sales are the limiting factor and the constraints on the budget. In other cases the limiting factors include the costs of raw materials.

Bureaucracy

A bureaucracy is a form of **organizational structure** which has highly routine tasks carried out by its workforce, who specialize in their area of work. These organizations tend to be grouped into functional departments, with centralized authority and a very narrow **span of control**. All decision making follows the **chain of command** and all activities within the organization are strictly controlled by rules and regulations.

See also **Weber, Max.**

Burnout

Burnout is best described as complications arising out of prolonged and substantial stress. It often exhibits emotional, mental or physical exhaustion in employees who have been exposed to unreasonable levels of stress which have not been picked up by the management or human resource department.

Burnout has been exacerbated by down-sizing of businesses and the streamlining of operations in the constant search for ways in which to economize and improve profitability. While these strategies are employed, businesses still seek to be as productive as they were with larger workforces. Inevitably this places more strain on the remaining employees. The reasons for burnout can thus be described as being a combination of increased work and the fear that the individual may be next on the list of dismissals.

Biggs, Richard K., *Burn Brightly without Burning Out: Balancing your Career with the Rest of your Life*. London: Thomas Nelson, 2003.

Burn rate

'Burn rate' refers to the pace at which a new business uses up its venture capital or money received from an **angel investor** before it turns a profit. In many new businesses, particularly those at the frontiers of technology, the burn rate is particularly high. In practice, many of these businesses literally burn out of funding long before there is any prospect of them being able to produce a profit for their investors. Increasingly, new businesses wishing to acquire venture capital are rated by an assessment being made of their investment requirement over time, so that a projection can be made, identifying the point at which they may make a profit.

Business administration

'Business administration' is often used as an alternative means of describing 'management', since management is concerned with the control and direction of a series of processes. Henri Fayol suggested that management was about the administration of work and the organization in terms of planning, coordination, command and control. Management is also concerned with the maintenance of procedures, record keeping and ensuring that the business adheres to relevant regulations.

Business administration, in its broadest sense, is also concerned with the control of activities, and not necessarily paperwork, with which it is most closely associated.

Business ethics

Business ethics has become a key aspect in ensuring success and, above all, a positive **corporate image**. In the aftermath of scandals and less-than-perfect business practice, in cases such as Enron and Barings, guidelines for acceptable behaviour by organizations and their employees or officers have been brought into sharp focus. In effect, business ethics implies a series of moral principles, including high standards of governance and the timely disclosure of information. Consumers expect businesses to be ethical and responsible and to make a commitment to those ethics in their conduct and operating principles.

Boatright, John R., *Ethics and the Conduct of Business*. New York: Prentice-Hall, 2002.

Business intelligence

See **competitive intelligence**.

B

Business practices model

A business practices model can be either an explicitly written set of rules, strategies and polices, or a series of informal and implied ways in which the business expects its operations to be carried out. Typically, the business will make clear statements within the model regarding quality specifications or safety regulations.

Business-to-business (b2b)

In its conventional form, 'business-to-business' describes communications and transactions between a supplier business and a purchasing business. In other words, the supplying business is only concerned with relationships between itself and other businesses, rather than with consumers. This describes the standard relationship between suppliers of raw, part-finished and consumable products and services used by other businesses.

More recently 'business-to-business' has been reframed as a term and is normally written as 'b2b'. This new alpha-numeric form is applied almost exclusively to the same relationships between supplying businesses and purchasing businesses, but with the additional concept that these transactions and communications are carried out over the internet.

Business-to-consumer (b2c)

The term 'business-to-consumer' is a shorthand means of describing the conventional relationship between a supplying business and its end-users or consumers. Bearing in mind that there is a difference between the terms 'customer' and 'consumer', in as much as the word 'customer' does not imply end-user, but 'consumer' does, this is a relationship between, typically, a high street retail store and conventional shoppers. In its alpha-numeric form, 'b2c', the term is applied specifically to communications, transactions and commerce carried out between a business and consumers using the internet.

Business-to-distributor (b2d)

'Business-to-distributor' refers to a third form of business transaction or relationship, as opposed to **business-to-business** or **business-to-consumer**. The term itself refers to communications and transactions carried out between a business and members of the distribution channel. These other businesses take the form of distributors, agents, resellers or retailers. These other members of the distribution channel are integral parts of the system which enables the original business's products or services to reach the consumer. Increasingly, the business-to-distributor relationship has been applied and successfully used on the internet, acquiring its alpha-numeric variant, 'b2d'.

Business-to-government (b2g)

'Business-to-government' is used primarily to describe economic commerce between businesses and government. In this respect businesses act as virtual suppliers to central government, local government and government agencies. However, b2g can also be used as a more generic term which describes the very large market related to providing government with products and services.

Call centre

A sales, customer-service and direct-marketing term used to describe a location or facility designed to take and make inbound and outbound telephone communications. Call centres are widely used for telemarketing by businesses aiming at direct sales contact with prospects.

Increasingly, call centres are located in areas remote from the regions they directly serve, largely because of the enormous cost differentials enjoyed by businesses prepared to relocate their call centres in less developed nations. Costs, in terms of both pay and premises, are considerably lower in countries such as India. Other notable call centre orientated countries include the Republic of Ireland, where pay rates and the fact that English is the primary language, as well as active canvassing towards businesses, has caused a considerable exodus to the country.

Another major trend in call centres is that many businesses have taken the step of **outsourcing** to dedicated call-centre facilities which are able to man the centre continuously. In addition, using the differentials in time zone, call-centre outsourcing allows the business to have total 365-day coverage in normal business hours, again reducing costs by not employing staff during unsocial hours.

Capacity

Simply, capacity is the maximum rate of output for a given process. It is usually measured in output per unit of time. Businesses will tend to use different units of time in order to calculate their capacity, such as per minute, per hour, per day or per shift. In truth, the maximum capacity is much better described as being the demonstrated capacity, as this is the true level of capacity which has been achieved. Some organizations and analysts will attempt to calculate a theoretical capacity, which is largely based on the capacity of the machines involved and rarely takes into account any variables which may affect the capacity. Businesses will attempt to operate at their optimum capacity. This means that they will attempt to reduce costs or loss of capacity associated with waiting time.

Capacity management

Capacity management is best described as producing the maximum output, content or performance of a given system or component. Capacity management is often applied to the information technology area, describing or defining in both business and technical terms the requirements of the business's information technology capacity. An efficient information technology infrastructure must deliver, at the optimum cost, the ability to deal with specified levels of capacity. 'Capacity', in its simplest form, describes the probable volume of activities which the information technology infrastructure must be able to cope with given normal circumstances. Clearly, capacity management needs to ensure that there is sufficient capacity, plus additional reserve capacity.

Capacity requirements planning (CRP)

Capacity requirements planning (CRP) is the process of determining short-term output demands, either on an organization or on one of its production processes. CRP is a computerized system that projects the load from a material requirements plan (MRP) onto the capacity of the system and then identifies under-loads and overloads. CRP is used by an organization to assess whether it can start new projects in the future, or whether it can produce an immediate order for a customer. Normally CRP will require information about when orders are required, details of equipment and labour, as well as orders which are already in the pipeline. The CRP will then be able to provide the organization with a profile for each operation in the production system. It will make an assessment of the work that needs to be completed and the work already in progress, in relation to the system's capacity. CRP relies on accurate information, defining capacity as a sum of the following formula:

Number of machines or employees × number of shifts × utilization of machines and workers × efficiency

CRP is therefore used to calculate the ability of the organization to meet its orders.

C

Capital employed

'Capital employed' is an accounting term describing the total of the fixed and current assets which a business has, less its current liabilities. It is a measure of the internal or self-generated investment which the business has provided for itself. Capital employed can also refer to the long term finance of a business, which consists of their loans, share capital and reserves. These are the funds which the business uses to obtain its assets; in other words the capital employed is equal to the assets employed.

See also **Return on capital employed (ROCE).**

Carrying value

Carrying value is the official amount, as detailed in a business's accounts, of the value of a particular asset or liability at the time. The carrying value is another means by which an assessment can be made as to the relationship between a business's assets and its liabilities.

Cash flow

'Cash flow' is a term used to describe the net funds which have flowed through an organization over a period of time. Traditionally, cash flow is usually defined as earnings. The identification of when those earnings were received and when payments had to be made defines the parameters of cash flow. Cash flow is often complicated by the actual value of the cash received in a given period. Cash flow does not take into account expenses which may have been incurred by the organization prior to the period the cash flow covers, yet during this period the organization is benefiting from those costs in the past. Equally, the reverse is true: payments may be due over the cash flow period on equipment or stock from which the organization has already profited and which have been noted on a previous cash flow account.

Cash flow also has a difficulty in dealing with outstanding debts and money owed by creditors. These do not appear on the cash flow as neither has been paid, yet they are important considerations, as they may have a negative or positive effect on the working capital of the organization. The available funds which are calculated and identified within the cash flow have enormous implications for the business, particularly as the available working capital determines the organization's immediate ability to pay subsequent debts and to make necessary investments.

C

Graham, Alistair, *Cashflow Forecasting and Liquidity*. New York: Amacom, 2000.

Cash operating cycle

The cash operating cycle of a business helps to identify the period of time which elapses between the point when the business must pay for products or raw materials which have entered its stock and the period when customers have paid for those products.

Casual labour

The employment of casual labour, or casual employees, is seen by many employers as a viable oprion to provide a degree of flexibility, particularly when demand may not be easy to predict. Casual labour is usually taken on for one job, or the individuals are placed on standby by the employer to come in and occasionally carry out work as and when required.

The term 'casual labour' also implies an employment situation where employees are given low pay, little or no training, no job security and no sick or holiday pay, and can be discarded as and when the business sees fit. Casual labour has attracted the unfortunate nickname of 'flexploitation', which refers to situations where the lowest, minimum-wage payments are made, often to individuals who are desperate for work and are prepared to ignore any dangers associated with the work they are asked to undertake.

Philips, Gordon and Whiteside, Noel, *Casual Labour: The Unemployment Question in the Port Transport Industry, 1880–1970*. Oxford: Oxford University Press, 1985.

Category management

Category management involves the identification of interchangeable or substitute products which could reasonably replace products required by the customer. The identified groups of products are brought together under one category so that they can be offered to the customer as alternatives, should the specific product demanded be unavailable, or if it has been superseded by another product in that category. Category management can be differentiated from an alternative means by which products are managed. In many cases businesses will manage products individually and they will have clearly identifiable differences from other products offered by the business. In this respect it is difficult for customers to perceive the level of substitution of alternative products offered by the same business.

Nielsen Marketing Research, *Category Management: Positioning your Organization to Win*. Chicago, IL: Contemporary Books, 1997.

C

CBI

See **Confereration of British Industry (CBI)**.

Centralization

Centralization is a measure of how concentrated the decision-making processes are within an organization. The greater the concentration, the more centralized the organization is considered to be.

See also **decentralization**.

Certificate authority

Businesses require secure systems for their **e-commerce** and data transfer. Certificate authority is a third-party version of this safeguard. A third-party business creates digital certificates which require users to have already been issued passwords, or keys, in order to access information. A certificate authority therefore guarantees a particular user's identity and gives that user the ability to access information, which will normally be encrypted to protect it from non-authorized users. In using the certificate authority the encrypted (coded) information is decrypted (decoded).

Certificate of incorporation

A certificate of incorporation is a document which brings a business into existence. In effect it is the birth certificate of the business.

Chain of command

The chain of command within an organization is typically associated with a business that has a hierarchical structure. The chain of command is the formal line of communication, beginning with the board of directors, or managing director, who passes instructions down to departmental managers, section heads and then to individual employees. The chain of command typifies a pyramid-shaped organization, where increasingly down the pyramid more individuals have to be informed of decisions and instructions. Effectively, the chain of command of the board of directors or the managing director encompasses every individual underneath them in the hierarchical structure. Similarly, the chain of command of a section head is merely the immediate employees who work under that individual's supervision. The term 'chain of command' is closely associated with **span of control**.

Keuning, Doede and Opheij, Wilfred, *De-layering Organizations: How to Beat Bureaucracy and Create a Flexible and Responsive Organization*. London: Pitman, 1994.

Challenge-handshake authentication protocol (chap)

Chap is a means by which a network connection can be validated using a secure procedure. A link is established between the user and the system. The server then sends a challenge message to the user, who must enter a user name or password as a form of encrypted **authentication**. The server then decodes the message (user name and password) and providing it matches with the data held at the server, the authentication is acknowledged. If the server fails to decipher the message, then authentication is denied and contact is terminated.

Change management

There are many theories regarding change management. Many focus upon the way in which a business thinks about change and the way it drives change. As there are a number of different theories, it is, perhaps, prudent to focus on just some of the ways in which change management can be achieved. Although change may not necessarily be driven by a human resource department, it is often the role of the department to manage the intricacies and complications arising out of change. There are innumerable theories on not only the way change affects individuals and groups within a business, but also the ideal ways of managing that change.

Doug Stace and Dexter Dunphy took the view that change management could be packaged in terms of its size and complexity and then organized accordingly, as can be seen in Figure 9.

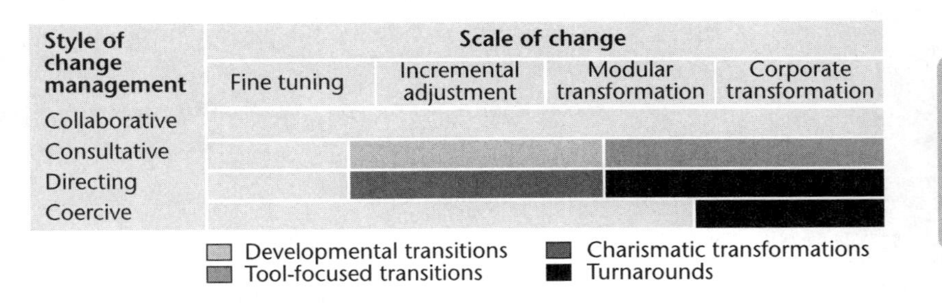

Figure 9 Stace and Dunphy's view of change management

Costello's approach sought to set the parameters purely by the size and scope of the change being envisioned and then to suggest strategies by which the change could be facilitated (see Figure 10).

Size of change	Planning and action implications
Developmental	Enables ideas to be generated from and developed by affected employees and involves them in implementation planning.
Transitional	Management needs to be clear about the change and identify similarities and differences between the current and the new procedures. Targets and objectives should be set and progress monitored and reported on. Employees should be acknowledged for their efforts and any successes.
Transformational	The change must be communicated throughout the organization with no possibility of ambiguity or misunderstanding. Employees must be educated as to why the change is occurring, how it will affect them and what the new vision is.

Figure 10 Costello's view of change management

Source: After Costello.

Paul Bate, on the other hand, considered the whole process of change to be a cycle which had clearly identifiable phases, as can be seen in Figure 11.

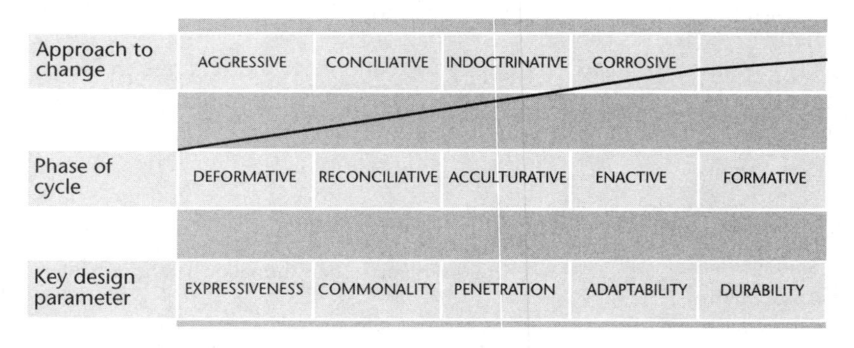

Figure 11 Bate's view of change management

Source: After Bate.

Bate, Paul, *Strategies for Cultural Change*. Oxford: Butterworth-Heinemann, 1995.
Costello, Sheila, *Managing Change at Work*. New York: Irwin Professional, 1994.
Stace, Doug and Dunphy, Dexter, *Beyond the Boundaries*. New York: McGraw-Hill, 2002.

Clicks-and-mortar

Clicks-and-mortar describes a business that has both an on-line and an off-line (physical) presence, as opposed to being a virtual business which only exists on the internet. Typically, the business may have an on-line presence in addition to its more traditional high street stores (such as Body Shop).

Clickstream

A clickstream is an internet advertising term which refers to the sequence of clicks or pages that are requested as a user explores the website. By establishing the most common clickstreams, the website owner is then able to identify premium pages when placing advertisements on that website. Alternatively, in the case of advertising on a business's own website, the identification of the clickstream can ensure that key advertising messages are placed on the most visited pages.

Click through rate

This is a web-related term used by advertisers to measure response to **banner advertising**. A 'click through' occurs when a user clicks on the advertisement and is sent to the advertiser's web page.

Closed shop

There are two different forms of closed shop, pre-entry and post-entry. Pre-entry closed shops require employees to already be a member of an appropriate **trade union** before they can work in a particular business. This form of closed shop is most closely associated with skilled, craft employees. A post-entry closed shop requires employees to join an appropriate trade union within a defined period of time after taking up employment. Closed shops are often referred to as Union Membership Agreements, which are joint agreements between the union and employers.

In Britain the number of closed shop arrangements has fallen steadily since the 1970s and is now believed to account for less than half a million employees. In 1990 the Employment Act removed the last protection for pre-entry closed shops, providing potential employees with the legal right not to be denied work for non-membership of a union. The earlier Employment Acts of 1980 and 1982 had also undermined closed shop arrangements, allowing employees with religious or conscience objections not to have to join a union and requiring that a majority of employees had to approve the Union Membership Agreement. The Employment Act of 1988 also removed all legal support for closed shops and stated that dismissal for refusing to join a union would always be considered by the court to be unfair.

CoBAM

CoBAM is an acronym which means Consortium of Bricks-and-Mortar. Typically, a number of businesses will collaborate in establishing a new **e-market**. The consortium often consists of more traditional businesses that have, in the past, been competitors. The creation of the group results from a realization that their existing business and, above all, market share, faces considerably more competition from **e-business** than it does from one another. By the early part of the new millennium, over 100 of these industry-based CoBAMs were in existence, but since many of them lacked the necessary technological expertise to develop and exploit e-markets, they were slow in combating the competitive effects of new e-businesses.

Collaborative commerce (c-commerce)

Collaborative commerce is a set of collaborative, electronically enabled interactions between a business and its employees, suppliers, trading partners and customers.

It has come about as a model for business **applications** by the development of the internet, hardware components and integration technologies. In effect, the c-commerce system creates what has been described as a dynamic eco-system, where businesses can integrate their business processes and information systems. Collaboration is the key and it has been estimated that over a third of US large businesses, accounting for $5bn of turnover, are actively piloting c-commerce programs.

The Deloitte Consulting Organization predicts that by 2005 some 85 per cent of all US businesses will have implemented some form of c-commerce initiative.

www.businessweek.com/magazine/content/01_35/b3746664.htm

Collaborative filtering

Collaborative filtering is a tool which is becoming increasingly used in **e-commerce**. Software is used to look at the profiles and the usage patterns of users who visit a particular website. Assuming that the software is aware of the identity of the user, it is able to make recommendations for purchases based on the purchasing habits and other preferences already identified and attributed to that user. The system has become increasingly sophisticated and is routinely used by businesses such as Amazon to recommend similar book titles, reflecting the purchasing patterns of other users who have purchased the same titles as the current user.

Communication barrier

A communication barrier is taken to mean a problem in the communication system or stream which effectively blocks either the communication itself or the understanding of that communication between the relevant parties. Communication barriers can take a number of different forms, such as:

- lack of sufficient or effective training of employees;
- lack of information needed to make a decision;
- personal relationship problems;
- faulty or inadequate systems or procedures.

Communication channels

The **organizational structure** will determine the channels through which communication is regularly made. Communication channels need to ensure that information flows freely throughout the organization in order that the right information meets the right person, at the right time. Open communication channels tend to take the following forms:

- notice boards;
- newsletters;
- minutes of meetings;
- non-confidential internal mail;
- multi-user computer systems;
- **email**.

Communication channels also have to pass information of a confidential or security-restricted nature and the organization will restrict the access to this information in a variety of ways, including passwords for computer systems.

Communication methods

An organization will select the most effective method of communication for transmitting information both internally and externally, taking into account considerations such as speed, cost, feedback requirements or written documentation needs. The illustration in Figure 12 identifies the main methods of communication, in both written and verbal format.

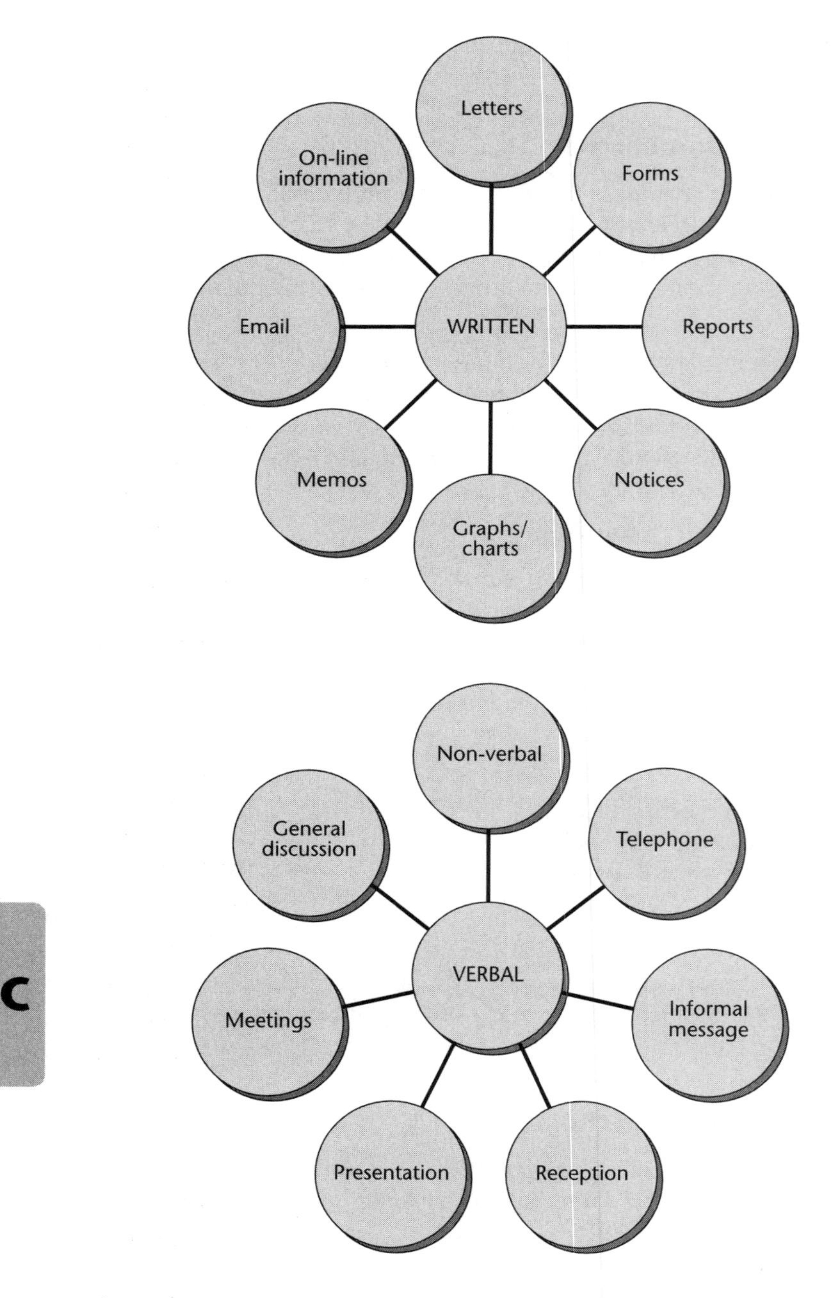

Figure 12 Methods of written and verbal communication

Communication standards

This is a formal protocol, often administered by the human resource department, which applies to internal communications within a business. The communication standards set the rules with regard to the elimination of racial, age, gender or other biases in communications within the organization.

Community relations

Community relations are programmes which businesses undertake in order to positively engage the local community. The businesses make a positive contribution in order to bring themselves into partnership with the local community, in exchange for their support. Community relations, also known as community involvement, is seen by many businesses as being an integral part of their social responsibility, particularly in relation to regeneration. Some larger businesses will second skilled employees to provide services to the local community, as well as engaging in training and educational initiatives. Other community relations projects can include sponsorship of sports and arts projects.

See also **public relations**.

Competency centre

This is an organizational structure used to coordinate IT skills within a business. Competency centres provide expertise for project or program support, where they act as a repository of knowledge and a resource pool for the various functional areas of the business. The most common type of competency centre in an information services organization tends to be used for **application** development, software language skills, data management, internet development and network design.

Within businesses it is becoming increasingly common to find competency centres (otherwise known as **shared services**) in travel, finance and human resources. Repository-based competency centres tend to act exclusively as sources of information.

Competitive intelligence

Competitive intelligence (CI) is increasingly seen as a distinct business management discipline, which provides an input into a whole range of decision-making processes.

There are four stages in monitoring competitors, known as the four 'C's:

1 Collecting the information.
2 Converting information into intelligence (CIA: Collate and catalogue it, Interpret it, and Analyse it).
3 Communicating the intelligence.
4 Countering any adverse competitor actions.

The Society of Competitive Intelligence Professionals website is at www.scip.org

Competitive orientation

Competitive orientation is often seen as measure of an organization's ability to recognize, consider and respond to the activities of competing businesses. A business which looks closely at the activities of the competition may be more inclined to make short-term adjustments to its own activities in order to offset any adverse effects on its operations.

Competitive orientation is another important factor in creating superior value for buyers. In order to create value for buyers which is superior to that offered by the competitors, a business must understand the short-term strengths and weaknesses as well as the long-term capabilities and strategies of both the main current competitors and the key potential competitors.

Slater, Stanley F. and Narver, John C., 'Does Competitive Environment Moderate the Market Orientation-Performance Relationship?', *Journal of Marketing*, 58 (1994), pp. 46–55.

Competitive pricing

Competitive pricing policy relates to a pricing strategy that takes into account periodic or permanent movements in the prices charged by competitors for similar products and services offered in the market.

A business will systematically monitor the pricing structures of the competition and, if necessary, bring its prices into line with those of the major competitors. The competitive pricing strategy approach is often closely allied to the overall **competitive strategy** of the business, linked to the stage that the product or service has reached in the **product life cycle**.

Campbell, Robert, *Competitive Cost-based Pricing Systems for Modern Manufacturing*. Westport, CT: Greenwood Press, 1992.

Competitive strategy

A potentially complex area of study, this includes all of the activities of a business aimed at gaining and/or maintaining a competitive edge in the market. The overall options of competitive strategy can be summarized as in Table 2.

Table 2 Competitive strategy options

Characteristics	Introduction	Growth	Maturity	Decline
Sales	Low	Rapidly rising	Peak	Declining
Costs	High per customer	Average per customer	Low per customer	Low per customer
Profitability	Negative	Rising profits	High profits	Declining profits
Customers	Innovators	Early adopters	Middle majority	Laggards
Competitors	Few	Growing number	Stable, but beginning to decline	Declining numbers
Marketing objectives	Create product awareness and trials	Increase market share	Maximize profits and defend market share	Milk brands and reduce costs
Competitive strategies				
Product	Basic product	Product extensions	Diversification	Eliminate weaker products
Price	Cost plus	Penetration	Competitive matching the competition	Price reductions
Place	Selective	Intensive	More intensive	Eliminate unprofitable areas of the distribution
Advertising	Build product awareness among early adopters and dealers	Build product awareness and interest in the mass market	Focus on brand differences and benefits	Reduce to level needed to retain loyal customers
Sales promotion	Heavy use to encourage trials	Reduce as mass market begins to make purchases	Increase to encourage and discourage brand switching	Reduce to minimum

C

Doyle, Peter 'The Realities of the Product Life Cycle', *Quarterly Review of Marketing*, Summer 1976.
Wasson, Chester R., *Dynamic Competitive Strategy and Product Life Cycles*. Austin, TX: Austin Press, 1978.
Weber, John A., 'Planning Corporate Growth with Inverted Product Life Cycle', *Long Range Planning*, October 1976, pp. 12–29.

Competitor Profile Analysis

Competitor Profile Analysis is a market research methodology which seeks to quantify the key success factors in a given industry or market, incorporating the same criteria for major competitors. By assigning a score to the importance or closest match for both the industry and the competitor, an aggregate score is derived (see Table 3). The industry score is calculated, then the competitor scores, and then aggregated to give the final score (C). These scores indicate the key determinants of success and show how well suited, or, perhaps, vulnerable, a given competitor may be. Obviously an extension of this profiling analysis would be to carry out a similar exercise with your own business.

Computer-aided design (CAD)

Computer-aided design enables engineers to create a design from predetermined specifications and then to view that design either in minute detail or from different angles. The software allows the designer to see how the changing of one value or variable has an overall impact on the design itself. Most CAD software is capable of being run on a standard computer.

See also **computer-aided engineering (CAE); computer aided manufacturing (CAM).**

C

Computer-aided engineering (CAE)

Computer-aided engineering is both a hardware and a software system which analyses engineering designs. These systems simulate how particular designs may work under different conditions. CAE can either be an integral part of a **computer-aided design** system, or it may be a stand-alone system which can analyse designs that have been produced by other computer-aided design systems.

Computer-aided inspection (CAI)

CAI uses systems such as infrared to detect defects in products passing along a production line. The computer is programmed to carry out an

Table 3 Competitor profile analysis key success factors

Success factor	To industry (A)	To competitor (B)	Score (C)
Product quality	1 2 3	1 2 3	1 2 3 4 5 6 7 8 9
Product mix	1 2 3	1 2 3	1 2 3 4 5 6 7 8 9
Price	1 2 3	1 2 3	1 2 3 4 5 6 7 8 9
Distribution dealers	1 2 3	1 2 3	1 2 3 4 5 6 7 8 9
Promotion ability	1 2 3	1 2 3	1 2 3 4 5 6 7 8 9
Manufacturing operations	1 2 3	1 2 3	1 2 3 4 5 6 7 8 9
Overall cost situation	1 2 3	1 2 3	1 2 3 4 5 6 7 8 9
Financial strength	1 2 3	1 2 3	1 2 3 4 5 6 7 8 9
Organization structure	1 2 3	1 2 3	1 2 3 4 5 6 7 8 9
General management ability	1 2 3	1 2 3	1 2 3 4 5 6 7 8 9
Human resource quality	1 2 3	1 2 3	1 2 3 4 5 6 7 8 9
Total weighted score			

A – The scale of importance is 3 = high, 2 = moderate, and 1 = low.
B – The scale for the rating is 3 = strong, 2 = moderate, and 1 = weak.
C = a × b.

inspection of particular features, specifications or parameters of the product throughout the production process. This enables the business to make the earliest possible detection of faults before the part-finished product proceeds further along the production line. Clearly the early identification of defects is cost effective in the sense that it eliminates the completion of products which subsequently prove to be defective.

Nambiar, K. R., *Computer Aided Design: Production and Inspection*. New Delhi: Narosa Publishing House, 1999.

Computer-aided manufacturing (CAM)

Computer-aided manufacturing is a hardware and software system which is used to automate the manufacturing process. It incorporates real-time control, robotics and material requirements – in other words, directing the whole manufacture of a product, as well as keeping track of the inventory of parts required.

Confederation of British Industry (CBI)

The Confederation of British Industry was established in Britain in 1965 when the Federation of British Industries, the British Employers' Confederation and the National Association of British Manufacturers merged. The CBI is effectively a pressure group for business. It is engaged in the promotion of business interests to the workforce, government and government agencies and overseas countries. The CBI attempts to make the voice of British business heard through events, press releases and lobbying activities throughout the world.

www.cbi.org.uk

Consolidation

The term 'consolidation' has various applied meanings in business. Consolidation can mean the bringing together of two or more organizations into a new organization which has a different structure. It is different from a merger in that it combines all of the assets and liabilities of the combining businesses.

Consolidation can also refer to loans and debts. It applies to loans in the sense that a large loan is taken out by a business to eliminate all of the smaller loans. A consolidated debt places together all monies owed into a more manageable and controllable single debt.

Businesses also use the term 'consolidation' to apply to invoices. A consolidated invoice covers all items which have been shipped to a particular customer over an agreed period of time. This eliminates the need to invoice individually for each purchase or set of purchases.

'Consolidation' is also used to describe the process by which a manufacturer or supplier will merge all of the products and raw materials bound for a particular geographical area. In international trade, for example, consolidation either occurs at the docks, where several individual orders are placed in a single container for shipment, or alternatively, transportation to a particular area may be delayed until such a time as it is economically viable to ship the various small orders as a single lot.

Consultant

A consultant, specifically a management consultant, is seen to be an expert in a specialized field or area of management technique. Consultants are brought in by businesses to provide independent, professional advice. Their remit may be to advise on a specific project or to advise generally on the running of the organization. Consultants tend to be brought in for a specified period of time, during which they will investigate, report and recommend. There are innumerable management consultants who operate as individual service providers in particular fields, or there are larger consulting businesses which have an array of different consultants to cover various areas of business practice. Primarily, management consultants differ from internal consultants, who may be non-executive directors on the board. An internal consultant, rather like a management consultant, is brought into the business to provide specific expertise, rather than the firm engaging an independent external specialist to give similar advice.

Consultation

Consultation implies a degree of amicability and discussion between employers and employees. Consultation can occur at various levels of an organization and seeks to involve the staff in arriving at a degree of consensus before decisions are implemented which may affect employees.

Consumer profiling

Consumer profiling aims to identify and quantify the habits and characteristics of the ideal or most common customer. As a primary market research and market segmentation methodology, it allows a business to more clearly match its products and services with the market, thus improving and influencing the buying habits of the customers.

Reliable data is required to create a consumer profile and this will tend to be derived from sources which can provide information on demographics which include variables such as age, gender and income level. Additional and more complex consumer profiling can also investigate and quantify such aspects as lifestyle and buying habits, but these measures need to be precise and match the basic criteria.

Consumer protection

Increasingly, governments have come to realize that consumers, or end users of products and services, require statutory support in relation to issues such as safety, price and quality. Since the rise of **consumerism** in the late 1950s, there has been an increased demand for consumer protection in order to gradually eliminate unscrupulous trading practices and the selling of unsafe products and services. In Britain, for example, statutory legislation exists to ensure that products and services are of a merchantable quality. This is a trend which has been replicated in many other countries across the world. Again in Britain, the Office of Fair Trading, established in 1973, considers the interests of consumers at a national level. There are also regulators, or **ombudsmen**, who are concerned with many of the utility businesses, such as railways, electricity suppliers and telecommunications. At a local level, regional or local authorities have Trading Standards Offices which act as a first stop in investigating consumer-protection-related issues and ensure that businesses are carrying out their operations within the statutory guidelines.

In 1975 The National Consumer Council was established. This organization essentially represents the views of consumers at local and central government level.

Consumer research

Consumer research is a branch of **market research** which, rather than analysing data which has been gathered regarding business or industrial customers, focuses on domestic or individual consumers. Typically consumer research would examine buying patterns, establishing a profile in terms of demographic factors, as well as assessing possible trends in demand and other aspects. The process of gathering and analysing this data is an integral part of ensuring that the marketing effort is directed primarily towards the needs and demands of the consumer and that any products or services, current or planned, address these issues.

Consumerism

In the 1970s, consumerism was taken to mean marketing and advertising which was specifically designed to create customers, in other words to make the product or service offerings as approachable and pertinent to the customer as possible. It is probable that consumerism can actually be traced back to the early 1960s when President Kennedy proposed that consumers should be accorded their rights in law.

Since that time, the term has taken on a radically different meaning in that it is more closely associated with the rights of consumers. Consumerism can be defined as illustrating to businesses in general that the customer is no longer to be considered an individual who can be manipulated by marketing and that customers' responses to advertising and other marketing activities are no longer as predictable as they may once have appeared. Consumers now flex their muscles and demand products and services that more closely match the claims made in marketing communications; they are supported by many non-governmental organizations or consumer groups coupled with local and national government bodies responsible for the advancement of consumer protection.

The two alternative definitions can be seen as being almost opposite in their meaning and it is the latter definition that tends to be applied to the term.

Aaker, David A. (ed.), *Consumerism: Search for the Consumer Interest.* New York: Free Press, 1982.

Consumer-to-business (c2b)

Consumer-to-business, or c2b, is in effect a reversal of the normal distribution channel. At present it is a small but significant and growing element of **e-commerce**. Consumers tell vendors what they are willing to pay for particular products or services and it is then incumbent upon the vendors to decide whether they will or will not accept that price.

Contact manager

Contact manager software programs are in effect traditional contact databases which hold information about past dealings with customers.

Contact management software is widely used in **business-to-business** sales and marketing, as it can be used as either personal contact management systems or centralized and automated sales tools. Typically, the program will allow the user to fill in particular fields in the database and set triggers or schedules in order to track future contacts with the customer.

Content management system (CMS)

'Content management' is an internet-related term which refers to the management of the text and graphics on a website. On larger, more complex websites, which may contain thousands of pages with innumerable words and images, it is essential that there is a content management application system in place in order to create and organize that content. Content management applications can also track traffic through the website and provide an analysis of how visitors use the website, which may reveal more efficient ways in which to organize the pages and the overall content.

Contingent workforce

A contingent workforce, as the term implies, is a flexible group of workers who can be hired by a business to add to the permanent staff as and when required. Contingent workers are often referred to as contract staff, who are taken on, on a temporary basis, either to assist with a specific project or during a period of high-intensity work. Businesses take the view that they do not need these employees on a permanent basis, but provided the workers have the necessary skills, the contingent workforce, having been assembled, is available on short-term contract terms, in order to plug much-needed gaps. Many contingent workers are former full-time employees of the business who may have chosen early retirement and are re-engaged by the business for limited periods, having the advantage of knowing organizational procedures and practices.

Continuous improvement

There are many ways of approaching the handling of continuous improvement. The fundamental concept however remains that in order for an organization to achieve long-term and sustainable improvements, there must be a continuous improvement process which leads them, over shorter periods of time. The whole continuous improvement system aims to achieve change in the longer term by carefully and consistently measured steps, which specifically address problems.

One of the many ways in which this process can be typified is a six-step process, as can be seen in Figure 13.

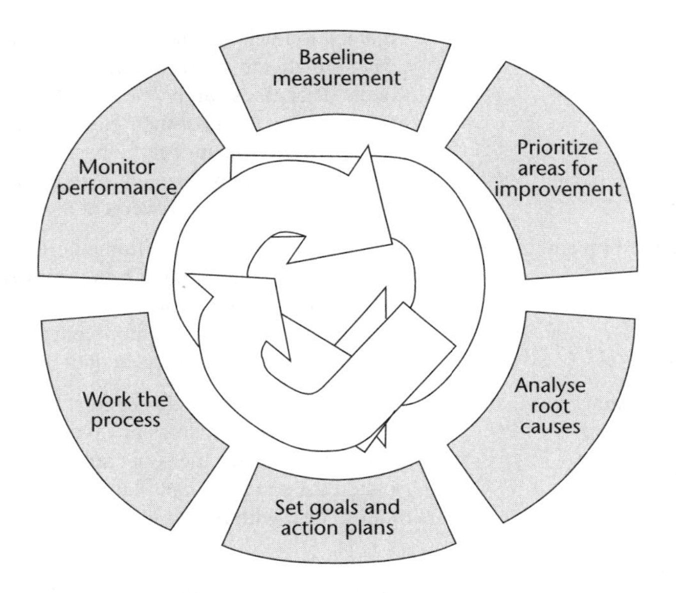

Figure 13 Continuous improvement model

The process begins with a baseline measurement system, which aims to guide the organization through the problem-solving process and identify the areas which require improvement. In the second and third steps the areas requiring immediate improvement are selected and the root causes of substandard performance are evaluated. Having achieved this improvement, goals are then developed, importantly both in the long and the short term, enabling the organization to systematically eliminate any barriers to improvement. The performance needs to be measured and tracked and the six-step process returns to the baseline measurement in order to redirect the organization's problem-solving efforts. The circle of related and interdependent issues is a continual one, which systematically addresses issues and barriers, discovering ways in which they can be surmounted.

In order to fully understand the implications of all of the processes, it is prudent to consider the implications of each of the six steps. The fundamentals are examined in Table 4.

Table 4 The six-step process of continuous improvement

Stage of six-step process	Description
Baseline measurement	The initial step is for the organization to determine its current operating situation. The organization will identify a number of areas which are affecting the overall operating system. Processes can be measured, analysed and tracked in terms of their effectiveness and productivity. In this model the baseline measurement can be likened to zero on the scale of continuous improvement.
Prioritize improvement areas	The organization will now frame performance standards, possibly through **benchmarking**. This will assist the organization in focusing on the major areas requiring improvement related to productivity, profitability, quality or safety.
Root cause analysis	Once the major areas have been selected the organization must address any barriers to improvement. Once the root causes have been isolated the solutions can then be framed in order to deal with them individually.
Goal setting and action planning	It is imperative that goals are incremental so that the organization and those involved can reap tangible benefits by seeing parts of the problem successively solved. Without the incremental factor, dealing with complex problems may lead to demotivation. A series of goals will make up a major goal, each of them progressing the organization along the way to dealing with a specific issue. Alongside the goals, clear, direct and specific action plans must be framed, but these need to be flexible enough to be changed as and when required.
Work the process	Definitive action plans will direct the organization in its efforts to implement the various improvements. The plans need to be logical, and revised if necessary. At this stage the organization is at the very heart of the problems it faces and the use of cross-functional teams and brainstorming to overcome issues can be essential tools.

⇒

Table 4 The six-step process of continuous improvement (continued)

Stage of six-step process	Description
Performance measurement	The final step in the first revolution of the continuous performance model seeks to measure the tangible results. By this stage, whatever problems have been tackled should now have been overcome, which will have had a positive impact on the operations of the organization. The goals should now be compared with the original baseline measurements in order to verify that they have been achieved. It may be the case that the improvements are more, or less, than had been desired. Therefore the process begins once again, as partially resolved issues may need further improvement.

See also ***kaizen*** and **total quality management (TQM)**.

Marsh, John, *The Continuous Improvement Toolkit: The A–Z of Tools and Techniques*. London: B. T. Batsford, 1998.

Nicholas, John, *Competitive Manufacturing Management: Continuous Improvement, Lean Production and Customer-Focussed Quality*. New York: McGraw-Hill Education, 1998.

Continuous professional development (CPD)

Continuous professional development is often driven by an individual employee and relies upon the support of human resource management. Continuous professional development is commonly seen as an integral part of the ongoing learning process, in which individuals can seek to attain additional skills and competences throughout their working life. CPD is often a requirement of professional memberships.

Norton, Bob and Burt, Vikky, *Practical Self-Development: A Step-by-step Approach to CPD*. London: Institute of Management, 1998.

Contribution

Contribution is equal to total revenue less total **variable costs**. In other words, contribution minus **fixed costs** is equal to the profit made by the business. Contribution is used as a means by which a business can calculate the contribution made by each product, service or department towards the **overheads** of the business. Once the overheads have been covered by the constituent elements, any further contribution is profit. Contribution is used to give a clearer indication of the situation of the business by effectively removing overheads, or other fixed costs, which are otherwise difficult to allocate.

Each product or service provides a unit contribution, which is taken to mean the selling price less the variable costs of producing it. From this excess the fixed overheads are removed. It is therefore possible to calculate the total contribution by summing the unit contribution and the number of units produced. The assumptions are that any marginal costs and final selling price will remain constant.

Cookie

A cookie is a computer code contained within a text file and is used to identify customers and analyse their on-line behaviour and website trends.

Corporate culture

Corporate culture is taken to be the beliefs, values, norms and traditions of an organization which directly affect the behaviour of its members. Each organization has its own unique culture and many businesses are conscious of this culture, which may be based on a sense of community or another fundamental driving force. It is widely believed that there are five different forms of corporate cultural diversity, as shown in Table 5.

Schein, Edgar H., *The Corporate Culture Survival Guide*. New York: Jossey-Bass, 1999.

Corporate identity

Corporate identity relates to the identifying marks of a business. This typically includes logos and brand names, which are then transposed onto all written communications, product markings, brochures, advertisements, websites, uniforms and vehicles etc.

Corporate identity is, in effect, a branding technique (corporate branding) applied to a business rather than a product or a service. This is an extensive part of the marketing industry as it also involves the creation of both visual and audio symbols, colours and strap-lines.

Carter, David E. (ed.), *The Big Book of Corporate Identity Design*. New York: Watson-Guptill Publications, 2001.

Table 5 Corporate culture

Corporate culture orientation	Explanation
Individual versus collective	How the business determines at which level behaviour needs to be appropriately regulated.
Power distance	How less powerful members of the organization accept and adhere to the distribution of power within the organization.
Uncertainty avoidance	The degree to which rules, long-term employment prospects and the possibility of progression exist and whether employees are unsure of how to deal with particular situations.
Dominant values	Whether a formal structure, based on well-defined roles, is at variance with employees' desire to have quality relationships, **job satisfaction** and work flexibility.
Short-term versus long-term	Whether the focus is upon short-term performance or longer-term relationships and the desire to take an extended view of achievement.

Corporate image

Corporate image is concerned with the associations made by customers, the general public or other **stakeholders** when they are asked to state their impressions of a business. The responses may be positive or negative and in some cases there may be no impression at all. Public relations activities are designed to either heighten or amend the corporate image of a business.

In itself, a corporate image is an intangible asset or a liability. A positive and strong corporate image can add immeasurably to the value of a business and in many respects is the embodiment of goodwill. A more practical and day-to-day purpose of the corporate image is to influence customers' likelihood of purchasing products or services and to attract investors or employees.

Argenti, Paul A. and Forman, Janis, *The Power of Corporate Communication: Crafting the Voice and Image of your Business*. New York: McGraw-Hill, 2002.
Fombrun, Charles, *Reputation: Realizing Value from the Corporate Image*. Boston, MA: Harvard Business School Press, 1996.

Corporation (US)

A corporation is a legally artificial entity. It is separate and apart from the directors, officers, employees or shareholders. It can, however, only act through these individuals. Corporations have limited liability; in other words, individuals who have invested in a corporation only have liability up to the amount which they originally invested. Corporations use a board of directors to control the short- and long-term policies of the organization, but are liable for their own debts and taxes.

The exact nature of a corporation and how it is created has slight differences from country to country, but in essence they have at least one owner, known as either shareholder or stockholder, and come into existence with a document known as an article of incorporation. They need to have at least one director, supported by other officers, which may include a treasurer or a secretary. In the US, corporations tend to have presidents and vice-presidents. It is the shareholders who effectively elect or appoint the directors.

See also **certificate of incorporation**.

Cost centre

Cost centres are units of a business, or a particular activity, to which costs are allocated. In normal circumstances individual parts of a business will make a nominal charge for their services when used by other parts of the organization. The allocation of costs to these centres allows the business to track the comparative expenses associated with each area of the business's internal activities.

Counselling

At its most basic, counselling involves discussing problems with an employee in order to assist them in dealing with situations which they are finding difficult. More broadly, counselling has been identified as an effective means by which emotional and stress-related problems can be addressed in order to offset the high costs of psychological problems encountered by employees, which inevitably lead to their low productivity. Effective counselling requires a careful and staged approach in order to avoid absenteeism, stress-related leave, **grievance procedures** and, in extreme cases, violence in the workplace:

- The counselling sessions should be planned in advance, allowing the employee and the counsellor to agree what issues should be discussed.
- The counselling session should encourage openness. The discussions should aim to share responsibility and build a relationship between the counsellor and the employee.

In many cases professional counsellors are not employed by businesses and the function is seen as an additional responsibility of a manager or supervisor.

Cracker

Crackers have, in the past, been described as little more than vandals or, in extreme cases, cyber-terrorists. Many crackers consider the breaking into a business's website to be a challenge and, as such, will seek by any means to gain access to the business's computer networks. They will intentionally breach the computer's security by bypassing licences or passwords. Some crackers, working as freelance security experts, are now deployed specifically to find weaknesses in a website's security system so that additional security features can be installed. Some crackers break into networks for profit, in the sense that there is valuable commercial information on a network which can subsequently be sold to a competitor. Others simply attack networks for malicious purposes, either because the business represents something abhorrent to them, or because they wish to highlight an issue they feel strongly about.

Crash

'Crash' or crashing is an attempt to shorten the duration of a particular activity. The implications are that the individual tasks involved, or at least some of them, can be concertinaed into a shorter length of time in order to reduce the overall time which the activity will take.

See also **crash time**.

Crash time

Once an organization or project team has decided to **crash** an activity, a re-estimation of the time the activity will take has to be calculated. This revised time span for the activity is known as crash time.

Credit control

Credit control is an essential function of most businesses, in as much as it ensures that outstanding debts are paid within a reasonable period. Credit control may, in fact, begin before any debts are incurred by customers, through a system which gives each customer a credit rating. This is based on a series of assumptions, investigations and checks which aim to determine the reliability of the particular customer.

Creditor

A creditor is an individual or a business to which another individual or business owes money. In accounting terms there is a distinction between creditors in as much as a balance sheet will reveal just the total amount which is owed to creditors. In reality, of course, some of these creditors will be paid during the forthcoming accounting period (short-term debts), while others will not be paid until much later (long-term debts).

A creditor can also be described as an individual or a business that has extended credit to another individual or business. The individual or business that owes the creditor money is known as a **debtor**.

Crisis management

For most organizations, crisis management is unavoidable when the business's survival or well-being is threatened by an unexpected problem. Most organizations will have established a series of contingency plans in order to ensure that specific steps have been outlined to deal with similar, predicted situations. In most cases the business will appoint an individual, probably from the board or senior management, to deal with the situation. This individual will be given the full support of the board and may be granted considerably more sweeping authority to deal with the crisis. In other cases, public relation companies are employed to deal with potential and actual crisis issues. Swift decision making is essential in crisis management as immediate remedies are required in order to ensure the business's continued survival.

C

See also **public relations**.

Fink, Steven, *Crisis Management: Planning for the Inevitable*. Parkland, FL: Universal Publishers, 2000.

Critical chain

A critical chain is a means by which an organization can look at the full duration of a particular project, and it can be considered to be somewhat more all-inclusive than a **critical path analysis**. The critical chain not only addresses the issues which a critical path considers, but also takes into account any factors relating to the supply of products or components prior to the commencement of the production process itself. A critical chain would consider the start and finish times, as well as any slack periods. The longest total time through these stages is known as a critical path. The critical chain seeks to assign the resources required for each part of the process and recognizes that the next stage cannot be undertaken until the resources required for that task are made available. The critical chain then identifies all of the stages in the process until the schedule has been completed. In this respect, a critical chain is somewhat longer than a critical path. In addition, the critical chain incorporates time buffers, which aim to protect the activities on the critical chain from beginning later than is desirable.

Alongside a critical chain, a non-critical chain would also be constructed, which ensures that activities which could have an impact on the critical chain are planned in such a way that they do not interrupt the critical chain.

Leach, Lawrence, P., *Critical Chain Project Management*. London: Artech House, 2000.

Critical incident

The critical-incident technique involves the identification and investigation of issues which have either a beneficial or a negative impact on customer satisfaction. Critical incidents can be typified as being either advantageous or desirable qualities which the business or its employees display, or factors which are continual causes for complaint and dissatisfaction. The critical-incident technique can be used to identify aspects not only of the organization's performance, but also of individual employees' performance, by recognizing aspects of how they handle customer service situations and provide a satisfactory or unsatisfactory outcome for the customer.

Latino, Kenneth, *Root Cause Analysis: Improving Performance for Bottom Line Results*. Boca Raton, FL: CRC Press, 2002.

Critical path analysis

A critical activity is a major event on a critical path. A **critical chain** is a means by which an organization can look at the full duration of a particular project, and it can be considered to be somewhat more all-inclusive than a critical path. The critical chain not only addresses the issues which a critical path considers, but also takes into account any factors relating to the supply of products or components prior to the commencement of the production process itself. A critical chain would consider the start and finish times, as well as any slack periods. The longest total time through these stages is known as a critical path. The critical chain seeks to assign the resources required for each part of the process and recognizes that the next stage cannot be undertaken until the resources required for that task are made available. The critical chain then identifies all of the stages in the process until the schedule has been completed. In this respect, a critical chain is somewhat longer than a critical path. In addition, the critical chain incorporates time buffers, which aim to protect the activities on the critical chain from beginning later than is desirable.

Alongside a critical chain, a non-critical chain would also be constructed, which ensures that activities which could have an impact on the critical chain are planned in such a way that they do not interrupt the critical chain.

A critical path is the longest possible path through which a project has to pass in order to be completed. A critical path identifies crucial activities in the stages of dealing with, or managing, a particular project, identifying in effect the worst case scenario in order to make a clearer estimation as to the time a project will take to complete. The critical path aims to focus the organization's attention on those activities which are essential to ensure the completion of the project.

The critical path method (CPM) begins with the start time for a particular project. It then proceeds to identify the earliest possible start times and finish times for each activity which is required to complete the overall project (see Figure 14). Once this has been completed, the CPM seeks to work backwards from the date by which the project needs to be completed and amends the start times of all of the activities in relation to this date. The critical path is the pathway that has the minimum

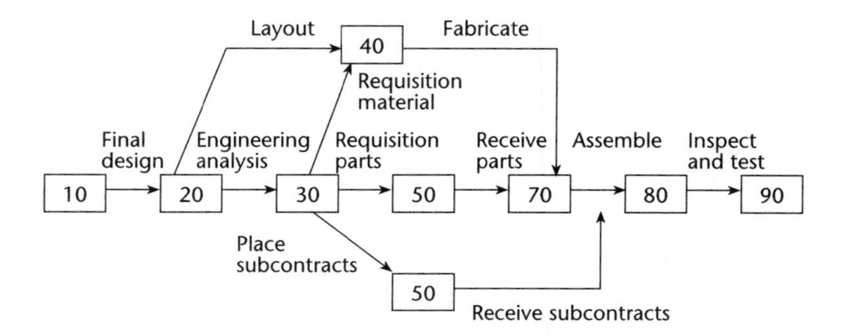

Figure 14 An example of critical path analysis

amount of slack time. This critical path is then given a priority in terms of attention and allocation of resources, aiming to reduce the overall project time.

The CPM should also assist the business in being able to identify aspects or activities in the process which can be either rolled together or speeded up in order to have a positive impact on the overall project completion time.

Busch, Dennis H., *New Critical Path Method: State of the Art in Project Modelling and Time Reserve Management*. Boca Raton, FL: Probus Publications, 1990.

Latino, Kenneth, *Root Cause Analysis: Improving Performance for Bottom Line Results*. Boca Raton, FL: CRC Press, 2002.

Leach, Lawrence P., *Critical Chain Project Management*. London: Artech House, 2000.

Critical success factors (CSFs)

A business may identify critical success factors (CSFs) as a means by which it helps determine its own strategic objectives. Each of the major objectives has associated CSFs, which in theory should be achieved *en route* to the principal objective or objectives. In other words, these CSFs criteria are major milestones along a continued process towards the objectives as identified by the business.

Sashkin, Marshall and Saskin, Molly G., *Leadership that Matters: The Critical Factors for Making a Difference in People's Lives and Organizations' Success*. San Francisco, CA: Berrett-Koehler Publications, 2003.

Cross-channel marketing

Cross-channel marketing is an increasingly effective means by which a business can use one of its existing sales channels to promote another, or a new, sales channel. A business may feature, in its printed catalogue, details of its on-line presence, perhaps showing sample pages of its website. In order to convince existing customers to consider the use of this alternative channel, the business may offer them an incentive, either to use it themselves or to recommend it to others.

Cross-functional team

A cross-functional team is set up within an organization, consisting of employees from similar levels in the hierarchy. Individually the members of the team can contribute specialist knowledge as they work in different areas of the organization. The teams tend to be established for a specific task or project and are then disbanded once this has been achieved.

Cumulative average time taken (CATT)

CATT is a measure which aims to establish the average time taken to produce each unit over a **product's life cycle** to date. Theoretically, assuming that the business is on a learning curve as far as production is concerned, the average time taken using the latest figures should be considerably less than the average time taken at the beginning of the production period. This is due to the fact that as the business gets into the swing of producing a particular product, the time taken to produce each unit should gradually reduce to an optimum time period.

Customer charter

Customer charters are a series of promises, guarantees or assurances to customers made by a business. They describe the aim to improve and maintain levels of service and quality to the customer, in clearly defined terminology. The charter may often take the form of a fair trading agreement and provides the backbone of business–customer relations and communications, including the methods for dealing with complaints, queries and other issues. In effect a customer charter is a commitment by the business to guarantee minimum levels of service across the full range of its operations.

Customer information control systems (CICS)

A customer information control system is an on-line transaction process in the form of a software program which was developed by IBM. It has become the most common program for creating customer transactions systems.

Customer interaction centres (CICs)

For many businesses customer interaction centres (CICs) have become an integral part of **customer relationship management**. These centres integrate all forms of customer contact by the business. In other words they are a control point for the collection and dissemination of customer data within the business. Typically, they will gather and disseminate information which has been derived from telephone contact, faxes, **email**, the internet and other marketing activities. The centres also function as the primary contact point for customers requiring or receiving information from the business.

Customer profitability analysis (CPA)

Customer profitability analysis is a management tool which is used to analyse revenue streams. Specific customers, or groups of customers, are examined in terms of the revenue derived from them and any associated service costs. In this way the business is able to identify and focus upon the most profitable customers or customer groups and put processes into action which seek to reduce the service costs for other potentially high-profit customer groups.

Customer relationship management (CRM)

Customer relationship management is based on the assumption that there is a relationship between the business or the brand and the customer. This is a relationship that needs to be managed both through the individual buying stages and in the longer term. CRM is very much related to fostering customer loyalty and, in the longer term, customer retention.

CRM can be used in **call centre** support and direct marketing operations. Software systems assist in the support of customer service representatives and give customers alternative means by which they can communicate with the business (such as mail, email, telephone etc.). Some sophisticated CRM software programs have **email** response systems which process incoming emails and determine whether they warrant a personal or an automated response. Recent figures indicate that systems such as this can handle around 50 per cent of the requests from customers (typically requests for additional information, passwords and responses to emails sent by marketing departments).

Other CRM software systems incorporate the facility for customer representatives to take part in live chat rooms or co-browsing, offering the business a less formal environment in which to make contact with customers. CRM software can also queue customers on the basis of their profiles, by requesting that the customer logs in to the website; it is then possible to pass the customer on to individuals in the customer service team who may be better suited to dealing with customers who share similar profiles. CRM software also provides the facility to maintain and update a database of information about each customer (in other words, a case history).

Customer relationship marketing

Customer relationship marketing is an integral part of **customer relationship management** as it is a marketing model which suggests that information should be gathered throughout the history of a customer's relationship with the business. This information can then be used in relation to that customer in such a way as to promote trust and loyalty, with the end objective being increased sales.

See also **customer relationship management.**

Customer satisfaction

Customer satisfaction is a measure by which businesses can assess how their actions have measured up to the expectations of their customers. Customer satisfaction requires a continued survey of how customers perceive the business and the level of service, including response times, value and other factors in their dealings with the business.

Customer service

In the past, customer service was simply restricted to the after-sales period, when the business would ensure that any issues arising out of a purchase could be dealt with effectively and efficiently by customer service staff. Increasingly, customer service has become an integral part of the whole relationship between a business and its customers. It therefore now incorporates pre-sale, during sale and **after-sales service** situations.

Effective customer service also incorporates the way in which customers are treated by staff and, above all, how far their wants or needs are satisfied. It has become abundantly clear to many businesses that the quality of their customer service largely determines how loyal customers remain. Customer service, therefore, extends beyond repair and replacement, the treatment of guarantees and other more regular, service-related issues. Most businesses now have clear complaints procedures, including freephone telephone facilities, and their customer support mechanisms have become integral to their **customer relationship marketing** activities.

Customer support/customer support real-time

Customer support incorporates a range of different services which a business offers to its customers in order for them to use its products or services in the most efficient and effective manner. Customer support may be delivered either at the place of sale, requiring the customer to return to that location, or increasingly through customer support telephone services or on-line assistance. In this respect customer support needs to incorporate the ability to troubleshoot problems, assist with the use of products and services, and offer other technical help. It has been apparent to businesses for some years that this form of **after-sales service** or complementary service is vital in order to ensure that good **customer relationship management** is achieved by the business.

The term 'customer support real-time' refers to customer support which is offered on a continual, round-the-clock basis, either by automated systems or more commonly through telephone support helplines.

Cyberfraud

As far as most conventional businesses are concerned, cyberfraud is synonymous with on-line credit card theft. The most common form of cyberfraud is the use of stolen or invented credit card numbers in order to purchase goods and services. Cyberfraud has become a considerable problem for businesses, which not only suffer the loss of income from the fraud itself, but also may achieve a reputation for their on-line ordering systems being insufficiently secure to risk making a purchase.

In order to acquire information from a business's database, the criminal needs to literally break into the business's system in order to steal that information. Increasingly, businesses are taking extreme measures in order to prevent this from occurring.

Cybersquatting

Cybersquatting is literally the purchase of a domain name in the knowledge that a business or organization with that name will subsequently wish to use that domain name. When internet commerce first became a reality, many speculators purchased well-known or potentially well-known domain names in the hope of being able to resell them to a business with that name. Many of the larger corporations discovered that domain names were already in the possession of private individuals, despite the fact that these had been registered using brand names or trademarks. Although some of the larger corporations subsequently purchased some of these domain names, others have chosen litigation in order to acquire them.

Data cleaning services

Given the fact that businesses rely on their databases for their marketing and other activities, they need quality data; new businesses have sprung up which offer data cleaning services. These businesses literally do what their name implies; they eliminate dirty data by removing errors, highlighting missing information and dealing with contradictions in the database. Data cleaning is an integral part of data management, which aims to ensure that the data is correct, validated and standardized. Many businesses, rather than using outsourced data cleaning services, now prefer to purchase software programs which cleanse their data.

Data protection

A term related to the storing of information, particularly customer details, on databases. Data protection, which differs in scope from country to country, seeks to protect individuals from the misuse of data which has been captured and stored by businesses or specialist data centres. In most cases, those with data files relating to them have the right to request sight of the material and to insist on amendments to it if it is inaccurate or misleading.

More broadly, data protection seeks to control the indiscriminate sale or sharing of data held on customers by businesses for the purpose of direct marketing and other marketing activities.

www.dataprotection.gov.uk

Carey, Peter, *Blackstone's Guide to the Data Protection Act 1998* (Blackstone's Guides). London: Blackstone Press, 1998.

Database management system (DBMS)

A database management system is a program which allows multiple users to store and access information on a given database. The database management system must be robust enough to make the information available in an organized fashion; in other words, to protect and maintain the integrity of the data stored in the system. A database management system will also be responsible for limiting access to the data to only those who have **authorization**.

Debenture

A debenture is a document which either creates or evidences a **debt** owed by a business. In many cases debentures are secured, giving the creditor a priority in terms of repayment compared with unsecured creditors.

Debt

A debt in the broadest sense is capital owed by a business to either investors or those who have provided the business with a loan. Long-term debts are usually lent to the business by investors, possibly in the form of loan stock or **debentures**. The investor receives interest, normally at a fixed rate, regardless of the financial performance of the business, until such a time as the full debt is repaid. Investors to whom the business owes the debt are the first to receive any funds available if the business is forced into **liquidation**.

Debtor

A debtor is either an individual or a business that owes a debt to another individual or business, known as the **creditor**. On a balance sheet debtors are denoted as those who owe money to the business and there is a distinction made between those debtors who are expected to pay their debts during the next accounting period and those debtors who will not pay until after that period.

Decentralization

Decentralization involves a gradual dispersal of decision-making control across an organization. Integral to the dispersal of decision making is the movement of power and authority from the higher levels of management, or a single headquarters unit, to various divisions, branches, departments or subsidiaries of the organization. At its very core, decentralization implies **delegation**, by transferring the responsibility and power from senior management to lower-level individuals. The purpose of decentralization is to encourage flexibility and, above all, assist faster decision making, which, in turn, means faster response times.

Decentralization is also strongly associated with the concept of **empowerment**, affording to frontline staff the power, authority and responsibility to make immediate decisions without reference to senior management.

See also **centralization**.

Decision support system

Decision support systems are usually a computerized series of flexible menus which include models and decision aids that can be used in conjunction with current and relevant data. These support systems are designed to assist managerial decision making at all levels of an organization.

Decision-making units (DMUs)

A decision-making unit is a group of people, usually taken to mean a business or perhaps a department, who make collective decisions with regard to purchasing. A DMU can, of course, be a household although the term is usually more closely associated with business-to-business marketing and sales.

Stereotypically, a DMU would have individuals who fulfil the following roles: a specifier, an influencer, an authorizer, a gatekeeper, a purchaser and a user.

Delegation

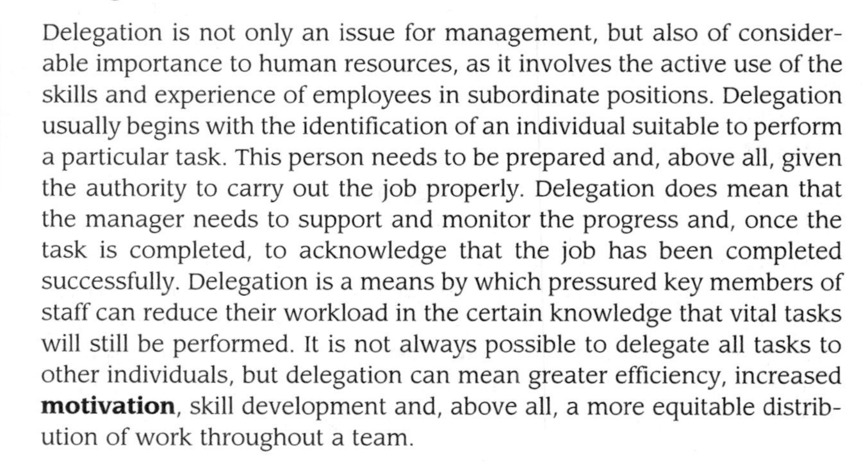

Delegation is not only an issue for management, but also of considerable importance to human resources, as it involves the active use of the skills and experience of employees in subordinate positions. Delegation usually begins with the identification of an individual suitable to perform a particular task. This person needs to be prepared and, above all, given the authority to carry out the job properly. Delegation does mean that the manager needs to support and monitor the progress and, once the task is completed, to acknowledge that the job has been completed successfully. Delegation is a means by which pressured key members of staff can reduce their workload in the certain knowledge that vital tasks will still be performed. It is not always possible to delegate all tasks to other individuals, but delegation can mean greater efficiency, increased **motivation**, skill development and, above all, a more equitable distribution of work throughout a team.

Smart, J. K., *Real Delegation: How to Get People to Do Things for You and Do Them Well.* New York: Prentice-Hall, 2002.

Denial of service (DOS) attack

A denial of service attack can be launched at a website or an **email** service either by someone with malicious intent or by those who wish to do it as a prank. In effect, the website or system is bombarded by messages so that either the system crashes or, more commonly, regular users cannot gain access.

Hackers and other individuals, often referred to as cyber-terrorists, will choose to target the website of a particular corporation in order to disrupt its normal activities on the website. By overloading the system with so many messages they hope to render the site or the system inoperative. As a protection system, the website or email service may then deny access or service to regular users.

Increasingly, these attacks are being seen as criminal acts and most national police forces have units set up to deal with and track down DOS attacks.

Departmentalization

Many organizations use departmentalization in order to concentrate specific expertise or operational functions into a single, common structure. Many departmentalized organizations have somewhat centralized authority and tend to have a rather bureaucratic attitude towards decision making. Within each department there is a recognized hierarchical structure, which controls aspects such as personnel or marketing for the whole of the organization. In effect, a department could be considered to be an individual operating unit which has full responsibility for its own management. This latter version of departmentalization implies that the organization is somewhat decentralized in as much as the department has more power and authority to carry out its functions, without necessarily referring to senior management.

Depreciation

Depreciation is a systematic reduction of the acquisition costs of fixed assets, such as machinery, over the period during which those assets were of benefit to the organization. Depreciation is, in effect, a paper-based accountancy exercise which seeks to take account of the fact that the value of fixed assets gradually decreases over a period of time and that those attendant losses should be written off against the expense accounts of the organization.

In the US this process is known as amortization, which is the systematic reduction of the value of primarily intangible assets, such as goodwill or intellectual property. The value of these intangible assets, such as a breakthrough in manufacturing processes, reduces in value over a period of time as they are either replaced or copied by other competitors. Amortization also applies to tangible assets.

Deskilling

Deskilling is the process by which division of labour and technological development may lead to the reduction of the scope of an employee's specialized tasks. Work becomes fragmented and employees lose the integrated skills and knowledge associated with a crafts person. Deskilling has been seen as a negative impact of technology where a process or machine can perform a task better than the human hand.

Harry Braverman wrote a Marxist critique of capitalism and in particular the organization of work under 'antagonistic' social relations. He was concerned with the loss of craft skills in the organization of work. He was one of the first theorists to define the term as 'deskilling', which he described as being the effective separation of mental work and manual work. Deskilling is closely associated with scientific management and is seen as a means by which management can closely control the labour process in the sense that it removes the skills, knowledge and science of the labour force and transfers these to management. An additional concern is that it can mean that manual and mental workers feel diametrically opposed to one another.

Braverman went on to suggest that deskilling leads to decomposition (the dispersal of the labour process across numerous sites and time) and that, as such, deskilling increases the opportunities for management to exploit labour and reduce the capacity of workers to resist their control.

Both Frederick Taylor and Henry Ford were deeply involved in early attempts to deskill and initiate decomposition. As scientific management practitioners they attempted to transform the organization of work to improve profitability and to reduce craft skills' control of work. The terms 'Fordism' and 'Taylorism' are closely associated with the use of the assembly-line. Fordism itself attempts to harmonize the dual desires of mass production and mass consumption.

Deskilling therefore involves the following:

1 the maximum decomposition of the labour process as a series of work tasks across time and space;
2 the separation of direct and indirect labour;
3 the minimization of skill in any work task;

4 the creation of standardized products;
5 the use of specialized machine tools (as opposed to general purpose machine tools);
6 the use of the assembly-line and methods of continuous production (at a pace set by management and not by the workforce).

Braverman, Harry, *Labor and Monopoly Capitalism: The Degradation of Work in the Twentieth Century*. New York: Monthly Review Press, 1999.
Taylor, Frederick Winslow, *The Principles of Scientific Management*. Atlanta, GA: Institute of Industrial Engineers, 1998.

Digital certificate

A digital certificate is, in effect, a digital version of an identification card. It is usually used in conjunction with a public key encryption system. This means that parts of a website or computer system are accessible to members of the general public, but in order to access other areas of the website, the business uses a digital certificate to restrict access. The digital certificates are usually issued by a third party, known as a **certificate authority**. It is the role of the certificate authority to ensure that the information included on the digital certificate proves that the senders are who they purport to be. Digital certificates aim to ensure that the parties exchanging information are who they claim they are. They have become vital parts of data security and **e-commerce**.

Digital employment advertising

Digital employment advertising, as the term suggests, is the on-line posting of job opportunities on the internet. Currently over 30,000 websites offer job posting services and these are the equivalent of conventional job agencies, often used instead of, or in conjunction with, conventional media job advertisements. There are a number of advantages attached to hosting job vacancies on these searchable databases of job posts, since the websites are able to suggest appropriate posts according to registered users' profiles, and they may also incorporate on-line application systems.

Digital or electronic cash

Digital or electronic cash at present is very much in its infancy. Not only are there few banks participating in digital cash experiments, but there are also even fewer businesses able to accept any form of digital cash. The principle of the system is relatively simple. It uses an electronic cash account which can be stored on the user's own computer, or alternatively on a Smart card. This allows the users to make purchases online from their account, streamlining the process of making an order and having the transaction confirmed by the bank. The system will require the user to transfer cash up to a given limit into their digital cash account. Once a purchase has been made it is automatically transferred from the customer's account into the supplier's account in a matter of seconds, automatically activating the shipping phase of the transaction.

Wayner, Peter, *Digital Cash: Commerce on the Net*. Burlington, MA: Morgan Kaufmann, 1997.

Digital shopping companions

A digital shopping companion is a piece of browser software which operates in the background until it is required to perform a task. Typically, the software will intercept junk **email**, provide passwords, manage personal information and compare prices. The software is designed to appear when the user is ready to make an on-line purchase, providing the supplier with instant shipping and billing information with one click from the user. The software accesses information which is kept either on a secure internet site or on the user's own computer.

Digital signature

Digital signatures are a means by which the sender of a message can be positively identified. Unlike a handwritten signature, the digital signature cannot be forged, and it also confirms that the message has not been altered in any way between the sender and the receiver. Digital signatures are used to authorize transactions, particularly payment systems. A merchant's digital signature ensures that through **encryption**, payment processes are protected on the internet.

Hammond, Ben (ed.), *Digital Signatures*. New York: McGraw-Hill, 2002.

Direct channel

A direct channel is essentially a direct distribution system in which products and services are delivered straight to the end-user, without the use of an intermediary. Notable direct channels include direct sales and, in some cases, standard mail order.

Direct cost

Direct costs are expenditures which can be solely allocated to a specific product or project. They are differentiated from **indirect costs** as these include unavoidable overheads which, in themselves, are not specifically related to the product or the project in question.

Direct labour

Direct labour is either the proportion of employees who are required to be intimately involved in the manufacture of a product, or the standard number of direct hours required to manufacture a given component or product.

Direct response

Direct response is a marketing tool in which manufacturers or suppliers have direct contact and communication with potential customers. Direct response does not use intermediaries and may take the form of advertisements in a variety of different media, including television, magazines and the internet, to elicit an immediate response from potential customers. There are clear advantages in using direct response forms of marketing and advertising in as much as products and services can be offered either at considerably lower prices, as there are no intermediaries, or at competitive prices, which means that the supplying business can enjoy a larger profit margin on each sale. Direct response campaigns seek to engage the consumers, rather like conventional advertising, but orders and fulfilment are handled by the supplying business itself. Many organizations have recognized the advantages of direct response and for many businesses this has improved their sales volume, whilst, for the first time, they have had direct contact with the end-users of their products.

Scherr, Leslie and Katz, David J., *Design for Response: Creative Marketing that Works.* Gloucester, MA: Rockport Publishers, 1999.

Disciplinary procedures

When an organization sets down its procedures for the handling of discipline within the workforce, it is imperative that:

- the procedures are written down;
- all employees have access to the procedures;
- all employees are aware of who operates the disciplinary procedures.

The **Advisory Arbitration and Conciliation Service (ACAS)** recommends that the disciplinary procedures should be both fair and impartial and should include the following features in addition to those listed above:

- The employer should clearly state who was involved in any particular disciplinary action.
- The employer should clearly state what kind of disciplinary action would be taken against particular types of infringements of the organization's disciplinary guidelines.
- The employee has the right to have a friend, colleague or **trade union** representative present during all disciplinary interviews.
- In most cases, the employee will not be dismissed for a first offence.
- The employee has the right to appeal against the decision made by the employer.
- All proceedings should be administered in a fair manner.
- The employee should not be unfairly discriminated against.

Normally an organization's disciplinary procedure would include the following stages of discipline:

1. *Verbal warning* – if the employee's conduct, behaviour or performance does not reach suitable and acceptable standards, then he or she will be given a formal verbal warning. This is the first official stage of the proceedings. Usually a time limit is set, and provided the employee reaches the acceptable standard within this time then no further action will be taken.
2. *Written warning* – if the employee persists with the same behaviour that resulted in the verbal warning, or if the offence was sufficiently serious, then a written warning will be issued. This is usually issued by the employee's immediate superior.

   The written warning details the complaint and clearly states what must be done by the employee to rectify the situation. The warning will also state how long the employee has to respond to the warning. If the employee persists, then the next stage of the process will follow. If, however, the employee complies with the requirements then the matter will not be taken any further. There is an opportunity at this stage for the employee to appeal.
3. *Final written warning* – if the employee continues to fail to improve conduct or behaviour, then a final written warning will be given. In some cases, employees may find themselves at this point in the disciplinary procedure as a result of a serious disciplinary offence. The employee should be aware that dismissal is imminent if there is no improvement in behaviour.
4. *Suspension* – as an alternative to, or in addition to, a final written

warning, an employer may suspend an individual for up to five working days without pay. This is known as disciplinary suspension.

5 *Dismissal* – the final stage of the disciplinary procedure is dismissal itself. To reach this point, an employee must have failed all the requirements laid down in the early stages of the procedure. The employee's most senior, but related, line manager will take the decision to dismiss the employee, usually in consultation with the human resource department. The employee will be given a written statement which includes the reasons for dismissal and the date of termination of employment. It will also include guidance for the employee in case of appeal.

Diseconomies of scale

Diseconomies of scale are said to be the point at which a manufacturing process simply becomes too large and the normal rule of **economies of scale** ceases to apply. In certain cases, as capacity continues to increase, the manufacturing organization may encounter the problem of average unit costs increasing, rather than falling. There are usually three reasons for this:

- The different processes within the manufacturing process may have already reached their optimum **capacity** and be unable to produce any more products, thus causing difficulties for other processes which are capable of a higher rate of production. This means that various parts of the production process are literally starved of parts and components by these **bottlenecks**.
- As the organization grows, there are attendant difficulties related to the coordination of activities. To support the production process there is an attendant increase in administration and a proliferation of bureaucratic procedures which may inhibit the production process itself, whilst adding indirect costs to each unit of production.
- Under the assumption that the capacity levels of the organization could, up to a point, be supplied by other organizations within a viable geographical area, as production increases, manufacturing organizations may need to cast their net wider in order to secure sufficient supply. They may also need to make compromises as to the **lead times**, quality and delivery costs of these supplies from the additional suppliers. All of these issues will add costs overall, which in turn are applied to each unit of production.

Diseconomies of scale, therefore, occur as a mixture of internal and external diseconomies.

Disintermediation

Disintermediation occurs when an organization in a supply chain is replaced by an alternative means by which the product or service passes down the supply chain to the end-user. Typically, this would involve a manufacturer's decision not to sell products or services through distributors and the retail trade, but to sell direct, possibly via a website. Alternatively, a distributor could be cut out of the supply chain, or disintermediated from it, by the manufacturers supplying retailers themselves.

Dispute resolution

Resolving disputes is one of the key functions of human resource management. The first stage of dispute resolution is trying to avoid disputes. This should be done through consultation with **trade union** representatives or employee associations, to form an agreement about working conditions. During these negotiations there will be discussions about the formation of a programme or set of procedures which will be followed in the case of a dispute, usually in order to avoid **industrial action**.

Although the procedures put in place will vary from organization to organization, the general content of such an agreement regarding dispute procedures will include the following guidelines:

- The dispute will initially be discussed between the employees and their immediate line manager.
- The employees' trade union representative will be called in to meet the line manager, or a member of middle management, should the initial discussion not resolve the issue.
- The trade union representative will meet with senior managers should there still be no resolution.
- If the dispute remains unsolved, senior national representatives of the trade union will meet with senior managers of the organization.

The next stage of the dispute resolution could involve the intervention of an independent arbitrator. It should be noted that the majority of dispute resolution agreements contain a clause stating that no industrial action will be taken until all the stages of the agreement have been undertaken.

See also **Advisory Conciliation and Arbitration Service (ACAS)**.

Disruptive technology

The term 'disruptive technology' was originally coined by Harvard Business School's Clayton Christensen and refers to new technologies which emerge and overthrow traditional business models. The internet, or more appropriately the widespread use of computers in business, has gradually overturned what may be called the age of paper, as these new technologies offer businesses the opportunity to have a 'paperless office'. It is believed that in due course business transactions via the internet will replace conventional business transactions, and examples such as the proliferation of supermarket on-line shopping will spell the end of retail parks and the need to purchase and maintain large supermarket premises.

Distance learning

The main advantage of distance learning is that it allows students to study at a time, pace and place convenient to their needs. Learning can therefore be integrated into existing commitments.

Distance learning is an increasingly popular method of course delivery for professionals, with most institutions offering students support through their programme or course of study. This is achieved in a variety of ways, from face-to-face or telephone tutorials to text-based or electronic study guides. Increasingly, students have the opportunity to network with other learners through a range of media options such as teleconferencing, video-conferencing and email.

The International Council for Open and Distance Learning (ICDL), operated by the Open University, promotes both open and distance education networks and systems at national, regional and global levels. The ICDL has a database which contains details of over 1,000 institutions worldwide offering distance learning courses.

www.icdl.open.ac.uk

Distribution

Distribution is the physical movement of products and services from the producer to the end-user and often involves the transfer of ownership through intermediaries between the producer and the end-user. A distribution channel ends when an individual or a business buys a product or service without the intention of immediate resale.

Part of the distribution channel involves organizations such as storage and transport companies and banks. They are integral parts of the distribution process, but they are outside of it in the sense that they never take ownership of the product or service; they merely aid the channel.

A business faces several different options when setting up the distribution system for its products and services. The key determinants of how this distribution channel is organized usually depend on the following:

- A determination of the role of the distribution and how it will help achieve the marketing objectives.
- The selection of the type of channel and whether intermediaries are required.
- An assessment of the intensity of the distribution, which allows the business to assess how many intermediaries will be needed at each level and in each area.
- The choosing of specific channel members which most closely match criteria set by the business.

Diversification

Diversification involves the movement of a business into a wider field of activity, with the primary objective of spreading risks and reducing its dependence on either a single market or a single product range. Diversification can be achieved in a number of ways, including the purchasing of other businesses already servicing targeted markets.

Businesses which are involved in diminishing markets (such as tobacco) or seasonal markets (such as ice creams) are keen to move into new areas in order to ensure their continued growth. Strategic decisions are made to either diversify through purchase or diversify through development of new areas within the business itself.

The key advantages include the improvement of the long-term survival prospects of the business, the movement away from a saturated marketplace in order to ensure sustained growth, and the provision of new opportunities for the business's existing skills and resources.

There are also clear disadvantages attached to diversification, which could include the business's failure to understand its new customers, the new market or the nature of the new competition. Diversification may also bring about **diseconomies of scale**, in as much as the business is involved in too many different areas to enjoy true efficiency in any one aspect of its operations. Businesses may also find diversification weakens their core business, as they may be required to divert resources away from their traditional areas in order to support the new business activities.

Division of labour

The term 'division of labour' refers to rigid and prescriptive allocation of work responsibilities. Formerly, skilled employees were allocated specific job roles and, because of the complexity of their work, it was difficult to assign individuals who did not have the same degree of skill to those particular roles. Equally, the skilled individuals were keen to avoid any moves by the management to deskill their work and thus undermine their position. Division of labour therefore became a system by which different employees within a manufacturing organization could be identified and compensated in different ways. As the process of **multi-skilling** has swept manufacturing, coupled with the introduction of more complex technology, many of these former divisions have either disappeared or become blurred over time. None the less, division of labour can still be typified as instances when specific groups or teams of employees are allocated specific roles, and where only these individuals carry out that work.

See also **deskilling**.

Document exchange service

For many years document exchange has taken place between businesses through secured distribution networks. Each business engaged in document exchange has its own distinctive code number and assurances from the distribution company that any documents entering the system will not only be secure but will also be delivered within a specified time frame. Increasingly, document exchange services have become digitized through secure **email** servers which ensure efficient document transfer over the internet, with equal reliance and peace of mind.

Document management

Document management is an integral part of many businesses' desire to set up a truly paperless, or document-less, office. Document management involves the transition of paper-based documentation into an electronic format. The system requires the availability of optical scanners and optical character recognition systems to convert paper-based documentation into an equivalent electronic format. Document management also requires a sophisticated form of **database management**, as an integral part of the transition from paper to digital document holding is the facility to search those electronic documents for key words, phrases and numerical sequences.

Dot-commercial

A dot-commercial is an emerging form of on-line advertising, as it incorporates interactive features and conventional television advertising. When the dot-commercial begins to run on a user's computer, the user has the option to investigate and, perhaps, change the focus of the dot-commercial in order to tailor-make it to his or her requirements, so that it provides the pertinent information required in order to make an informed choice. The key aspect of dot-commercials is their interactivity. For example, users would be able to specify precisely which tracks they would require on a compilation CD, or the format in which they would require a book title.

Dumping

Dumping is a sales-related term which has considerably negative connotations. Dumping is the practice of selling obsolete products and services into an overseas market at a lower price (often) than had been charged in the home market. Normally products and services which have reached the decline stage of their **product life cycle** are identified as being ideal candidates for dumping procedures. Dumping is not entirely restricted to obsolete products as the practice can be seen as a means by which a business can achieve a significant influx of income by reducing its margins on a product or service overseas, whilst retaining the margins at home. Typical examples of products which have been dumped in this way are those in the consumer electronics industry, notably from Japan and South Korea. The US and the European Union have begun to set up protectionist measures to prevent this practice.

A rather more sinister form of dumping involves the selling of products which have not met safety standards or other criteria in the home market. Overseas markets are chosen which have less protection for their consumers, notably in the pharmaceutical market, where potentially dangerous drugs are sold openly overseas, whilst they have been either banned or restricted in use in the home market.

Dupont formula

The Dupont formula is used to show the rate of return on gross assets. Using this formula, gross assets is the product of total asset turnover and the net profit percentage. There are two accepted forms of the Dupont formula: both refer to return on investments and are:

$$\textit{Net profit margin} \times \textit{Total asset turnover}$$

or

$$\frac{\textit{Net profit after tax}}{\textit{Sales}} \times \frac{\textit{Sales}}{\textit{Total assets}}$$

Earnings per share

Earnings per share is a ratio which shows after-tax profits that are available for ultimate distribution to shareholders. The difference between the after-tax profit and the distribution to shareholders usually equates to money that will be ploughed back into the business. Typically the business would use the following formula to calculate the earnings per share:

$$\textit{Earnings per share} = \frac{\textit{Total profit after tax}}{\textit{Number of shares}}$$

E-business

The term 'e-business', or 'electronic business', was probably coined by IBM in 1997. It used the term as part of a major advertising campaign. In effect, e-business is the process of conducting business using elements of the internet. E-business is a more generic term than **e-commerce** because it transcends the acts of buying and selling to include the collaboration with business partners and the servicing of customers. In effect, e-business is a fusion of business processes, applications and organizational structure. The vast majority of businesses are now incorporating e-business as part of their overall planning procedures. Typically, in manufacturing for example, the internet can be used to buy parts, components and supplies. Providing the organization is satisfied with the quality of products (which would certainly entail the receiving of samples), the global implications for supply are enormous. It is perfectly feasible for a manufacturing organization to now access, interrogate and evaluate organizations remotely in ways that would have been impossible in the past. The convenience and availability of suppliers, notwithstanding the attendant delivery costs, may continue to revolutionize the supply and fulfilment functions of the manufacturing industry.

Chaffey, Dave, Bocij, Paul, Greasley, Andrew and Hickie, Simon, *Business Information Systems: Technology, Development and Management in the E-business.* London: Financial Times, Prentice-Hall, 2002.

E-commerce

'E-commerce', or 'electronic commerce', is a term specifically used to describe the buying and selling of products and services via the internet. In many respects the term has been superseded by **e-business**, as the latter description is taken to encompass more aspects of trade using the internet. In effect, e-commerce is a paperless exchange of information via **emails**, bulletin boards, the electronic transfer of funds, and fax transmissions. These tools allow on-line buying and selling in a wide variety of consumer and industrial sectors.

E-community

An e-community is a virtual version of a traditional community where similarly minded individuals with common interests, or shared purposes, gather on the internet. The creation of e-communities requires a number of key criteria, including:

- the sustaining of interest by continually updating websites and sending out **email** letters and circulars;
- the request for feedback in order to understand the membership;
- the provision of useful information, advice and connections;
- the creation of a strong brand and focal point;
- the opportunity to support all activities by earning revenue from on-line registration and advertising.

E-communities have begun to draw the interest of marketing professionals, as they represent a ready-made target market which is fully profiled and receptive to relevant advertising and marketing messages. Several businesses have indeed established their own e-communities, providing for themselves a captive audience whose members are not only mutually dependent upon one another (particularly in the case of freelance workers), but will also purchase tools, products and services from the sponsoring business.

Economic order quantity (EOQ)

EOQ aims to identify the optimum size of an order which will minimize the cost of holding that stock, as well as the cost of ordering the stock from a supplier. The formula for calculating the economic order quantity is:

$$\sqrt{\frac{2SA}{ic}}$$

where A = annual demand; S = order cost; i = carrying charge or warehousing costs; and c = unit cost

In reality, businesses rarely bother to calculate the economic order quantity, as the tendency is always to order expensive items more frequently in smaller quantities. EOQ is, however, useful in understanding the fact that in trying to minimize the costs associated with placing orders with suppliers, this has to be measured against the organization's immediate demands for that product.

Economies of scale

Strictly speaking, 'economies of scale' is an economics-related issue. However, it has considerable implications in terms of marketing and general business operations. The basic concept revolves around the fact that a business needs to build up a critical mass. In other words, it must be large enough or powerful enough relative to the market to be able to influence it and to enjoy any degree of success. It is notoriously expensive to establish a presence in anything but the smallest markets. The concept suggests that small businesses are simply too small to register any impact on larger markets. Businesses need to be able to assign a certain percentage of their turnover towards product development and marketing activities. However, in the case of small businesses, this percentage, in real terms, will inevitably be minuscule. Once a business has reached a point where it is a larger trading entity, it can enjoy many of the benefits associated with larger-scale production or distribution. In other words, as the size and scope of the business increases, the generally held view is that the unit costs are driven down. The corollary is that having achieved economies of scale, a business has more funds available to further improve its market position.

See also **diseconomies of scale.**

E-distribution

E-distribution is an emerging alternative to conventional distribution methodologies. E-distribution aims to deliver digitized products, such as magazines, newspapers, software, films, books and music, direct to the consumer via the internet. This system is often referred to as 'e-fulfilment'.

Effective capacity

Effective capacity can be differentiated from design capacity in as much as it describes the actual achievable output of a manufacturing organization. The design capacity refers to the optimum output given optimum circumstances. However, effective capacity is a more realistic measure as it takes into account any operational issues which may affect the output as experienced by the organization.

Efficiency

Efficiency is a means by which an organization can compare the average time taken to carry out a particular process on a production line against a standard processing time. In other words, if a particular process normally has a standard time of 30 minutes per production unit and the current production time is actually 25 minutes, then the efficiency of that part of the process is 30/25 = 1.2, which is normally expressed as a percentage, in which case this would be 120%.

Coelli, Tim, Prasada Rao, D. S. and Battese, George E., *An Introduction to Efficiency and Productivity Analysis*. Dordrecht: Kluwer Academic Publishers, 1997.

Wheelwright, Steven C. and Clark, Kim B., *Revolutionizing Product Development: Quantum Leaps in Speed, Efficiency and Quality*. New York: Free Press, 1992.

Eingetragener vereim (Germany)

This is the German equivalent of a non-profit making organization.

E-lancers

E-lancers are the internet equivalent of freelancers. They are computer-literate individuals who are able to provide a wide variety of services to businesses worldwide and are paid on an hourly or contract basis. There are a number of organizations to which e-lancers can belong in order to give them a sense of community.

E-learning

E-learning incorporates both **intranet**- and internet-based training opportunities. The development of computer-based technologies is now widely applied by many human resource and training departments to internally train and enhance employees. Clearly, the establishment of an Intranet training system incorporates the need to extend the security of the internal system from unauthorized use.

Businesses are gradually moving towards using computer-based training materials which are stored either on an intranet system or on the internet and, in some cases, on CD-Roms or DVDs. For most businesses the development of computer-based training (CBT) is not yet cost-effective in areas other than general training, which can be applied to most employees. The costs associated with the creation of CBT often require a business to consider the purchase of general training aids, rather than producing or outsourcing bespoke materials.

One of the major developments has been the creation of an entirely new form of trainer and learning system. Those professionals who are able to train employees via web-based training programmes are often referred to as e-trainers and the CBT as e-learning. It was generally believed, when CBT was first developed, that it would eventually lead to businesses not requiring the services of trainers, as the systems would be smart enough to accommodate the needs of individual learners. Generally this has not proved to be the case and e-trainers are integral parts of e-learning systems. There is still a requirement, no matter how remote each individual learner may be from the e-trainer geographically, that there is a degree of interaction. This need not necessarily be verbal, or, indeed, face-to-face, yet the provision of chat room and discussion forums has become vital to ensuring understanding, commitment and instruction throughout the programme.

Computer-based training can be seen as the successor to more traditional forms of **distance learning**, which has tended to rely on paper-based materials, supported by occasional seminars or tutorials. Admittedly many distance learning courses did use CD-Roms and websites as backup and as a potential means by which individual learners and deliverers could interact.

The implementation of CBT requires a business to consider the following issues:

- What are the criteria for success? Does the training have a link to specific business objectives and how will the effectiveness of the training be measured?
- How will the CBT communicate with the trainee, the human resource department and those responsible for overseeing the training on a day-to-day basis?
- How will the CBT be implemented? Where will it appear and how portable will the system be, given the fact that some of the trainees may be in remote locations?
- How will human resources departments ensure that the trainees are committed to the learning?
- What will the system be to ensure progress and completion?
- How will results be measured? Will the trainees be required to undertake specific examinations, either internal or external, in order to provide proof of their acquired knowledge and skills as a result of the CBT?

Cartwright, Steve R. and Cartwright, G. Phillip, *Designing and Producing Media-based Training*. Oxford: Focal Press, 1999.
Horton, William, *Designing Web-based Training*. Chichester: John Wiley & Sons, 2000.
Lockwood, Fred and Gooley, Anne (eds), *Innovation in Open and Distance Learning: Successful Development of Online and Web-based Learning*. London: Routledge Falmer, 2001.

Elective resolution

An elective resolution is a resolution passed by members of a private company in the UK under the terms of the Companies Act (1986). This form of resolution requires the unanimous consent of all of its members. The resolution seeks to achieve one of the following:

- To give the directors authority to issue shares.
- To dispense with the need to provide accounts before the Annual General Meeting.
- To dispense with the need for the annual reappointment of auditors.
- To dispense with the need to hold an Annual General Meeting.
- To reduce the majority of shareholders whose consent is required for the holding of an Extraordinary General Meeting.

Electronic bill presentment and payment (EBPP)

Electronic bill presentment and payment is a major step towards true on-line banking. It enables the user to send, receive and pay bills. Most banks allow customers to pay their bills on-line; however, EBPP will allow the whole process to become electronic. The customers will be able to review their bills and approve the payment on-line. Although the system will have marked benefits for the customer, the real advantages will be accorded to businesses that at present need to maintain large numbers of employees to produce and distribute paper-based bills. Equally, the banks will benefit from the system as, while the customers are reviewing and authorizing on-line payments, the banks will have the opportunity to market other services to them.

E

Electronic communications networks (ECNs)

The term 'electronic communications network' relates to all forms of fixed and mobile transmission of signals across telephone, internet and satellite networks. In March 2002 the European Parliament passed draft guidelines for the control of electronic communications across Europe. This was reinforced in Britain by the Communications Act (2003).

Electronic Data Interchange (EDI)

Electronic Data Interchange (EDI) is application-to-application transfer of business documents between computers. In essence, EDI is the paperless movement in electronic form (often automated) between or within businesses, to reduce the need for administrative documents. EDI has revolutionized the way in which businesses conduct their trading activities by allowing a fast, efficient and accurate means of electronically exchanging business transactions. Traditional documents are converted into a structured, machine-readable format so that a remote computer can receive and process data from another computer belonging to the same or to another business. Typically, documents will relate to purchasing, sales, inventory management, accounts received and accounts payable. EDI offers a faster trading cycle with greater speed and accuracy between the ordering and invoicing systems. EDI has also assisted businesses to adopt **just-in-time (JIT)** techniques, cutting the time between an order and delivery (see Figure 15), often a key determinant in winning or losing a contract. EDI also enables businesses to reduce their stock levels, improve their cash flow, increase security and reduce errors. Automated confirmations of delivery are integral and recent developments allow the system to be extensively used by customers electronically via the internet.

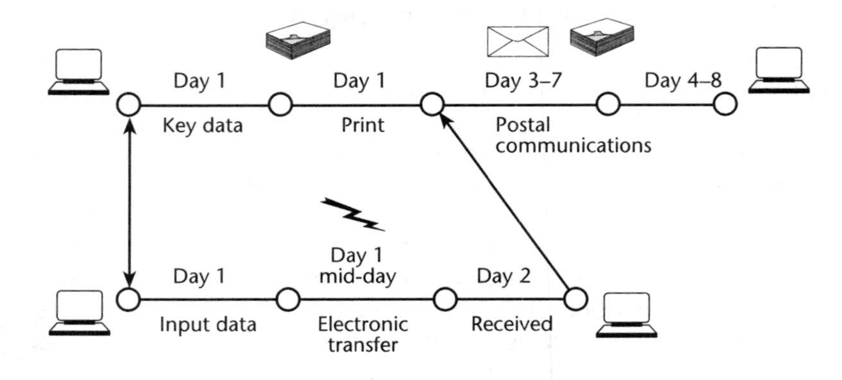

Figure 15 Electronic versus postal systems

Busby, Michael, *Demystifying EDI*. Texas: Wordware Publishing, 2000.

Electronic human resources (e-HR)

Electronic human resources, or e-HR, incorporates new ways of carrying out, managing and maintaining traditional human resource functions. Inherent within e-HR is on-line recruitment, the **outsourcing** of human resources, the communication between human resources departments and employees via the internet and **email**, the establishment of a human resource **intranet** and the provision of **e-learning** facilities. Much of the e-HR can be delivered through the internet, allowing employees to access information at any time and in any location. Employees can also update their own details, such as a change of address or bank account, which saves human resources administration time. Above all, businesses which operate in a number of different remote locations can communicate and share information.

One of the increasing trends for organizations which have incorporated e-HR is the concept of self-service, which empowers employees and management to grant specific pay and benefits packages on an individual basis.

Electronic marketplace

'The electronic marketplace' is a generic term which is used to describe web-based trade between suppliers and customers. It is dependent upon the continued development of information and telecommunication technology, enabling worldwide information exchange and trade. In effect the electronic marketplace is served by **e-commerce** operations, which for the first time allow businesses in completely different parts of the world to engage in trade with one another and also to operate as suppliers to customers in markets they could not have hoped to have access to using conventional methods of trade.

Increasingly the e-marketplace is becoming regulated in order to ensure basic standards are upheld. Equally the development of the e-marketplace is dependent upon secure payment methods, which are slowly being put into place in many countries, but are still in their infancy in many others.

The e-marketplace offers an enormous opportunity for trade and the ability to satisfy demand on a global basis. Once the issues of security, payment, electronic cash, transaction management and communications have been dealt with, there is theoretically no limit to the scope of the e-marketplace.

Electronic payment systems

Electronic payment systems are, in effect, the **business-to-business** equivalent of **electronic bill presentment and payment**. They allow payments to be made electronically on receipt of a bill from another business, greatly streamlining **e-commerce**. It is assumed that as the systems become more sophisticated and reliable and, above all, secure, they will obviate the need for conventional cheques to be sent by post in response to similarly posted paper documents in the form of invoices or statements of account. The system requires a seamless and secure system between the business paying for the products or services, the bank or banks involved and the supplier or merchant who has presented the electronic invoice.

Electronic point of sale (EPOS)

EPOS or electronic point of sale is data which is captured electronically when a sale is made. The system relies on the presence of a bar code and an appropriate bar-code reader. When the sale is made the salesperson scans the bar code, or in some cases, the shoppers do it themselves by using a portable reader. The bar code itself contains information including an identification of the item sold, the price and the store location. When coupled with a customer loyalty card, EPOS is able to match the purchases to the individual customer, thus enabling the business to target special promotions in line with the customers' buying habits.

The other major purpose of EPOS is to send the information to a computer which is linked to the purchasing facilities of the business. Having registered the fact that a product has been sold, the EPOS system, in conjunction with purchasing software, generates a re-order once a minimum order level has been reached. In this way businesses can be assured that they have largely accounted for the stock which has left their shelves and that a process has been put in place in order for them to restock.

Brook, James, *Payment Systems: Examples and Explanations* (Examples and Explanations Series). Phliadelphia, PA: Aspen Publishers, 2001.

Electronic ticketing

Electronic ticketing and its slightly less sophisticated telephone ticketing alternative allow a purchaser to select and pay for a service using a credit card or debit card and then pick up that service at the supplier's location. Typically, these transactions for tickets are used for air travel, live events such as football matches, and cinema tickets. Once the purchase has been made, either on-line or via the telephone, by keying in the appropriate credit card details, the purchasers can present themselves and their credit card at the establishment and insert their credit card into a ticket machine with verification software, which then matches the credit card details with the tickets purchased. In the area of air fares, whilst e-ticketing systems often offer lower prices than conventional means of payment, customers are still proving reluctant to pay for even a ticket which they do not instantly have in their hands. Equally, many e-ticketing systems do not allow tickets to be transferred, although the airline industries are upgrading their systems in order to establish a universally accepted system.

Electronic wallet

An electronic wallet is in essence a storage system which facilitates **e-commerce** transactions. It contains personal information, including shipping and billing addresses, as well as credit card numbers. The wallet itself is stored either on the user's own computer or on the server of a web payment service. An electronic wallet is also known as a digital wallet.

Email

Email is a shortened version of 'electronic mail', which is the internet equivalent of a letter, postcard or similar communication, which exists only in electronic form. Emails can be sent from any remote location via servers to a specified email address anywhere in the world. In the past 10 years emails have become one of the most dominating forms of global communication, vastly surpassing more traditional forms of communication. In this respect emails can be considered to be a **disruptive technology** as they have had a marked impact upon traditional mail delivery systems.

Email encryption software

One of the principal problems with **email** is that technically anyone with **authentication** could access the content of the message. Email encryption software, therefore, encrypts or scrambles the email so that regardless of authentication, it is unreadable unless the person accessing the email has the relevant mathematical key to decrypt or unscramble it.

Email marketing

E-marketing involves the utilization of electronic communications technology in order to achieve specific marketing objectives. This is often referred to as email marketing.

Using the internet as a way of collecting market research information offers two different methods: email research and internet (or website) research. Email research is just like a more modern method of carrying out a postal survey. The questionnaire is emailed (posted) to the respondent and they email it back. Internet research involves putting the questionnaire on a website and hoping that people will take the time to fill it in.

Belch, George E. and Belch, Michael A., *Advertising and Promotion: An Integrated Marketing–Communications Approach.* New York: McGraw-Hill Higher Education, 2000.

E-market

See **electronic marketplace**.

Employee self-service (ESS)

Originally, this was a system which allowed employees to access the human resource department to review or update their benefits, or to seek information which had previously been under human resource management control.

The definition of this service has now expanded to allow access to many other areas, such as employee time tracking, account changes for payroll, as well as skills and training updates. It is expected that this open-access human resource management system will continue to expand as businesses demand increased productivity and both the business and the employees require real-time information exchanges.

www.websterb.com

Employee turnover

Labour turnover, or employee turnover, is a measure of the rate at which employees are leaving a business. There are two effective measures in calculating labour turnover. These are:

Number of employees who left the organization ÷ the total (average) number of employees in the organization × 100

This provides a percentage figure. Alternatively, turnover rate can be calculated as:

Number of employees who left the organization ÷ total number of employees in the organization

Turnover rates can differ widely from business to business and, indeed, from industry to industry. It is particularly common for younger and newer employees to leave a business rather than older or more established members of staff.

Having identified the labour turnover rate, a business now needs to address why the turnover rate is at the level it is. There are obvious circumstances in which management has no control over the turnover rate. These typically include factors such as illness, pregnancy, marriage, or the relocation of a partner or spouse. Most other reasons can actually be avoided by effective human resource policies and procedures and, in many cases, a considerable change in outlook by management itself. In order, therefore, to work out the underlying trend of labour turnover, it is imperative that a further calculation is made using the following formula, which counts only those who have left for unavoidable reasons. The formula is:

Total number of employees leaving for unavoidable reasons ÷ total number of employees

This figure provides the business with the underlying trend. The loss of employees or a business's inability to retain its staff or deal with attrition represents a considerable expense, as not only are there interruptions in productivity, as employees who have learned to do the job efficiently may be those who have chosen to leave, but there is also the additional expense of having to launch a recruitment drive to replace them. Typically, reasons for high turnover may relate to comparatively low pay, low morale, ineffective or authoritarian leadership or more attractive job opportunities elsewhere.

Empowerment

The term 'empowerment' applies to individual employees who are allowed to control their contribution within an organization. This means that they are given the authority and responsibility to complete tasks and attain targets without the direct intervention of management. The benefits to the organization of empowerment are that it reduces the importance of repetitive administration and the number of managers required at the various levels of the structure. By streamlining management levels this often increases the effectiveness of communication. From the employees' point of view, empowerment increases their creativity and initiative, as well as their commitment to the organization, by allowing them to work with **autonomy**.

Encryption

Encryption is the process of scrambling **emails**, credit card numbers, documents or other digital data into an unreadable format which is known as cipher text. Cipher text cannot be unscrambled unless the user has the necessary mathematical algorithms.

End-user

An end-user, or consumer, is an individual who actually uses the product after it has been fully developed and has passed down the distribution channel. End-users are differentiated from others who may use the same product or service for developmental purposes.

Enterprise engineering (EE)

Enterprise engineering is essentially an integrated approach which aims to build or improve a business, its processes and its systems. EE aims to be a powerful change methodology, harnessing both the human and the technological elements into a partnership which creates maximum efficiency, where learning takes place at every level of the organization. Typically, enterprise engineering would use enterprise modelling software and examine case studies of organizations that have been through similar processes in order to dynamically reposition themselves in the face of competitive challenges.

Enterprise performance management (EPM)

Enterprise performance management is a strategic approach to answering the age-old question of how a business is performing. It aims to align business strategy with existing technology by considering all of the technological components which are aligned with new or existing business processes. EPM is often used as a synonym for **balanced scorecard**, but it actively measures and manages the performance of a business through analysis in order to bring about change. The focus of EPM is to provide proactive triggers, rather than simply providing the business with standard executive information.

See also **balanced scorecard.**

Enterprise resource planning (ERP)

ERP is an integrated software system which is often used by manufacturers. It incorporates accounts, payroll and **manufacturing resource planning (MRP2)**, as well as other related systems.

Gunn, Tom, *In the Age of Realtime Enterprise: Managing for Sustained Performance with Enterprise Resource Planning.* Essex Junction, VT: Oliver Wight Publications, 1994.

Shtub, Avraham, *Enterprise Resource Planning (ERP): The Dynamics of Operations Management.* New York: Kluwer Academic Publishers, 1999.

Entrepreneur

An entrepreneur is an individual who is associated with a degree of risk taking and a flair for identifying potential business opportunities. Entrepreneurs exist in almost every area of business activity and seek to identify gaps in present market provision which can be filled using new means by which the products or services can be delivered, often in a radically different way from the one in which the market already operates. Entrepreneurs place a great emphasis on innovation and will seek to design an entirely new business model, rather than relying on tried and tested business practices.

Entreprise unipersonnelle à responsabilité limitée (France)

This type of business organization is the French equivalent of a **sole trader** or **sole proprietor**, but with limited liability.

E-procurement

E-procurement is the process of obtaining supplies via the internet. Usually a software system is incorporated into the purchasing operations, which handles specifications, authorization and the acquisition of products and services. E-procurement can involve the customer requesting supplies to specific specifications, deliveries, price ranges and other factors, and requesting that suppliers quote to fulfil the order.

Equal opportunities

The importance of complying with equal opportunity legislation has increased dramatically in recent years. Certainly, it is imperative that human resource department employees are fully aware of all UK and European legislation, for which they should receive suitable training and updates. The control of equal opportunity spans every stage, from recruitment to the termination of employment, and no decisions can be made that are prejudicial to anyone on the basis of their race, colour, religion, gender or national origin.

E-recruitment

E-recruitment is the use of an organization's website, or an on-line recruitment agency, to attract potential employees for current vacancies. It has been estimated that in the UK alone some 6.3 million individuals use various e-recruitment agencies to seek work. In countries where internet penetration is high, it has been estimated that e-recruitment is growing at a rate of 50% per year. E-recruitment can be both proactive and reactive from the point of view of the potential employee. Many websites now offer the facility to upload CVs or résumés, which potential employers can browse to find a close match to their requirements. Alternatively, employers may post their vacancies either on their own company websites, or via an e-recruitment agency, seeking to attract potential employees and from that point institute a normal recruitment procedure.

Again, in the UK alone around 1.4 million on-line job seekers have uploaded their CVs to recruitment sites each year. The efficiency of e-recruitment has become such that many businesses now believe that on-line recruitment is more effective than placing advertisements in local or national newspapers and trade magazines, or using conventional recruitment agencies.

Ergonomics

The term 'ergonomics' relates to the study of the design of equipment and the working procedures and environment in order to promote employee well-being and organizational efficiency and effectiveness. Ergonomic design can trace its history back to the Second World War, when tank designers acknowledged the fact that a human being should be considered in the design of tanks, guns and planes. Now it is active in the use of computers and their related equipment, such as the design of tables and chairs, and screens, but ergonomics now also incorporates the human being in many of the commonly found items of equipment and machinery on the production floor, providing the user with the ability to:

- obtain a stimulus in the use of machinery – by the incorporation of instruments, flashing lights and buzzers so that the tedium is removed to a degree;

- perceive, through touch, smell, sight and sound, whether there is a problem that needs addressing;
- make a decision about what action to take if there is a problem;
- respond, by operating controls on the machinery or by communicating with others.

Ergonomics also takes into account the working environment of the employee and addresses issues such as:

- the suitability and level of lighting;
- noise levels;
- the suitability of heating and ventilation systems.

Ergonomics seeks to address both the capabilities and the limitations of the human body, aiming to reduce the cumulative impact of motions or forces which may be applied to the human frame.

Wilson, John R. and Corlett, E. Nigel (eds.), *Evaluation of Human Work: A Practical Ergonomics Methodology*. New York: Taylor & Francis, 1995.

Evaluated receipt settlement (ERS)

Evaluated receipt settlement allows a business to settle goods receipts without having received an invoice. Payment is based upon the order price specified in the purchase order and the quantity entered on the goods receipt. The system determines the current invoice amount. Evaluated receipt settlements reduce the number of steps in the standard purchasing procedure, receipt, invoice, the payment cycle, and reduce the chances of clerical errors. Several businesses have moved over to this form of transaction, which requires a log which can be printed out and sent to the vendor as an indication of settlement. ERS can only be used for goods which have been purchased using a purchase order and only purchase orders with a known exact price at the time of issue can be incorporated into the ERS system.

Expectancy theory

See **Vroom, Victor.**

External service provider (ESP)

An external service provider is an **outsourced** organization that provides actual or virtual support systems and services to a business. External service providers are one of the key growth areas in the outsourcing area of business. It has been estimated that by around 2005 approximately 40 per cent of Europe's IT and business process functions will be provided by external service providers. The value of using an ESP can mean that the services actually cost less than providing the services in-house. For many businesses concerned with cost-cutting exercises in increasingly competitive markets, this has been a prime mover towards taking on ESPs. ESPs also provide instant expertise when a business moves into a new area or recognizes the need to incorporate a particular service within its operations. Although ESPs are third-party organizations, the relationship between the business and the provider is one of mutual dependence, confidentiality and commitment.

Fayol, Henri

In 1916 Henri Fayol, a French industrialist, wrote his views and theories about the problems commonly encountered by organizations. His view was that many of the root causes of industrial failure were down to management and personnel. Fayol was a 'top–down' theorist (see Figure 16), who believed that change must begin with the board of directors or the managing director.

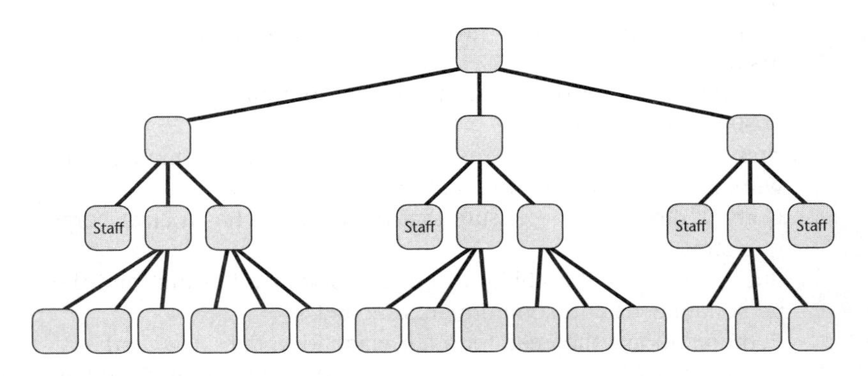

Figure 16 A top–down business hierarchy

Fayol began by identifying the three main aspects of management, which are:

- the activities of the organization;
- the elements of management;
- the principles of management.

Fayol identified the six main categories of activities of an organization as being:

- Technical activities – which include production, manufacture and adaptation.

- Commercial activities – which include buying, selling and exchanging.
- Financial activities – which include the seeking of finance and deciding the best use of that finance.
- Security services – which include the protection of the organization, its employees and its property.
- Accounting services – which include the production of balance sheets, costings, statistical data and stock inventories.
- Managerial activities – which include forecasting and planning, organization, giving instruction, coordinating and controlling employee activity.

Fayol then identified 14 elements and principles of management which were key qualities and functions:

- Division of work – ensuring that all employees know what their duties are.
- Authority – the ability to give clear, complete and unambiguous instruction.
- Discipline – to be rigid and firm when appropriate but always to ensure understanding.
- Unity of command – to ensure that all aspects of management within the organization are uniform.
- Unity of direction – to ensure that the business has a clear corporate strategy.
- Subordination – the ability to put the organization first and their personal needs and commitments second.
- Remuneration – the need for a fair wage for a fair day's work.
- Centralization – to ensure that tasks are concentrated and not duplicated in order to maintain cost effectiveness.
- Clear scalar chain – to ensure that all individuals within the organization know their position. Fayol suggested that this could be achieved through the production of an organization chart.
- Internal order – to strive to avoid internal conflict.
- Equality – to ensure equal opportunity within the organization and avoid discrimination by age, sex, sexual orientation, disability or religion.
- Stability of tenure – to ensure that employees feel their job is secure, so that they are not concerned about their own security.
- Initiative – to encourage idea creation and to accept ideas from employees, without, necessarily, enforcing senior management input.
- Esprit de corps – to encourage a company spirit where individuals are proud to support the objectives of the business.

Fayol also identified some rules which he considered management should follow. He wrote that an individual who specialized would become more skilled, efficient and effective, but also considered that the manager should have the ultimate accountability for the employees.

Boje, David and Dennehy, Robert, *Managing in the Postmodern World* (3rd edn), September 2000, at http://cbae.nmsu.edu/~dboje/mpw.html

Summary of Fayol's work at www.comp.glam.ac.uk/teaching/ismanagement/manstyles1f.htm

See also **span of control**.

Feedback loop

The feedback loop is the final part of the communication process. Feedback is essential during communications as the message itself is returned to the communication system in order to ensure that there have been no misunderstandings in the communication process.

Fiedler contingency model

Fiedler wrote on the style of leadership and the relationship between that style and particular situations. His model depends upon the leadership style being described in terms of task or relationship motivation. The form of leadership depends upon three factors:

- the relationship between the leader and the members, which is concerned with how the leader is accepted and supported by the members of the group;
- the structure of the tasks and whether they are well defined, with clear goals and procedures;
- position power, which details the leader's ability to control subordinates through punishment and reward.

Fiedler suggested that high levels of these three factors give the most favourable situation, and low levels the least favourable. Leaders who are relationship-motivated are most effective in moderately favourable situations whilst task-motivated leaders are most effective at either end of the scale. Fiedler recognized that whilst it is difficult for leaders to change their style, what they must attempt to do is to change their situation in order to achieve effectiveness.

Filter

'Filter' is a web-related term refering to a program which accepts incoming data and processes it on the basis of programmable criteria.

Once it has done this, it moves the user to the most appropriate next location. A typical example would be an on-line insurance quote, which would ask the age of the applicant and then move the applicant on to the next question which is appropriate to their age group.

Email programs also use filters, which can automatically re-route certain emails into particular folders. This filtering system is based on the sender's information. Filters can also be used to automatically delete particular emails related to certain subjects.

Firewall

A firewall is a program, or series of programs, which aim to protect a private network from users of other networks. The firewall is placed at the network gateway server and is essential for businesses that allow their employees wider internet access, as it prevents external users from accessing the business's own private data resources. It also aims to ensure that the business's own users have access only to relevant resources outside the private network.

Firewalls are often installed on a particular computer, separate from the remainder of the network, but used as the contact point between the private network and the internet in general. Firewalls allow remote access, provided the user inputs the correct log-on procedures and has the appropriate **authentication** certificate. Most firewalls offer logging and reporting systems, alarms which indicate attack, and a user interface to control the firewall.

First in, first out (FIFO)

First in, first out is used in both stock valuation and stock rotation. When FIFO is applied to stock valuation an assumption is made that the oldest stock will be consumed first, and that stock is valued at the oldest relevant price. When FIFO is applied to stock rotation it is used to ensure that the oldest stock is sold first, or consumed first, in order to make sure that the business is not left with stock which may become obsolete, or, in the case of perishable items, out of date.

See also **Last in, first out (LIFO).**

First-mover advantage

The term 'first-mover advantage' is most closely associated with the competitive edge gained by a business which is first, or early, into a new market. Whilst businesses moving into a new market face the risk of failure, since they and no other businesses have experience of that market or those modes of operation, assuming success, they have a substantial competitive edge over those who may wish to emulate them.

In internet business terms, both ebay and Amazon were keen to not only establish clear distribution, promotion and fulfilment, but they were also concerned with measures to successfully combat competitors who would seek to enter or emulate their market. In both cases these businesses have successfully used their first-mover advantage, being first into the market, and remaining the most dominant businesses.

Five Forces (SLEPT/PEST/STEEPLE)

This concept originally began with just four criteria, with the acronym PEST (Political, Economic, Social and Technological). These forces are seen as being the principal external determinants of the environment in which a business operates. In later years the four forces became five under the acronym SLEPT (Social, Legal, Economic, Political and Technological). The concept has now extended to include seven forces, using the acronym STEEPLE (Social, Technological, Economic, Educational, Political, Legal and Environmental protection).

The purpose of the Five Forces, or its variants, is to examine or audit where threats originate and where opportunities can be found. In other words, the broader STEEPLE acronym applies to the macro-environment (factors outside the organization). The main areas of interest within each letter are listed in Table 6.

Porter, Michael, *Competitive Advantage*. New York: Free Press, 1985.

Fixed budget

In many cases fixed budgets are essential for a business to be able to successfully plan its financial requirements. Normally a fixed budget is set prior to the beginning of a particular accounting period. Once the budget has been agreed and set, it is not changed as a result of other changes in activity, or changes in costs and revenues. Whilst fixed budgets are rather inflexible, they provide businesses with a means by which they can clearly estimate their financial requirements, unlike businesses that use **flexible budgets**, which change in response to unexpected occurrences or opportunities.

Fixed cost

Fixed costs incorporate all the costs attached to a manufacturing process which do not change, regardless of the volume of production.

Table 6 The Seven Forces (STEEPLE)

Letter	Description
S	Social and cultural influences, including language, culture, attitudes and behaviour, which affect future strategies and markets.
T	Technological and product innovations, which suggest how the market is developing as well as future developments in research and arising opportunities.
E (E1)	Economics and market competition, which considers factors such as the business cycle, inflation, energy costs and investments. An assessment is made as to how they will affect the level of economic activity in each market.
E (E2)	Education, training and employment – primarily the trends in these areas which may impact upon the availability of trained labour as well as the potential demands of new generations and probable expectations.
P	Political, which focuses on current and proposed policies which will impact on the business and the workforce.
L	Legal, which focuses on current and proposed legislation. Of equal importance is the business's adherence to current laws and regulations.
E (E3)	Environmental protection, which addresses the business's current and future impact on the environment, working on the basis that environmental protection will continue to be a major issue in restricting and amending the ways in which a business operates.

Typically, fixed costs can be related to overheads, such as the rent of the premises, lease payments on equipment, or other predictable costs which remain static. Fixed costs can be applied to any type of industry.

Flat structure

A flat organizational structure is a **hierarchical structure** in the sense that it is in the shape of a pyramid, but has fewer layers. Often a hierarchical structure can be de-layered in order to create a flat structure. This de-layering process often allows decisions to be made more quickly and efficiently because the layers are able to communicate more easily with one another. This enables the organization to become less bureaucratic and is a simpler structure often used by organizations operating from a single site. The directors and other major decision-makers are more available for consultation with employees, who often find that they feel more a part of the process. This encourages motivation, particularly amongst junior managers, who are likely to be given more responsibility through delegation from the senior management level of the structure.

Flexible budget

Flexible budgets can be differentiated from **fixed budgets** as they incorporate a mechanism which recognizes and responds to different cost patterns. Flexible budgets are designed to change in response to activity changes, such as increased volume or competition.

Flexible staffing

Flexible staffing aims to provide businesses with a responsive approach to the deployment of their employees. Flexible staffing implies that the business will have a small number of core employees supported by a number of available part-time workers or contract workers. Part-time workers' hours can be changed or amended in order to fit with additional pressures of work or demand, whilst contract workers can be brought in or outsourced from employment agencies. Temporary contracts can be offered to individuals for fixed periods of time and, once the immediate problem period has passed, staffing levels can then return to their normal pattern.

Focus group

A focus group is a selected collection of individuals who are consulted as specialists during the **market research** process. As experts in their field they are considered to have useful and up-to-date information which could be of value to a business. In internet terms a focus group is a collection of on-line individuals who carry out on-line market research for organizations. The research can be in the form of e-questionnaires, e-testing and mystery shopping.

Forecast

There are a number of associated terms related to forecasting, but forecasting itself is an attempt to predict the future of a variable. Businesses will attempt to forecast the demand for their products or services in order to plan both their stock and manufacturing requirements. The accuracy of a forecast very much depends upon the reliability of the data upon which the forecast has been based and, indeed, the length of time into the future which the forecast is expected to encompass. Generally a manufacturing organization will seek to forecast demand slightly in excess of its average manufacturing **lead time**. The further into the future a forecast is projected, the more chance there is of a significant error, as variables become far more unpredictable as a result of other, unknown variables having an influence upon them.

Formal group

In most organizations formal groups are designated work groups, comprising a number of individuals under a clear command, which may take the form of a section or department. Within the formal group there is a clear structure, not only of responsibility, but also of authority. Within the formal group the clear hierarchy and division of responsibility indicate to each individual their relevant position within the formal group and to whom, if any, they are ultimately responsible under most normal circumstances.

Formal network

Formal networks are task-related communication systems within an organization which follow the predominant chain of authority. Formal networks are the means by which the majority of instructions and responses to requests for information move up and down the organizational structure, passing through the various levels of authority.

Formalization

Formalization is the degree to which jobs, processes and procedures are standardized within an organization. The greater the degree of formalization, the higher the likelihood is that the organization is a hierarchical bureaucracy. Lack of formalized systems within an organization may mean that the business is more flexible and can adapt both its workforce and its processes quickly.

Franchise

A franchise is a form of business in which the franchisor enters into a business relationship with the franchisee. The franchisor grants the franchisee a licence to use their common trade name, or trademark, in return for a fee, and during the association the franchisor will render assistance to the franchisee. It is essentially a licensing system which affords the franchisor the opportunity to expand, with the capital required to enable that expansion being provided by external sources.

In the US alone franchising generates some $800bn per year and employs around 9 million people. Franchisees enjoy considerable benefits, which include:

- the ability to open a franchise business which is already a proven success;
- receipt of full training and continued support from the franchisor;
- the ability to enjoy the benefits of national advertising;
- a guarantee that the franchisor will not sell a similar business to a competitor in the immediate area.

The bulk of fastfood outlets are franchises.

Free-pricing model

The term 'free-pricing model' is generally used with reference to internet service providers. The most common model of the relationship between internet service providers and their customers offers a low-fee dial-up connection. Free-pricing models are often used by particular internet service providers in order to provide a no-cost internet access to their customers, which is offset by advertising revenue. By attracting considerable numbers of users, the system becomes attractive to advertisers, which offsets the costs to the internet service providers of internet connection and their other overhead costs.

Freezing/unfreezing

'Freezing' and 'unfreezing' are terms most closely associated with the management of change. A business which adopts this form of change management takes the decision that all necessary changes to the organization, its policies, procedures and processes, will take place at a specified point in the future. Until that time the business determines to remain operating as it currently does, without instituting any changes to take it towards its new operating principles. In other words, change during this period is frozen and the organization continues to operate in its familiar ways, without the danger of disruption from gradual change. During this period employees and management are trained to understand and run the new systems which will be put in place at the given date. Once all necessary preparations have been undertaken the business ceases trading under its current operating structure and immediately begins the unfreezing process and the institution of the new changes.

Fulfilment

Fulfilment is the process of completing a transaction with a customer. Fulfilment does not necessarily simply entail sales, as the transaction can include information requests, premiums, refunds and a variety of other interactions between the business and its customers. Fulfilment can often be **outsourced** to a separate business, which handles all transactions with the customers on behalf of the organization. This aspect is particularly true of businesses involved in **e-commerce** as many of the sales-related web businesses simply act as a means by which products and services can be offered to internet users, but without the business itself holding any stock. This process and relationship between the **e-business** and its outsourced fulfilment partners is an integral part of e-fulfilment. The partners offering the e-fulfilment cope with the warehousing, process orders and maintain a database which ensures accurate inventory and quality-control systems.

Full-time equivalent (FTE)

Part-time workers are increasingly being used by businesses in order to provide a more flexible workforce. The term 'full-time equivalent' is used when calculating the total number of part-time workers' hours as a whole and then dividing that total by the average hours of a full-time worker, in order to obtain the equivalent number of full-time employees. In other words, if the total work carried out by part-time workers is equal to 120 hours per week, and a full-time worker's hours is 30, then the full-time equivalent of all the part-time workers is 120/30 = 4.

Functional structures

A functionally based organizational structure is designed around specific sections of the organization, usually those that produce, market and sell the organization's product or service. Functional structures can be a sub-structure of **hierarchical** or **flat structures** and similarly will be controlled by a managing director, supported by relevant senior function or departmental managers. The creation of positions and departments around specialized functions is an integral part of the functional structure. There will be common themes, in terms of function or process within each department, enabling management to concentrate on specific issues within their own technical area of expertise. This form of organizational structure has a number of advantages and disadvantages over other types of structure, as shown in Table 7.

Table 7 An evaluation of functional structures

Advantages	**Possible disadvantages**
Promotes skills specialization and reduces duplication of resources.	These organizational structures tend to limit the organization to having a relatively short-term horizon.
There is a clearer career progression route.	Managers of each department could become parochial, thus limiting career advancement.
There are clearer lines of communication which could lead to higher productivity and performance within the department.	There is a chance of restricted communication between departments.
	If one department does not reach expectations, this has a knock-on effect on other departments.

Sutherland, Jon and Canwell, Diane, *Organisation Structures and Processes*. London: Pitman Publishing, 1997.

F

Gaap

'Gaap' is an acronym which means 'generally accepted accounting procedure'. Its use implies that the business uses standardized accounting methodologies, including the relevant checks and balances.

Gantt chart

The Gantt chart was developed as a production control tool by Henry L. Gantt in 1917. Gantt was a US engineer and social scientist and developed this type of horizontal bar chart, which is now commonly used to illustrate many different types of schedule.

Gantt charts are also used in project management. They provide a graphical illustration of a schedule, which assists the planning, coordination and tracking of each task within an overall project. Gantt charts can be simplistic horizontal bar charts, drawn on graph paper, or, as is more common, can be created using proprietary software, such as Microsoft Project or Excel.

Gap analysis

'Gap analysis' is both a general management and strategy term as well as having its applications in marketing.

Gap analysis attempts to identify what is known as the performance gap. It does this by comparing current objectives, which have been defined in the corporate goals, against forecasts (particularly of sales) which will arise from existing strategies. Businesses often encounter performance gaps when they switch their objectives, or when environmental conditions change, as well as through the relative success or failure of competitors.

It is standard practice to illustrate gap analysis in terms of a graph. This measures sales against time. Both the existing strategies and the new strategies are plotted and the difference between the two highlights the performance gap.

General ledger

The general ledger is at the core of a business's financial records. They are sometimes referred to as the 'central books' as every transaction is detailed in the general ledger. They remain as a permanent record of the history of all financial transactions carried out. Most accounting systems will have a series of sub-ledgers and the entries in these sub-ledgers will be placed on the general ledger account. Some items are not put onto sub-ledgers, such as capital contributions, loans, loan repayments and proceeds from the sales of assets; these are linked to the balance sheet. The general ledger provides the information which assists the business in creating its balance sheet and its profit and loss statement.

General meeting

The term 'general meeting' usually refers to meetings of equity shareholders of a business, either at an Annual General Meeting (AGM) or at an Extraordinary General Meeting (EGM). Public companies are required to hold an AGM where shareholders have the opportunity to listen to and question officers of the business and to vote on issues which may affect the running of the business and its profitability.

There are, of course, several other different forms of general meeting. Formal meetings take place and are governed by the constitution of the organization. The rules determine the procedures for formal meetings and include board meetings and statutory meetings. General meetings have a number of associated forms of documentation which begin with the Notice of Meeting, which alerts relevant parties to the fact that a meeting has been called on a specific date. This allows those who are invited to the meeting to present Agenda items and documentation for consideration by the meeting. Once these communications have been processed, a formal Agenda will be drawn up, incorporating any communications which have been received by those who intend to be present. Typically the meeting will also include reports from relevant officers of the business, such as the Finance Director and the Managing Director, who will present and deliver a summary of activities up to the date of the meeting.

Information papers will have been circulated to those who intend to attend so that they are fully apprised of any issues which will be presented or discussed at the meeting. An individual taking the role of the Minutes Secretary will make concise and precise notes regarding what was discussed and any decisions that were made during the meeting. These Minutes of the Meeting will be ratified as a true account of the meeting at a subsequent meeting.

Gesellschaft des bürgerlichen rechts (Germany)

This is the German equivalent of a partnership, which is mainly used for non-commercial purposes. Partners have full liability as owners of this form of organization.

Gesellschaft mit beschränkter Haftung (Germany)

This form of German company translates literally to 'company with limited liability'. It is often shortened to GmbH, which means that the company is incorporated, but not publicly traded. GmbHs are partnerships – in effect, requiring that there be at least two partners.

Goal congruence

Goal congruence occurs when the objectives of two stakeholders in an organization have been met. In other words, the goals or objectives of those two stakeholders, such as the management and the shareholders, have both been reached through the joint or several actions of the two parties.

Going concern

The term 'going concern' implies that a given business will continue to operate for the foreseeable future. The inference is that the business is sufficiently established to be able to justifiably claim that it will, under normal circumstances, still be operating for a considerable period of time. Normally the board of directors of a business will make a statement that the business remains a going concern for the next financial period.

The term 'going concern' is also used as a description of a business which may be for sale to a third party. Again the inference is that rather than simply buying the stock or premises of the business, the third party is actually buying a successful and ongoing business which is a going concern. Clearly the value of a going concern is in excess of the total assets of that business and is sometimes referred to as **goodwill**.

Gomei kaisha

This is a Japanese form of business which is the rough equivalent of a partnership, with unlimited liability.

Goodwill

'Goodwill' is a term which is often included on a balance sheet, or listed as an asset, in the event of an organization being sold. Goodwill suggests not only that the business is a **going concern**, but also that there is an additional premium in terms of its value compared with the business's existing and identifiable assets and liabilities. Goodwill therefore implies that not only is the business a going concern, but the potential purchaser is buying the work which has gone into building up the business over a number of years and will have access to and will enjoy the benefit of the business's existing customers.

Goshi kaisha

This is the Japanese equivalent of a partnership with limited liability.

Grievance procedures

Frustration and change can often result in a grievance from an employee against the organization. Often this can be as a result of a misunderstanding or lack of appropriate communication. Usually these simple day-to-day grievances are dealt with by supervisors and line managers, but on occasion they require further intervention.

A well-constructed and well laid out grievance procedure will enable the human resource management to resolve grievances quickly, without the need for further intervention or industrial action. A formal grievance procedure is a set of agreed rules that have been drawn up to provide strict guidelines as to how grievances are dealt with. Organizations have found that it is in their own interests to have formal grievance procedures established, particularly in cases where legal intervention has been necessary; this is primarily due to the fact that an employer has to be seen to be attempting fairness. A formal grievance procedure would include the following:

- An attempt to ensure that both parties involved in the issue are impartial and behave responsibly.
- Measures to ensure that both parties understand the process and progress of the procedure.
- Written procedures to allow the consistency needed to be applied even when **trade union** or employee representatives, or senior managers from within the organization, have been replaced by new individuals.
- Clarification of the authority for decision making.

- A clear timescale for registering a grievance.
- The opportunity, and deadline involved, for lodging an appeal.
- A formal procedure allowing the content of the hearing to be minuted, which allows for comparison in future disputes.
- Measures to increase employee security and peace of mind.

Gross profit

'Gross profit' is an accountancy term for a calculation of the profitability of a business. The calculation is made by establishing the total turnover of the business, less the cost of sales. Gross profit does not take into account other expenses, such as the purchase of products, any holding costs, taxes or other overheads which can be attributed to the products or services sold. It is a measure of the total business performed by the organization over a given period of time.

Group demography

'Group demography' is a term applied to the study of the component parts of a business's workforce. Group demography looks at factors such as age, race, gender, educational level and length of service and tries to identify members of groups which share common demographic attributes. The identified groups are then compared in terms of their impact on the operations of the organization, particularly the effect on the **turnover**.

Group think

The term 'group think' was coined by Irving Janis, who related the term to a phenomenon within groups. Janis considered that group think occurs when a group of individuals are so determined to make a decision that they ignore all major considerations and alternatives, as well as any disagreements within the group, in order to achieve this. Groups suffering from group think are often thought to be over-cautious and to lack necessary creativeness. They bond with each other and the individuals see themselves as secure because they belong to the group. The group members have little doubt about the effectiveness or vulnerability of the group and consider the views of anyone not involved within the group to be those of insignificant outsiders. According to Janis the symptoms of group think are:

- Invulnerability, in that they consider they cannot be touched.

- Inappropriate rationale, in that they consider things are unlikely to happen to them.
- Morality, in that they think they know what is best.
- Stereotyping other groups by considering them all to be less effective than their own group.
- Pressurizing other groups.
- Exerting an element of self-censorship by not communicating all, but selecting what they consider to be appropriate, information to other groups or relevant individuals.
- Unanimity, by assuming a consensus when individuals do not speak.
- Mind-guards – referring to the fact that they do not allow any other thoughts to contradict what they have already decided.

Suffering from group think can make groups ineffective. Janis considered that management would have to encourage the individuals within the group to:

- consider and examine all alternatives;
- feel able to express their own doubts within the group;
- listen to criticisms from outside the group;
- challenge those who have firmly held beliefs;
- actively seek feedback, advice and information from outside the group;
- create subdivisions within the group;
- avoid grapevine communication.

Group think can lead to ineffective decision making through insufficient attention to alternatives and risks.

Guarantor

A guarantor is an individual or an organization which guarantees the repayment of a loan should the borrower default or be otherwise unable to pay back the loan.

Guerrilla marketing

Essentially, guerrilla marketing techniques are unconventional marketing activities that are designed for maximum impact with the use of scarce resources.

Jay Conrad Levinson is considered to be one of the originators of the concept, having written *Guerrilla Marketing* (1984). He states that:

The need for guerrilla marketing can be seen in the light of three facts:

1 Because of big business downsizing, decentralization, relaxation of government regulations, affordable technology, and a revolution in consciousness, people around the world are gravitating to small business in record numbers.
2 Small business failures are also establishing record numbers and one of the main reasons for the failures is a failure to understand marketing.
3 Guerrilla marketing has been proven in action to work for small businesses around the world. It works because it's simple to understand, easy to implement and outrageously inexpensive.

An ideal example of guerrilla marketing was carried out by Best Offer.com who received excellent free media coverage as a result of their unconventional marketing activities. When they launched in San Francisco, they promoted a 'Painfree Parking Day' and gave away free parking, and when they launched in Los Angeles they had a 'Painfree Commuting Day' and gave away 20,000 gallons of petrol (gas). As a result of their activities they were able to generate over forty-five minutes of free television news coverage.

Levinson's site is www.gmarketing.com

Hacker

In the past, the term 'hacker' was a positive description of a programmer who was used to create solutions to programming problems. The term's current usage, however, is far more negative as it describes programmers who use their abilities to break into computer networks, perhaps with the intention of destroying or disrupting the service provided.

Health and safety

Health and safety is primarily concerned with the well-being of employees. In most large organizations all health and safety issues are coordinated by a particular individual who is concerned with the maintenance of a safe working environment and safe working practices. Businesses are required by law to ensure that their employees' health does not suffer detriments as the result of their work. Various statistics are collected, primarily detailing fatal injuries, major injuries and other injuries. There is a continued concern that accidents at work are under-reported by employers.

The Health and Safety Commission estimates that there are at least 80,000 new cases of work-related disease occurring each year and that half a million people suffer from continuing damage to health at work. The principal legislation in Britain is the Health and Safety at Work Act (1974), requiring, as far as is practicable, that employers ensure the health, safety and welfare of those who work for them. Britain's national legislation has been modified in recent years to incorporate European Directives on health and safety. The initial framework directive led to the Management of Health and Safety at Work Regulations (1992), which detailed more specific duties for employers, requiring them to carry out risk assessment, appoint competent individuals to develop preventative measures, and ensure that employees and others have sufficient information.

The Health and Safety Executive is a public agency responsible for the inspection and the enforcement of health and safety legislation. Its powers include the issuing of improvement notices and prohibition notices. The inspectors may initiate criminal proceedings if the regulations are continually flouted.

Hierarchical structure

A hierarchical organization structure is best imagined by use of an image of a pyramid. At the top are the major decision-makers, who are few in number, and further down the pyramid the shape of the organization broadens as more employees become involved at the lower levels. At the base of the pyramid are the majority of the workers.

Power, responsibility and authority are concentrated at the top of the pyramid and decisions flow downwards from the upper layers. An organization would choose this form of structure when decisions need to be made by those who have expertise and experience, together with the authority to ensure that decisions are implemented.

The most common version of this form of structure is the steep pyramid, where there are many different layers of management, possibly within an organization that operates in several different locations, needing to fulfil different administrative functions. Equally, organizations of a complex nature may choose this structure.

There are some disadvantages to those lower down the hierarchical structure in that if the pyramid is too multi-layered and complex, they often find difficulty in understanding how and why decisions are made. The organization may also find itself too bureaucratic in nature and the result could be that the decision-making process becomes too complicated and time-consuming because there are too many layers involved.

See also **chain of command.**

Home networking

Home networking is the inevitable extension of the increasing trends which businesses show in employing workers in remote locations. Theoretically, the system allows multiple users to connect to the internet using a single account. The most common forms of home networking are, however, in single-site businesses where, once again, multiple users can use the same account to connect to the internet, but importantly share peripherals, such as printers.

Horizontal integration

Horizontal integration occurs when a business establishes new markets for its existing products or introduces new products into its current market. The business is not necessarily doing anything particularly new, but is playing to its strengths in order to achieve **economies of scale** or scope.

The term is also used to describe the purchase of a business which broadly operates in the same area of industry. Specifically it would refer to a retailer purchasing a competitor retailer, or a manufacturer purchasing another manufacturing firm. This is a more common form of takeover or merger, or **acquisition**, as the business is still effectively operating at the same level in the distribution chain. If a retailer was to purchase a manufacturer, then this would be known as **vertical integration**, as they have moved up or down the distribution chain.

Human capital management (HCM)

Human capital management is an embedded strategy to manage the performance of employees, recognizing that they are the key to a competitive advantage, rather than the utilization of physical assets. HCM identifies and facilitates the needs and aspirations of individual employees and then delivers a tailor-made benefits package in terms of training, compensation and working arrangements. This aims to ensure that key members of staff are retained and motivated.

Mello, Jeffrey A., *Strategic Human Resource Management*. Mason, OH: South Western College Publishing, 2001.

Human resource management system (HRMS)

A fully integrated human resource management system is, in effect, a suite of applications which aims to cover all aspects of human resources. At its heart is a flexible database which maintains full details and history regarding each employee. Reports and letters can be written from the database, set against a human resource diary, with training updates, performance appraisals and other routine human resource issues. The HR database is usually integrated with a payroll calculator, which also features the range of benefits, holiday entitlements, bonus payments and other human resource calculations.

Idle time

'Idle time' is a term used to describe the time between periods of work, usually at a **work station** while the operator or employee reconfigures the machinery for the next job. Technically the work station is available for production, but it is not being used. This may be because the work station is not ready to accept new work as it needs to be reconfigured, or there may be a shortage of materials, or, indeed, the work station may lack an operator.

Inc. (US)

See **certificate of incorporation.**

Incentives

The term 'inducement' covers pay, benefits and other intangible incentives which are part of an overall package offered by an organization in order to attract potential employees. The inducements represent the total benefits or compensations which the employee would expect to receive as a result of accepting a job offer from a particular organization.

The term 'fringe benefit' refers to any incentive given to employees as a reward in addition to their wage or salary. Fringe benefits can include:

- a company pension scheme;
- employee sick pay schemes;
- subsidized meals;
- company products or services at a discounted price;
- company cars;
- private medical health insurance;
- counselling or mentoring services;
- occupational health screening;
- social and recreational facilities;
- legal and financial service support.

Fringe benefits are not necessarily related to merit, but often increase with the employee's status and length of service. They do not necessarily benefit all employees but are established and monitored after the initial analysis process. Once they are established, however, it is difficult for the organization to remove them as this could affect employee retention. Fringe benefits are considered important because they improve job satisfaction provided they are consistently and fairly administered.

Incubator

An incubator is an office facility for a new business which has a clear direction and sufficient capital to begin its operations, but not enough to make a significant impact upon the market, due to lack of finances. Increasingly, office facilities for these new businesses are shared so that administrative support, equipment, telephones and advice can all be used. Some of the most successful incubators are funded by venture capital organizations and are used to test the business and iron out potential difficulties which may arise. In this way the venture capital organization can make a more informed decision as to which businesses within the office facility are most likely to succeed once they are fully rolled out into the market.

Independent variable

An independent variable is a variable whose value is not affected by any other variable. The independent variable is important in the sense that it may well have an impact upon one of the other key variables. The most common independent variable used when plotting potential effects upon a project or a product is time. Independent variables are usually shown on the horizontal axis of a graph or chart.

Index-linked

The term 'index-linked' refers to changes in a value as a result of changes in the retail price index (RPI). In Britain the RPI is the standard measure of inflation, and index-linking has been used in the past to determine wage increases. It was considered prudent that wage increases were index-linked in order to ensure that wages did not rise above the current rate of inflation. In practice, however, index-linking proved not to work as wages increased in line with inflation, which left real incomes effectively unchanged, but, at the same time, industry costs were increased, triggering a rise in the price of products and services.

This was then picked up in the next RPI, which triggered another wage rise, and so the spiral continued. Index-linking was thus seen as not a solution to combating inflation, but very much a cause of it.

None the less, in Britain and several other countries pensions still remain index-linked, in order to maintain the buying power of the retired.

Indirect costs

Indirect costs are costs which cannot be directly attributed to a specific product line or indeed a particular **cost centre**. Usually they are **fixed costs**, such as general maintenance in an office or a factory. Using absorption costing, indirect costs are nevertheless allocated to product lines of cost centres.

See also **direct costs**.

Indirect hours

Indirect hours are time which has been worked by **indirect labour** and the time spent by direct labour on indirect activities, which include cleaning or training. A business needs to be aware of the cost of these indirect hours, how they may collectively impact upon the overall costs of a given product or project and whether there are any means by which these **indirect costs** can be reduced in order to achieve greater profitability.

Indirect labour

The term 'indirect labour' encompasses all employees whose work aims to support those directly involved in the production process. Indirect labour would therefore include warehousing staff, inspection, maintenance, machine setup and product testing. The normal rule of thumb is that the level of indirect labour should not exceed those involved in direct labour activities, and that wherever possible indirect labour tasks become part of the overall function of workers directly employed on the production process. This is usually achieved by **job enlargement**.

Industrial action

Industrial action is often the result of lack of agreement in **dispute resolution**. Industrial action can take a number of different forms, all of which will have been the centre of discussions between **trade union** members, their representative and the management of the organization. If, after a series of negotiations, there is no resolution to the issue, then trade union representatives have the following options to present to their members:

- To withdraw cooperation with management by ending negotiation and assistance in future dispute resolution and the compilation of agreements until the industrial action issue has been resolved.
- To insist on formal rights – this means that the trade union representative would bring to the attention of management every issue that arises, however trivial. Normally such trivial incidents would have been dealt with in a less formal manner.
- To withdraw willingness to work overtime – this means that employees would not be prepared to work additional hours to those stipulated as their normal working hours. This form of industrial action can have serious implications for an organization that relies on employee cooperation to meet production output targets.
- To work a 'go-slow' – this means that employees will continue to adhere to the requirements of their contract of employment, but will not carry out any additional duties, nor respond to urgent requirements or rush jobs as they may emerge.
- To withdraw labour – in effect this is strike action, when either a trade union calls for an *unofficial strike*, which could be for short periods of time until the dispute is finally resolved, or in some cases, an *official strike* is called, usually when the dispute has remained unresolved for a length of time or a collective agreement is thought to have been broken by the employer.

Industrial relations

The term 'industrial relations' has largely negative connotations since it is often preceded by the words 'poor' or 'bad'. As a general term, industrial relations refers to the ongoing dialogue or relationship between employers and employees, which may, or may not, involve aspects of collective bargaining, discussions regarding working conditions, rewards, job structures and a variety of other human resource topics. Industrial relations also implies an underlying conflict between those who own and control industry and those who provide the labour in order to fuel it. In most countries industrial relations have had periods during which the relationship between employers and employees (largely represented by **trade unions**) has been extremely poor, confrontational and irreconcilable, on the basis that their objectives are mutually exclusive.

The term 'industrial relations' is also interchangeable in many respects with the term 'labour relations', which again refers to the ongoing attitudes of employers and employees towards one another and their ability or willingness to cooperate on various matters. There is an underlying suspicion for both parties that decisions and stances are taken without regard to the other's desires.

Infomediary

This term was originally coined by John Hagel and Marc Singer in their book *Net Worth*, published in 1999. They describe an infomediary as being an information and intermediary on-line middleman. The infomediary operates between the seller and the consumer, receiving income from the seller in exchange for internet data. Typically an infomediary is a website which facilitates business-to-business **e-commerce**. It operates as a one-stop shop, with information about various suppliers and businesses, allowing the potential customer to make an informed choice before placing an order.

Hagel, III, John and Singer, Marc, *Net Worth*. Boston, MA: Harvard Business School Press, 1999.

Informal group

An informal group is a number of employees who operate in an unstructured manner in order to carry out their tasks at work. Informal groups are typified by a lack of formal organizational structure, where the relationships are based on mutual dependence and support. In informal groups there is no necessary or recognized hierarchy and the scope of work and interaction between the members of the group is dependent upon their need for one another and the level of work involved.

Informal network

An informal network is, in effect, the communication grapevine in an organization. Grapevine communication is an informal method of communication which allows the passing on of messages to be one of the speediest forms of communication. Often considered to be gossip and rumour, grapevine communication can be extremely unreliable. Snippets of information get passed from one individual, or group of individuals, to another and the message can become extremely distorted. Grapevine communication is not a method to be encouraged by managers, who should attempt to inform employees of the subject of the communication in a more formal way, stating facts rather than part-truths. A high degree of grapevine communication within an organization, if it is not adequately dealt with by management, can lead to low morale. Although this method of communication is quite natural and prevalent in all organizations, it should be tackled in a suitable manner so that employees hear the message from the appropriate level and through the appropriate channels.

Initial public offering (IPO)

An initial public offering, or IPO, is the sale of equity in a business, generally in the form of sales through an investment bank. IPOs are usually ideal for both start-up and established businesses. In the former case the business will have to demonstrate its potential to deliver profits and that it will enjoy increases in sales and earnings over a given period. An initial public offering implies that up until this point the business was not offering its shares on the stock market, but has now decided, in order to expand or provide funds for a specific project, that for the first time shares will be available for investment. Normally an initial public offering is a relatively expensive way of attracting finance as, working through an investment bank, fees can be as high as 20 per cent. In the US alone over 1,000 companies have IPOs each year; they are largely comprised of businesses which need to raise at least $5m. The IPO is ideal when permanent capital is required which does not take the form of a loan.

The business needs to find an investment bank which will effectively underwrite the offering and this is why the fees are as high as they are, as the investment bank is effectively guaranteeing that the share on offer will be sold and that the funds will consequently become available.

Insolvency jurisdiction

The term 'insolvency jurisdiction' refers to the power of a particular court to make a **winding up** order in respect of a business.

Institutional investor

An institutional investor, such as a pension fund, insurance or life assurance company, an investment trust or similar organization, makes fund investments on behalf of its savers, depositors or clients. Institutional investors look for both long- and short-term investment opportunities in businesses and, as such, are one of the main investors in shares in most leading stock markets around the world.

Instrument of transfer

'Instrument of transfer' is an alternative term used to describe a stock or share transfer form.

Integrated services digital network (ISDN)

ISDN is an alternative means by which a communication network can be established using a standard telephone line. ISDN requires equipment to be set up at either end of the connection, and when it was brought into operation standard modems could only transfer 14.4 kbps against the ISDN's impressive 128 kbps. Unfortunately, ISDN was largely ineffective and failed to dominate the market because of poor customer services and high telephone and equipment costs. ISDN has been largely replaced with DSL (digital subscriber line) or Broadband connections but, in areas where Broadband connection is not available, ISDN remains the only high-speed access option.

Interactive marketing

This is a relatively new branch of marketing, enabled by advertising media such as the internet or CD-Roms. The purpose of interactive marketing is to allow consumers to interact with the source of the message. Consumers are encouraged to actively seek information and respond to questions, thus allowing the business to send specifically targeted messages back to the consumer.

Sargeant, Adrian and West, Douglas C., *Direct and Interactive Marketing*. Oxford: Oxford University Press, 2001.

Inter-group development

'Inter-group development' is a term most closely associated with organizational dynamics, as it seeks to amend the ways in which different groups within an organization perceive one another. The process involves looking at the actual attributes, stereotypes and perceptions of each group and then comparing them with how those groups are viewed by other groups. At the end of the process it is intended that the perceptions of each group are radically changed and that there is a far greater degree of understanding between each of the groups involved in the exercise. Ultimately, of course, the intention is to make various groups within the organization more cohesive and to allow a higher degree of coordination between those groups.

Internal development

Internal development is often a viable alternative to potentially more expensive and disruptive developmental needs. On the one hand a business may acquire new skills simply by employing additional expertise from outside the organization. Equally it may turn to a **consultant** to advise it on how to develop its business. Internal development rests very clearly on the in-house provision of education and training, together with encouragement to bring forward ideas. Critics of this form of development suggest that it is neither cost-effective nor valuable, in the sense that the business is operating within a relatively small pool of expertise which, in some cases, may be a sterile atmosphere. They will also not be able to compare their internal development progress as clearly as would be achieved if new blood or external ideas were incorporated. Internal development requires a sophisticated analysis of process and employee status and an identification of deficiencies in any area of the business. Once these deficiencies have been identified, then internally the business can deploy its resources in order to deal with these potential shortfalls.

Internet business services (IBS)

The concept behind IBS is that it gives smaller businesses inexpensive access to many forms of sophisticated enterprise software, including purchasing, **customer relationship management**, recruitment and retention, project management, travel and expense reporting and other applications. It is internet-based and provided by a number of organizations which describe themselves as business solution services. The key function and purpose of the IBS is to allow automation, integration and control of a business's main processes. The IBS providers have a centralized database and series of preloaded applications resident on their server in order to support the needs of their client businesses and individual users.

Internet message access protocol (IMAP)

This **email** tool was originally created at Stanford University in 1986 and allows email recipients to search for key words amongst received email while those emails are still on the mail server. Having searched the emails for appropriate key words within the messages they can then choose to download those messages to their own computers.

Internet protocol (IP)

The internet comprises of a vast network of other networks. Internet protocol is the technical specification and rules which ultimately enable those networks to exchange data. Internet protocol defines how data can be sent, which route it uses and how it arrives at the intended destination.

Internet service provider (ISP)

In order for a business or an individual user to connect with the internet, they require an internet service provider. Some ISPs charge per minute for internet access, whilst others offer a flat monthly fee, regardless of the level of use. ISPs also provide **email** facilities and website building and hosting. Many ISPs are now global concerns, such as AOL, whilst others are country specific or even regional. All, however, offer their customers the facilities to connect with the internet and therefore to any website or email facility in the world.

Internet telephony

Theoretically, internet telephony offers a viable and perhaps cheaper alternative to conventional telephone communication. Technology now exists for users to add a telephone capability to their personal computer and therefore make international or long distance calls while on-line. The telephony board, which is inserted into the computer, has multiple functionality as it incorporates a traditional modem, a sound card, a speaker phone and voice mail. It is therefore possible for users to transmit faxes or communicate by voice. Internet telephony should also allow customers to talk to sales people while viewing products on-line and to be able to have a real-time conversation with customer service departments of a business.

Interoperability

'Interoperability' is an internet-related term which refers to various systems conforming to interface standards. By ensuring that the various different products conform to these standards, they should, in theory, be enabled to work together without technical problems. There are standards for the internet which include html (hypertext markup language), http (hypertext transfer protocol) and tc/ip (transmission control protocol/internet protocol). Provided the websites conform to the necessary interface standards there should be no difficulty in users being able to automatically access specific facilities.

Intranet

An intranet is a private and enclosed network which uses internet tools. The resources contained on the intranet are physically protected from external contact by either a **firewall** or literally an unconnected physical network. Intranets can also be defined as a geographically limited network of computers, usually in a single building. Intranets do have access to the internet in general, but are usually protected from access from the internet and may have restrictions on what can and cannot be viewed or downloaded.

The key benefits of an intranet are the following:

- Employees can get accustomed to the same kind of approaches and working practices as they would encounter if they were dealing with external groups.
- All employees have access to a wide range of applications.
- Employees can be more flexible and mobile since applications and information are readily shared on the intranet.

The key disadvantages are:

- Performance limitations, in as much as employees will not have access to enhanced internet technologies.
- Presentational limitations, in the sense that information is far more attractive in web-page format, rather than standard printed equivalents.

Intrapreneur

The term 'intrapreneur' was originally coined in the early 1980s and literally means an entrepreneur within an organization. The term is used to describe an individual with responsibility for developing new enterprises within the organization itself. Unlike standard start-up businesses, any new enterprise can enjoy the protection and financial benefits of the existing organization and usually has a far better opportunity to succeed.

Inventory

'Inventory' is another term for stock and is the preferred term used in the US. In essence, an inventory is the sum of all finished goods, raw materials and **work in progress** held by a business. Typically a business will count its inventory at the end of a financial year in order to confirm that these figures are broadly in accord with what it expects to own.

There are a number of ancillary uses of the word 'inventory', which include the following:

- *Anticipatory inventory* – which refers to stock held by a business in anticipation of a later increase in demand. This usually only occurs when the costs of storage are less than the costs of changing production levels.
- *Buffer inventory* – this is a level of stock which is held to protect the business against variations in supply, demand and **lead times**. It is in effect, a stock safety margin.
- *Cycle inventory* – which seeks to minimize inventory and the costs of setting up production by minimizing these costs using **just-in-time (JIT)** techniques.
- *Pipeline inventory* – which is stock items that are at various stages in the production process or the business's system. In themselves, although they have a monetary value, they have already been earmarked for particular projects or production processes.
- *Uncoupling inventory* – these are stock items which are currently in transit from one machine to another, or perhaps from a manufacturer or raw material supplier to the manufacturer or customer.

Investor relations (IR)

Investor relations can be either a function or a separate department within an organization which is publicly traded, and which operates as an intermediary between the business and investors and the general financial community. The investor relation function deals with all of the communications between the business and its shareholders, market analysts, the media and potential investors. This is achieved by disclosing information, preparing reports (both annual and quarterly), taking responsibility for organizing annual shareholder meetings, and cooperating with the business's public relations department. Collectively, investor relations and public relations will seek opportunities to show the business in the most positive light in order to attract interest in the business and, hopefully, additional investors.

Invoice or bill presentation

Invoice or bill presentation is the stage at which the supplying business requests payment under its normal trading terms from the business or customer it supplies.

IP address

An IP address is the specific identifier for a computer or device on the TC/IP (transmission control protocol/internet protocol) network. Without an IP address it would be impossible to route messages. The IP address has two distinct elements. The first identifies a particular network on the internet and then the second element identifies a particular device on that network. Businesses request a network number from the Network Information Centre (NIC) and then each individual device on that business's network is assigned an identifier.

ISO 9000

This is a certification standard which was created by the International Organization for Standardizations (1987). ISO 9000 plays a major part in establishing the documentation standards for global manufacturers. The standards are recognized in many countries around the world and the ISO standards can be summarized as being an externally driven methodology which aims to persuade organizations to 'document what you do – and do what you document'.

As far as many countries are concerned, the ISO standards are only seen as a way of barring them from markets (notably Europe), whilst others see the system as being a **benchmarking** process by which overseas businesses can aspire to match the best standards of the leading European and North American organizations.

The latest versions of the ISO 9000 very much focus on ongoing improvements rather than striving for a specified goal and then remaining there.

ISO 14001

ISO 14001 is a certification standard created by the International Organization for Standardizations and related to environmental impacts of business. The standards require organizations to have an environmental management system as a driver to formulate a policy (and objectives) on their environmental impacts. The standards also require the organization to take into account any relevant legislative requirements derived from countries and/or areas in which the organization operates. The certification is reliant on the organization effectively controlling the environmental aspects over which it can reasonably be expected to have a degree of control.

Job costing

The term 'job costing' refers to the process of identifying a specific cost unit and then identifying the costs attributed to that cost unit. This process is imperative as it is the basis upon which a business sets its selling price, whilst ensuring that costs incurred on that job are kept within a fixed price band. It is also useful in identifying labour or machine time. Job costing requires a cost record for each individual job, incorporating time analysis and material-usage records. Whilst it is difficult to incorporate individual job accounts into financial books, a separate job cost ledger is usually kept, which is then reconciled with the financial books. Many businesses now use an integrated system, which is a responsibility of the production control department. It deals with five key issues:

- It accounts for the costs of materials and **direct labour** and how these are charged to the job account.
- The job account is also debited with its share of the factory overheads, usually based on the absorption rates.
- The job account is also charged with other overheads, including administration, cost of sales and distribution.
- A calculation is made to compare any agreed selling price with the total actual cost of the job and this is expressed as either a profit or a loss.
- Finally, the costing procedure also requires a statement of how scrap will be treated and to whom it will be debited.

Job description

The main purpose of a job description is to define the job role and the intended tasks to be carried out within that role. It is vital to the success of the selection process of recruitment that the job description is exact in its nature, both for the benefit of the organization and for the new employee. Typically, a job description would include the following:

- the title of the job;
- the location at which the work is to be carried out – this might be a branch of the organization or the department or section within which the new employee will be based;
- the title of the new employee's immediate line manager;
- the grade of the job;
- the job titles of any subordinates of the new employee;
- the purpose of the job;
- the tasks to be carried out within the job role;
- details of any equipment, machinery or other job- or skill-specific information;
- details of any travel that may have to be undertaken as part of the job role;
- details of any additional work requirements, such as overtime, weekend work, shift work or dangerous working conditions.

Job design

The implementation of a system of job design can assist an organization in increasing employee **motivation**. An organization that carries out job analysis during the process of job design aims to improve its employees' **job satisfaction** and ultimately their performance. Job design does not, however, simply involve motivation, but has the added determining factors which may restrict or limit the job. These are:

- technology;
- the cost of providing essential equipment or materials;
- resistance from current employees or their representatives;
- the organizational structure of the business.

If a job has significantly changed, then an organization might choose to amend the job by using **job enrichment**, **job enlargement** or **job rotation** and accordingly amend the employees' **job descriptions**, rather than go through the costly and time-consuming process of a new job design.

Wall, Toby and Parker, Sharon, *Job and Work Design: Organizing Work to Promote Well-Being and Effectiveness*. London: Sage Publications, 1998.

J

Job enlargement

As an alternative to designing a new job, an organization might decide to redesign the parameters of an existing job to incorporate additional required tasks. Job enlargement involves an employee having to expand into carrying out additional but similar activities. Although it is often hoped that this enlargement of tasks will lead to a higher level of **job satisfaction** and **motivation**, it has to be remembered that once the enlarged job has been orientated, then there is a risk that this job, too, will become boring. An organization would need to ensure that this job enlargement process does not simply incorporate into a tedious job yet another set of equally tedious tasks. However, it has been concluded that the job enlargement process does give employees a greater degree of job satisfaction and that their performance improves as a result of the process as compared with those who remain in restricted job roles. From an organizational point of view, however, the job enlargement process can be a costly exercise, with few guaranteed benefits.

Job enrichment

Job enrichment is, effectively, another form of **job enlargement**, but one in which the employee often finds a higher degree of **job satisfaction** and **motivation**. The closest type of job enrichment to job enlargement is known as 'horizontal job enrichment', which involves the incorporation of similar tasks into the job for the employee. This has proved not to be as satisfactory as the more successful form of job enrichment, known as 'vertical job enrichment'.

Vertical job enrichment involves an individual employee being given the opportunity to see the task in hand through to its completion. This allows the employee to become involved in related, but not necessarily similar, tasks, allowing a higher degree of motivation. Research has identified that this type of job enrichment has both short-term and longer-term effects. After approximately three months the employee's performance levels have been shown to decrease, possibly as a result of the difficulties they have been facing in taking on board the added considerations in their enriched role. However, after approximately six months these employees show an improvement in their original performance levels, possibly because they have had the time to develop confidence in what they are doing.

Peters, Tom, *Projects 50: Or, 50 Ways to Transform Every 'Task' into a Project that Matters.* New York: Alfred A. Knopf, 1999.

Savall, Henri, *Work and People: An Economic Evaluation of Job-enrichment.* Oxford: Oxford University Press, 1981.

J

Job evaluation

An organization can undertake a process of job evaluation in a number of different ways, the three most common being:

- by ranking the different jobs in order so that the value of each job can be identified;
- by grading the job from the **job specification** point of view;
- by giving each job a points rating, again from the job specification point of view.

The considerations of each of these job evaluation methods are given in Table 8.

Table 8 Job evaluation methods

Job evaluation method	Considerations
Ranking	A committee will often be established to rank different jobs according to their worth to the organization. This is an inexpensive and speedy process for smaller organizations to use, provided they have a sensible pay structure in place. Larger organizations may have difficulties using this method as experience has proved that issues regarding pay inequality have been the outcome.
Grading	Normally this process is taken from the job descriptions, with the job requiring the lowest degree of skills or the highest level of supervision being the starting point. Jobs are then graded from this starting point according to the skills, knowledge and responsibility involved. This is a straightforward way of carrying out the job evaluation process, although there are significant numbers of routine jobs that are difficult to categorize in this way, particularly again in larger organizations.
Points Rating	This is possibly the most popular way of carrying out job evaluation. Several factors contribute to the measurement of the job, including the skills and degree of effort required, the responsibilities undertaken and the working conditions within which the job is performed. These basic starting points are often expanded on by creating subdivisions within each factor with a number of points being allocated for each. Where one particular skill or level of expertise is imperative to a job, then this score is doubled, trebled or quadrupled to reflect its importance.

The job evaluation process is carried out by the human resource department, in collaboration with functional managers, in order to ensure that the pay structure matches the demands and conditions of jobs. The process looks in detail at:

- the tasks involved in each job;
- the responsibilities and obligations of each of the post holders;
- the skills used in each job;
- the knowledge required for each job;
- the initiative required by each of the post holders;
- the ability of each individual post holder to cope with stress;
- the organization's requirements to plan for the future;
- the organization's need to control employees;
- the overall coordination of the organization's environment.

Having established a need for the job evaluation process and categorized each job using the most suitable method, the organization would place a monetary value on each of the jobs. They would do this to ensure that:

- the pay administration process is as uncomplicated as possible;
- internal rates of pay can be harmonized;
- each of the jobs receives a reasonable rate of pay;
- each of the post holders can see the possibility of promotion to a higher job grade.

Quaid, Maeve, *Job Evaluation: The Myth of Equitable Assessment*. Toronto: University of Toronto Press, 1996.

Job rotation

Job rotation is a way of extending or enlarging the tasks carried out by employees. It involves training, or retraining, employees so that they are capable of exchanging jobs with one another, often on a regular and predetermined basis. Job rotation can often lead to increased **job satisfaction** because employees feel that they have a fuller picture of the related jobs and feel more involved in the organization as a whole. The employees also feel more versatile and consider that the scheme gives them a wider variety of tasks, as well as eliminating the need for them to carry out difficult or disliked tasks regularly, instead of only having to confront these tasks on an infrequent basis.

The main benefits to an organization of introducing a job rotation system are that there is constant cover for periods of holiday or sickness. Individual employees can, however, feel that they are constantly on the move and not given sufficient time for the development of specific skills, particularly if the process is carried out during times of high demand, when they often consider they have left a job with too many loose ends still intact. Additionally, levels of competence also have to be reasonably parallel; otherwise individual employees could find themselves completing the bulk of the tasks involved in the job whilst the next employee finds little to do.

The question of **motivation** through job rotation is a questionable one as often employees are motivated at the introduction of the system, but once they have grasped the aspects of the new tasks involved, they find little reason to continue to strive. The job rotation scheme is an ideal system to be put in place by an organization employing large numbers of unskilled or semi-skilled workers.

Job satisfaction

The term 'job satisfaction' refers to the attitude the employees have to the work they carry out. Clearly a positive attitude is more favourable for all concerned than a negative one. Sometimes the degree of job satisfaction that individual employees have depends on the degree of involvement they have in the organization as a whole. Research has revealed that employees tend to have a higher degree of job satisfaction if they:

- are in a job which suits their personality and expertise;
- carry out a balanced number of mentally challenging tasks;
- feel they are being justly rewarded by receiving a fair day's pay for a fair day's work;
- have the appropriate resources available to them within a good working environment;
- have supportive managers and colleagues.

Research has also discovered, however, that job satisfaction does not necessarily lead to increased productivity, particularly for unskilled and semi-skilled workers.

Robbins, Stephen and Coulter, Mary, *Management*. New York: Prentice-Hall, 2001.
Robbins, Stephen, *Organizational Behaviour*. Englewood Cliffs, NJ: Prentice-Hall, 2003.

Job sharing

Job sharing is one of the ways an organization can arrange **alternative working arrangements**. This working arrangement has become more popular in recent years as managers have discovered that job sharing can be beneficial to the organization and employees often find it more convenient. Job sharers find that they can approach the job in a fresher and more positive manner because they are only working for a part of the week, as opposed to a complete week. Commonly employees embarking on a job share scheme are able to choose the hours that they work and this is often arranged via negotiation with their partner job sharer. This gives each of the job sharers time to deal with domestic issues whilst maintaining a percentage of their income from the organization. There can be drawbacks for an employee, however, particularly if one of the job sharers is more organized than the other, or if one of the days worked is the busiest time of the week for the organization. Like all part-time workers, job sharers have the same employment rights as full-timers.

From an organizational point of view, employers often benefit from the fact that there are two individuals, each with different ideas, available to input into the activities of the business. Job sharing can increase flexibility when used to meet peak demand, for instance by both sharers being present when workloads are heavy. There is greater continuity because one sharer can carry on with at least half the work if the other partner is absent through sickness, holiday or maternity leave.

Disadvantages can include the extra costs of induction, training and administration. There may also be problems if the individuals sharing a job perform differently and thus produce an inconsistent output or level of productivity. Job sharers may also find it difficult to communicate with each other as they are not usually at work at the same time. If one job sharer leaves, it may be difficult to find someone to complement the hours worked by the remaining sharer. If the job share involves the managing or supervising of staff, this may create difficulties for the employees involved as they may find the two sharers have differing styles of management.

Job specification

A job specification would be drawn up by an organization in order to identify a number of key issues related to a post. Initially a job analysis would be completed and, from this research into the nature of the job, the job specification would define:

- the qualifications required;
- the experience, knowledge and skills required;
- the personal qualities required;
- any other special demands the job might have.

The purpose of the production of a job specification is to enhance the interview stage of the recruitment process and to enable the interviewer to ask appropriate and enlightening questions of the potential new employee. It is vital that the level of qualification required is precise in the job specification and that the requirements are not pitched at either too high or too low a level. There are two recognized ways of analysing the information on a job specification: the seven-point plan and the five-point plan.

The seven-point plan was developed by Alec Rodger and covers:

- Physical make-up required – this looks at health, physique, appearance, bearing and speech issues.
- Attainments – this is where the education, qualifications and experience required will be stipulated.
- General intelligence – this is the intellectual level required.
- Special aptitudes – this is where considerations such as manual dexterity, communication or number skills or those in the use of particular equipment or machinery will be included.
- Interests – this section would identify whether the individual needs to be physically active, practical, artistic etc.
- Disposition – this section would identify whether the individual has to be of a certain nature, for example, steady, reliable, self-reliant, able to influence others.
- Circumstances – this would relate to the individual's domestic circumstances and family occupations.

Munro Fraser designed the five-point, or five-fold grading system, which is often considered to be simpler and concentrates more on the previous career of the applicant. The five-fold system looks at:

- Impact on others – this looks at issues such as the potential employee's physical make-up, appearance, communication skills and general manner.
- Acquired qualifications – education, training, qualifications and, where appropriate, work experience carried out.
- Innate abilities – this aspect considers the potential employee's aptitude for learning and quickness of comprehension.
- Motivation – this aspect considers whether the potential employees have set goals, aims, targets or objectives for themselves and whether or not they have achieved them.
- Adjustment – this considers issues such as emotional stability, ability to deal with stressful situations and the individual's nature with regard to getting along with others.

Brannick, Michael T. and Levine, Edward L., *Job Analysis: Methods, Research and Applications for Human Resource Management in the New Millennium*. Thousand Oaks, CA: Sage Publications.

Job ticket

A job ticket is used to record the labour time and the machine time which is spent on each process or operation during the production of products.

Joint venture

A joint venture implies a long-term agreement by two or more separate business entities to cooperate and jointly control a separate business entity. Typically, a joint venture would involve a manufacturer and, perhaps, a distributor, in developing a new business venture which affords both parties the potential for profit and a more secure share of the market. A contractual arrangement, setting out the terms of the joint venture, forms the basis of the association between the two separate founding businesses.

Just-in-time (JIT)

JIT is a philosophy which was developed in Japan emphasizing the importance of deliveries in relation to the processing of small lot-sizes. The philosophy emphasizes the importance of set-up cost reduction, small lot-sizes, pull systems, level production and importantly, the elimination of waste (*muda*).

JIT is designed to allow the achievement of high-volume production, whilst ensuring that minimal inventories of raw materials, **work in process** and finished goods are held by the business. Parts arrive at the manufacturing plant from suppliers, just in time to be placed into the manufacturing process and, as the products are processed along the line, they arrive at the next work station just in time, thereby moving through the whole system very quickly.

JIT relies on the management ensuring that manufacturing waste is kept to a minimum and that nothing is made or brought on to the premises that is not immediately required. JIT requires precision as the right part needs to be in the right place at the right time. Waste is described as being the results from any activity that adds cost without adding value (which includes moving and storing).

JIT is also known as lean production or stockless production and the theory is that it should improve the profits and the returns on investment by the following means:

- reducing inventory levels;
- increasing the inventory turnover rate;
- improving product quality;

- reducing production and delivery lead times;
- reducing other costs (machine set-ups and equipment breakdown).

JIT also recognizes the fact that any under-utilized capacity can be used to build up a small stock of products or components (buffer inventories) in order to ensure that in the event of a problem the production process will not be interrupted.

JIT is primarily used in manufacturing processes which are repetitive in nature and where the same products and components are used and produced in relatively high volumes. Once the flow has been set up, there should be a steady and even flow of materials, components and finished products passing through the facility. Each work station is linked in a similar way to an assembly line (although the exact layout may be a jobbing or batch-process layout). The goal is to eliminate queuing and to achieve the ideal lot-size per unit of production.

Delbridge, Rick, *Life on the Line in Contemporary Manufacturing: The Workplace Experience of Lean Production and the 'Japanese' Model.* Oxford: Oxford University Press, 2000.
McInnis, Kenneth R., *Kanban Made Simple: Demystifying and Applying Toyota's Legendary Manufacturing Process.* New York: Amacom, 2003.

Kabushiki kaishi (Japan)

A *kabushiki kaishi* is the Japanese equivalent of a joint stock company.

Kaizen

Kaizen is a Japanese term which implies the adoption of the concept of aspiring towards gradual, but orderly, continuous improvement. The *kaizen* business strategy seeks to involve individuals from across the organization at any level of the organization.

The goal is to work together in order to achieve these improvements without having to make large capital investments. Each change or improvement collectively complements and moves the process onwards. *Kaizen* requires a culture of sustained continuous improvement, whilst focusing on the elimination of waste in areas, systems and processes of the organization. Above all, the cooperation and involvement of all of the employees is vital to the overall success of the philosophy.

www.kaizen-institute.com/kzn.htm

Colenso, Michael, *Kaizen Strategies for Successful Organizational Change: Enabling Evolution and Revolution in the Organization* (Kaizen Strategies). London: Financial Times, Prentice-Hall, 1999.

Imai, Masaaki and Heymans, Brian, *Gemba Kaizen: Collaborating for Change*. San Francisco, CA: Berrett-Koehler, 2000.

Knowledge management

Knowledge management can be seen as one of the key factors of organizational development. Knowledge management recognizes that information and ability are among the most valuable assets an organization possesses. In the past, organizations have not been able to quantify or recognize this aspect as being one of their prime assets, as it is intangible. Knowledge is not just information or data; it needs to have a meaning and a purpose, and in human resources this means the ability to apply and use information. In other words, knowledge management is all about people and the process of using information. There is no compelling definition of the term 'knowledge management' and it has been variously described as intellectual capital or property, amongst a variety of other different attempts to explain its purpose and worth.

The key concern for human resources managers is the retaining of individuals who are able to impart knowledge as an essential function of their relationship with the business. This knowledge management is a complex process, but includes questions as to how to share knowledge, how to find it, how to use it and how to convert it or transfer it from one individual to another.

Davenport, Thomas H. and Prusak, Laurence, *Working Knowledge: How Organizations Manage what they Know*. Boston, MA: Harvard Business School Press, 2000.

Von Krogh, Georg, Ichijo, Kazua and Nonaka, Ikujiro, *Enabling Knowledge Creation*. Oxford: Oxford University Press, 2000.

***Kommanditgesellschaft* (Germany)**

This is the German equivalent of a partnership in which there must be two partners; one must have limited, but the other unlimited, liability.

***Kommanditgesellschaft auf Aktien* (Germany)**

This is a German form of limited partnership in which the partnership has shares.

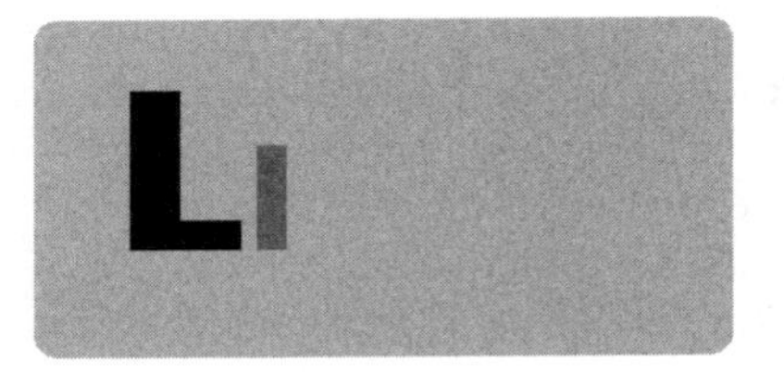

Last in, first out (LIFO)

LIFO is an inventory policy in which the last item added to an organization's inventory is the first one that is used or charged out. It is of interest for tax purposes in that in a time of rising raw material prices, taxable profits are postponed.

See also **first in, first out (FIFO).**

Lead time

There are a number of definitions related to lead time. The term 'lead time' refers to the length of time that an organization takes to produce a product or a component. The planned lead time is a time parameter which is used in a planning and control system to determine the start date for an order.

The planned lead time for a manufacturing order is the sum of the planned lead times for all of the necessary activities in the assembly of that order. For a single operational step, this typically includes:

- the queue time before the production process begins;
- the set-up time for the machine for production;
- the run time to process the order;
- the post-production waiting time for the product to continue to the next stage.

From a customer's perspective, the promised customer lead time is the length of time they can expect to wait for the product, and refers to the planned difference between the times of order placement and order receipt.

All lead times have random variables: means, modes, medians, standard deviations, minimums, maximums, etc. Therefore, it is important that organizations are clear about when to use the word 'lead time'.

Learning curve

A learning curve shows the relationship between an individual's performance and the amount of time spent learning, but can also be inter-

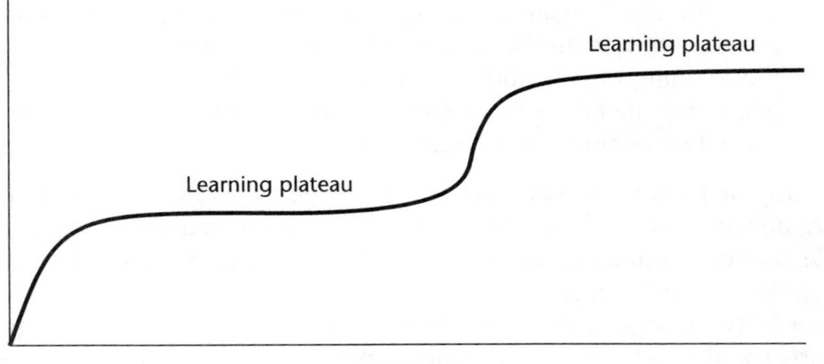

Figure 17 The learning curve

preted as an individual's level of ability or motivation. Very often the individual will reach a stage known as the *learning plateau* (see Figure 17), where little progress is seen to be made. However, this tends to be a temporary stage, sometimes due to a lack of motivation, but also likely to be a result of the need to refresh or revise what has been learned to date before further progress can be achieved.

The rate of learning very much depends on the difficulty of the task involved and often the learning plateau is reached on more than one occasion.

Learning environment

A learning environment occurs in an organization which is deemed to be a learning organization. In other words, the organization has put in place both facilities and a culture for learning. An exact definition of the term 'learning organization' is somewhat problematic since there are a number of different categories of learning organization. The essential encompassing concept is that the organizations learn from external stimuli and, as a result, alter or amend their internal framework to match new opportunities. This requires a re-evaluation of goals and, in extreme circumstances, a change in **organizational culture**, **organizational structure** and patterns of work in order to take advantage of these new opportunities.

The main recognized categories of learning environment are:

- the knowing organization – which tends to be a business in a static or mature market;

L

- the understanding and thinking organization – which is prepared to adapt its culture and structure within certain parameters;
- the learning organization – which accepts change as being both necessary and desirable. These are ultimately the businesses which drive their competitors to mimic them.

Clearly, a human resource department which operates in a learning organization, of whatever type, has to be far more adaptable and flexible, as well as effective and efficient, in driving changes within the organization. It has been recognized that there are two stages of evolution in a learning organization, of which human resources are an integral part. The first is known as a single-loop or adaptive learning organization, where new techniques and ideas are assimilated. The second type of learning organization is known as a double-loop or generative learning organization. In this case the business continually evaluates its goals and objectives, as well as its organizational culture, to suit any emerging external opportunities. Both forms of learning organization offer considerable challenges to human resources managers, who have to quickly learn that they are in an ever-shifting and adaptive organization.

Chawla, Sarita, *Learning Organizations: Developing Cultures for Tomorrow's Workplace*. Shelton, CT: Productivity Press, 1995.

Kline, Peter and Saunders, Bernhard, *Ten Steps to a Learning Organization*. Arlington, VA: Great Ocean Publishers, 1998.

Lease

A lease is often a viable alternative for a business in respect of equipment or property, compared with rental or outright purchase. A lease is a legal agreement between a lessor and a lessee in which the lessee obtains the right to use an item or asset owned by the lessor in exchange for periodic payments. Leases are differentiated from rentals as the lease may in fact be an arrangement by which the lessees can opt to make additional payments which will mean that the asset, at the end of a given period, has passed into their ownership.

Lewin, Kurt

Kurt Lewin, in the 1950s, identified three stages which individuals, groups or organizations pass through when dealing with change. These are listed in Table 9.

Lewin, Kurt, *Field Theory in Social Science: Selected Theoretical Papers*. London: Tavistock Publications, 1967.

Lewin, Kurt, *Resolving Social Conflicts and Field Theory in Social Science*. Washington, DC: American Psychological Association, 1997.

Table 9 Kurt Lewin's three stages of change

Stage	Description
Unfreezing	This stage calls on the management and human resources department to make it clear to employees that there is a requirement to make a change in the business. Employees are consulted, changes are planned, organized and scheduled and appropriate training is arranged.
Changing	This is the actual implementation of the changes, which rests upon the flexibility of the planning process and steps which have been taken during the unfreezing stage.
Refreezing	Now that the change has been implemented, an assessment needs to be made of how effective and satisfactory the change has been. Whatever the new systems or procedures which have now been put in place, these are effectively the new ways of doing things and should now be fully accepted by the employees and the organization as a whole.

Liability

Liabilities are both the current and long-term debts of a business. Debts which have to be paid within 12 months are classed as current liabilities, whilst those payable after 12 months are known as long-term liabilities. Other liabilities include shareholders' funds, for which there is no specified repayment time or period. Liabilities are usually acquired as the result of a purchase of assets.

Limited company

A limited company is a business which has limited liability. The owners or shareholders of the business risk only the amount that they have invested in that business. In Britain many small to medium-sized businesses are known as **private limited companies**.

Limited liability company (US)

This is a form of US business, otherwise known as an LLC, which has a blend of some of the better characteristics of **corporations**, partnerships and **sole proprietorships**. Like a US corporation, it is a separate legal identity, but for tax purposes it is treated like a partnership. It is also a very flexible and simple business to run as there are no statutory requirements to hold meetings, keep minutes or make resolutions. Relatively speaking, LLCs are a new form of business to the US and the first legislation only came into effect in Wyoming in 1977. Since 1988, however, all of the other states have enacted LLC laws; the initial hold-up was the fact that the Inland Revenue Service would not give LLCs partnership tax classifications while the owners of those businesses were exempted from personal liability for the business's debts.

An LLC is formed by the completion of a form, known as the articles of organization. Some US states require an LLC to have an operating agreement which states how it will be managed.

Limited liability partnership (UK)

Since 2001 businesses in the UK can be run as limited liability partnerships. In a similar way to **private limited companies**, the partners' liability is restricted to the amount that they originally invested in the business and any other personal guarantees they may have given to providers of loans. A limited liability partnership, or LLP, operates much like a limited partnership. The Limited Liability Partnership Act allows two or more individuals to form a business once the incorporation document, together with appropriate fees, has been registered at the Registrar of Companies.

Limited liability partnership (US)

In a limited liability partnership, in US terms, the exposure of the partners is limited to the investment they originally made in the business, or any personal guarantees made by the partners. The partnership is a separate legal entity which enters into contracts, incurs debts and pays taxes, being separate and apart from its employees, stockholders or directors. It can only act through its directors, stockholders or agents.

Line authority

The term 'line authority' is applied to individuals who have a direct management responsibility for a number of subordinates. The concept of line authority is integral to the **chain of command**, in which successive levels of management have line authority (responsibility) for all those individuals who are technically, in the hierarchy, lower than them in the organization. Line authority is distinguished from staff authority in the sense that the latter refers to management or supervisors, who have a specific responsibility for an aspect of an employee's work. Examples of staff authority would include human resources personnel, who, technically, have authority in certain respects towards all employees, regardless of grade or position in the hierarchy. Line managers, however, have line authority and can, on a daily basis, exert their decisions upon those for whom they have responsibility.

Liquidation

Liquidation literally means turning a business's assets into readily available cash. This process normally begins when the business ceases to trade in its current form as a result of insolvency. Liquidation is often described as **winding up**, usually as a result of a creditor finally taking the business to court for non-payment of debts. In these cases an individual known as a receiver or liquidator will be appointed to raise enough cash to satisfy the creditors. This is achieved by the disposal of the business's assets or the selling of the business as a **going concern** to a third party.

In many cases businesses will choose to go into voluntary liquidation, deciding to cease trading as they are currently organized. In these cases the business appoints a liquidator who then calls a meeting of creditors to endorse the liquidator's powers. The liquidator then assumes control of the business and collects assets, pays debts and, if there is surplus, distributes it to the company's members according to their rights.

Local area network (LAN)

A local area network is a network of **work stations** which share either the same server or processor. The work stations are located in a relatively small geographical area, usually a single office or building. The work stations share **applications** and peripherals and allow the sharing and interchanging of files between work stations.

m2m

M2m is a variant form of **business-to-business (b2b)** and refers to the relationship and transactions between different manufacturers. In its shortened form, m2m, the implication is that the manufacturers have electronic exchanges, rather like the internet-based b2b.

Macro-marketing

Macro-marketing is a marketing approach which takes a broader view, encompassing the whole economy. It seeks to understand the way in which products and services flow from producers to consumers in a manner that most closely matches the actual supply and demand in that economy, or that market. In this respect, macro-marketing recognizes that in effectively matching supply and demand, it accomplishes the objectives of society in general.

Management accounting

Management accounting is the collection, collation and appraisal of financial information in order to assist management in the decision making, planning, control and performance appraisal of the business. Management accounting also ensures that **gaaps** are followed and that the business is creating, protecting, preserving and increasing value during its operations, in order to deliver that value to the **stakeholders**. Management accounting is an essential element of management as it identifies, generates, presents and interprets information relevant to the formulation of business strategy. It is also essential in all planning and control activities, including various decisions which need to be made. It provides essential data for the examination of performance improvement, as well as safeguarding both the tangible and intangible assets of the business. A business will also use the management accounting function as a form of corporate governance and internal control.

Keown, Arthur J., Martin, John W., Petty, William D. and Scott, David F., *Financial Management: Principles and Applications*. New York: Prentice-Hall, 2001.

Management board

A management board is usually chaired by the managing director or chief executive officer, within a two-tier board-of-directors' structure. The chairperson of the management board reports directly to the chairperson of the supervisory board. The executive managers of the management board have a direct responsibility for the operational performance of the business.

Management by exception

This is a form of management which states that an efficient manager should concentrate primarily on dealing with situations which significantly deviate from plans. In other words, they focus their attention upon exceptions to the normal procedures, standards and quality and effectively ignore performance which is in accord with normal plans.

Management by objectives (MBO)

The concept of management by objectives was developed by Peter Drucker in the 1950s. The management concept relies on the defining of objectives for each employee and then comparing their performance, and directing that performance, against the objectives which have already been set. MBO requires that clear objectives are set, and that every employee is perfectly well aware of what is expected of them, a factor which often means that the employees themselves have a considerable input into the setting of the objectives. Also at MBO's heart is **delegation**, as it requires employees to take a responsibility for the achievement of objectives. It is recognized that employees are much more able and willing to seek to achieve their objectives if they have some degree of independence in how those objectives are achieved, rather than being led or directed overtly by management. MBO has at least one fatal flaw, in as much as the objectives of individuals within different departments can be different. When they are required to act together collaboratively, the objectives of one of the individuals may override those of another individual, who has a different set of priorities and a different set of objectives. Inevitably, conflict or inertia may occur, which will clearly have an impact on productivity. Provided the business has thought the whole process through, objectives need not be mutually exclusive, but can be compatible, which would seek to impel all collaborative projects forward and facilitate inter-disciplinary cooperation.

Management buy-out

A management buy-out involves the acquisition of a business by its existing management. In many cases the management group will establish a new holding company which then effectively purchases the shares of the target company. There are variations of management buy-out, notably management buy-in (where external management buys the business) and buy-in management buy-out (which is a combination of the two).

Management buy-outs may arise as a result of any of the following:

- a group may decide to sell a business because it has become a non-core activity;
- a business may find itself in difficulties and needs to sell part of its business;
- the owner of a business may choose to retire;
- a receiver or administrator may sell the business as a **going concern**.

The normal sequence of events in a management buy-out are:

- an agreement of the management team as to who will become the managing director;
- appointment of financial advisors;
- assessment of the suitability of the buy-out;
- approval to pursue the management buy-out;
- evaluation of the vendor's asking price;
- formulation of business plans;
- selection of suitable equity investors and obtaining written offers;
- appointment of legal advisors;
- selection of lead investor;
- negotiation of best equity deal;
- negotiation of purchase of the business;
- implementation of a due diligence test with the aid of an auditor;
- obtaining finance and other equity investment;
- preparation of legal documents;
- legal ownership achieved.

Andrews, Phildrew, *Management Buy-Out*. New York: Kogan Page, 1999.

Management by walking about (MBWA)

The driving force behind this approach to management was the belief that senior managers, in particular, were perceived by employees as being elitist and unwilling to expose themselves to the realities of day-to-day business operations. In effect, the managers sought to isolate themselves in their offices and dispense orders from a distance, without any real conception as to the realities of shop-floor life. The concept probably derives from Japan and was originally applied primarily to manufacturing industries. As the term suggests, managers are encouraged to visit the shop floor and see what is happening, solve problems on the spot and interact with normal employees. In Japan, management by walking about is actually termed *gemci genbutsu*, which literally means 'go and see'.

There are a number of human resource management implications arising out of the adoption of a management by walking about system. The fact that senior managers are out and about in the factory or offices of an organization means that they may inevitably interfere with normal lines of communication, authority and supervisory management decisions. Clearly a senior manager becoming involved in what would normally be a situation that could be handled using day-to-day management and procedures could cause unnecessary friction within the organization. Human resource management would, therefore, need to ensure that a clear notion of cooperation, communication and demarcation is established.

Management control

Management control is a general term which is used to describe all of the processes and procedures used by management to ensure that organizational goals are achieved. Ultimately, management control seeks to ensure that the organization responds in an effective manner to changes, both internally and externally, which may impact upon the business's overall efficiency and success.

Management information system (MIS)

A management information system, or MIS, is a computer **application** which is used to record, store and process information that can be used to assist management decision making. Generally, a business will have a single integrated MIS into which data from various functional areas of the business is fed and to which senior management has access.

There are two additional sub-types of MIS, which are decision support systems and executive information systems. Decision support systems also collect, store and process information accessible by management. They contain data on the business's operational activities and allow managers to manipulate and retrieve data using modelling techniques to examine the results of various different courses of action. An executive information system (EIS) provides similar facilities for senior management, combining internal information along with external data. It is used to support strategic decision making and presents the information in a variety of formats, primarily aimed at enabling the users to identify trends.

Laudon, Kenneth C. and Laudon, Jane P., *Management Information Systems*. New York: Prentice-Hall, 2003.

Manufacturing resource planning (MRP2)

Manufacturing resource planning (MRP2) is a method to effectively plan all the resources of a manufacturing company. It is a natural development of material requirements planning (MRP) but is broader in concept and application. MRP2 links functions such as business planning, sales and operations planning, production scheduling, MRP, capacity requirements planning and support systems for both capacity and materials. An MRP2 system is designed to make maximum utilization of the resources available to the business. The underlying principles of MRP2 require:

- An aggregate sales and operations plan, to create a framework for the master production schedule to be produced, including all major inputs from each functional area of the business.
- A master production schedule – the critical element of MRP2 – which specifies what is to be made and when, fitting within the aggregate and financial plans and the capacity constraints. This schedule requires updating to take into account **lead time**.
- A materials resource plan, which gives a detailed listing of all the materials and resources required for each order.
- A capacity requirement plan, which analyses the processes, helping to anticipate difficulties, thus allowing for short-term adjustments to the master production schedule.
- Shop Floor Control (SFC), which maintains, evaluates and communicates data.

MRP2 improves production timing, cuts inventories, improves customer service and staff productivity and allows the business to plan across all its operations. The system requires, however, the availability of accurate data and expertise in implementation and enforcement.

Wallace, Thomas F., *MRPII: Making it Happen: The Implementer's Guide to Success with Manufacturing Resource Planning*. Essex Junction, VT: Oliver Wight Publications, 1990.

Margin

A margin can be applied either to the total business carried out by an organization, or to a specific product, range or service. In its more general use, margin is expressed as the gross profit as a percentage of the turnover of the business. When applied to specific products, it refers to the difference between the total costs (including overheads) attributed to the product compared with the selling price of that product. In this respect 'margin' is not dissimilar to **markup**, which may be based on a fixed percentage addition to the costs of a product in order to ensure a sufficient margin.

Margin of safety

A margin of safety is usually expressed as being the difference between the **breakeven point** and the current or forecast level of sales. Usually the margin of safety is expressed as a percentage of turnover, but it can also be expressed as sales revenue or units.

Market research

There is considerable confusion as to the comparative definitions of 'market research' and **marketing research**. Market research is, in effect, a subset of marketing research as it most usually describes consumer interviews and other procedures involved in marketing research. Whilst the generally accepted definition of marketing research encompasses all of the collection, recording and analysis of data related to the marketing of products and services, market research has a somewhat more limited definition.

Birks, David and Malhotra, Naresh, *Marketing Research: An Applied Approach*. London: Financial Times, Prentice-Hall, 2002.

Birn, Robin J. (ed.), *The Handbook of International Market Research Techniques*. London: Kogan Page, 2003.

Market segmentation

Market segmentation involves the identification of specific target markets for broader based products and services, in order to enable businesses to develop suitable marketing mixes for each of their target segments.

Market segmentation probably came into existence in the 1950s when product differentiation was a primary marketing strategy. By the 1970s, however, market segmentation had begun to be seen as a means of increasing sales and obtaining a competitive advantage. In recent years more sophisticated techniques are being developed to reach potential buyers in ever-more specific target markets.

Businesses will tend to segment the market for the following reasons:

- To make marketing easier in the sense that segmentation allows the business to address the needs of smaller groups of customers which have the same characteristics.
- To find niches, typically unserved or under-served markets, and to be able to target these buyers in a less competitive environment.
- To increase efficiency in being able to apply resources directly towards the best segments, which have been identified by the business.

There are some common rules regarding market segmentation which determine whether the identified segments are significant enough or measurable. These are listed in Table 10.

In effect, there are two ways of segmenting a market. These are known as either *a priori* or *post hoc*. These two approaches are typified in the following manner:

- *A priori* segmentation is effectively based on a mixture of intuition, use of secondary data and analysis of existing customer database information. *A priori* segmentation takes place without the benefit of primary market research and may well produce relatively simplistic segmentation, such as male or female, young or old, regional segments or buyers and non-buyers.

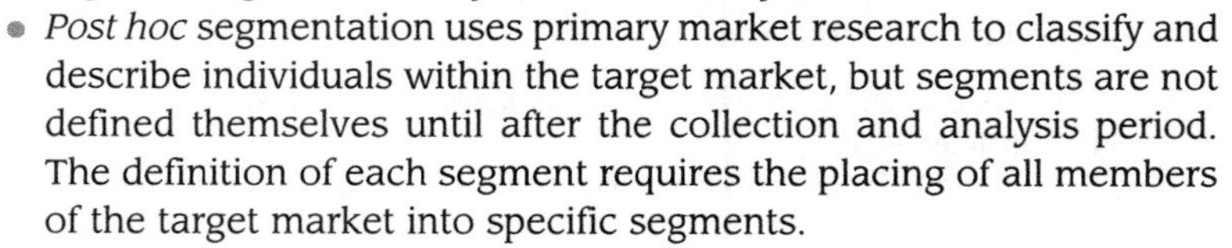

- *Post hoc* segmentation uses primary market research to classify and describe individuals within the target market, but segments are not defined themselves until after the collection and analysis period. The definition of each segment requires the placing of all members of the target market into specific segments.

There are a number of different types of information which are used extensively in market segmentation. These can be best described by category as in Table 11.

McDonald, Malcolm and Dunbar, Ian, *Market Segmentation*. Basingstoke: Palgrave Macmillan, 1998.

Wedel, Michel and Kamakura, Wagner A., *Market Segmentation: Conceptual and Methodological Foundations*. New York: Kluwer Academic Publishers, 1999.

Table 10 Market segmentation

Segmentation criteria	Description
Size	The market itself needs to be large enough to warrant segmentation. Once a market has been segmented, it may be revealed that each of the segments is too small to consider.
Differentiation	There must be measurable differences between the members of the segment and the market in general.
Responsiveness	With the market segmented, marketing communications need to be developed to address the needs of each segment. If a business cannot develop marketing communications which can contact the segment and have an impact upon it, there is little value in knowing about the segment in the first place.
Reachability	Marketing communications need to be able to get through to the segments in order to be effective. There may well be a single best advertising medium or promotional device which can reach the segments and tell them the business's message.
Interest	Having established what benefits the segment is looking for, the business needs to be assured that this is precisely what the potential customers require and that the product or service matches these needs.
Profitability	A decision needs to be reached as to whether it is cost-effective to reach these segments, considering the cost which may be incurred in running multiple marketing programmes alongside one another. Existing products or services may need to be redesigned in order to match the specific needs of each segment.

Market share

Sales figures do not necessarily indicate how a business is performing relative to its competitors. Changes in sales simply may reflect changes in the market size or changes in economic conditions. The business's performance relative to competitors can be measured by the proportion of the market that the firm is able to capture. This proportion is referred to as the business's market share and is calculated as follows:

Market share = Business's sales/total market sales

Table 11 Information used in market segmentation

Measured variable	Description
Classification	Broadly speaking, classification actually encompasses demographic, geographic, psychographic and behavioural characteristics. It requires a system of classifying individuals and placing them into segments by using a mixture of these variables.
Demography	Demography features age, gender, income, ethnicity, marital status, education, occupation, household size, type of residence and length of residence, amongst many other demographically based measures.
Geography	This broad range of variables includes population density, climate, zip or postcode, city, state or county, region or metropolitan/rural district.
Psychography	Another broad range of variables which include attitudes, hobbies, leadership traits, lifestyle, magazines and newspapers read, personality traits, risk aversion and television or radio programmes watched or listened to.
Behaviour	These variables encompass the current ways in which the target market views, buys and responds to products, services and marketing. The category includes brand loyalty, benefits sought, distribution channels used and level of usage.
Descriptors	Descriptor variables actually describe each segment in order to distinguish it from other groups. The descriptors need to be measurable and are usually derived solely from primary research, rather than secondary sources of information. Descriptors will typically explain in shorthand the key characteristics of each segment and the members of that segment, so that these characteristics can be more readily exploited by subtle changes in the marketing mix. A descriptor variable may be featured as under 30, single, urban dweller, rented accommodation, medium to high income etc.

Sales may be determined on a value basis (sales price multiplied by volume) or on a unit basis (number of units shipped or number of customers served). While the business's own sales figures are readily available, total market sales are more difficult to determine. Usually, this information is available from trade associations and market research firms.

Often, market share is associated with profitability and thus many businesses seek to increase their sales relative to competitors. Businesses may seek to increase their market share for the following reasons:

- economies of scale – higher volume can be instrumental in developing a cost advantage;
- sales growth in a stagnant industry – when the industry is not growing, the business can still increase its sales by increasing its market share;
- reputation – market leaders have the power which they can use to their advantage;
- increased bargaining power – a larger market share gives an advantage in negotiations with suppliers and channel members.

The market share of a product can be modelled as:

Share of market = Share of preference × Share of voice × Share of distribution

According to this model, there are three drivers of market share:

- share of preference – this can be increased through product, pricing and promotional changes;
- share of voice – the business's proportion of total promotional expenditures in the market; thus, share of voice can be increased by increasing advertising expenditures;
- share of distribution – this can be increased through more intensive distribution.

From these drivers market share can be increased by changing the variables of the marketing mix.

- product – the product attributes can be changed to provide more value to the customer, for example, by improving product quality;
- price – price elasticity means that a decrease in price can increase sales revenue; this tactic may not succeed if competitors are willing and able to meet any price cuts;
- distribution – new distribution channels can be added or the intensity of distribution in each channel can be increased;

- promotion – increasing advertising expenditures can increase market share, unless competitors respond with similar increases.

Miniter, Richard, *The Myth of Market Share*. London: Nicholas Brealey Publishing, 2002.

Marketing research

Marketing research attempts to adopt a scientific approach to building a clear picture of customers, the market and the competition and latterly it has been extended as an investigation into the wider environment in which the business operates.

Marketing research aims to discover, in a systematic manner using reliable and unbiased questions, the ideas and intentions as well as trends which may affect a business, its markets and its customers. Marketing research processes data, analyses the data and interprets the facts, and is employed extensively in marketing management to help plan, evaluate and control marketing strategy and tactics.

Marketing research is often confused with **market research**, which has a considerably narrower definition. For the most part, market research simply refers to consumer surveys, normally questionnaires, carried out face-to-face or over the telephone. Marketing research, therefore, can be seen as a broader church in terms of information gathering, collation and analysis.

Marketing research must provide information to a business to help it understand its situation more clearly. In other words, it needs to have a real value. The value, of course, is based on a number of different determinants, which include the following:

- The business must be willing and able to act on the information received from marketing research, no matter what its conclusions may be.
- The researchers and the business need to be assured that the information which has been gathered is accurate.
- The business needs to recognize that its moves would probably be indecisive without the benefit of the marketing research information.
- The business also needs to be clear that whilst accepting the validity of the information gathered, there may be a degree of variation or a margin of error.
- The business can also recognize that accurate and pertinent marketing research can reduce risk.
- The business needs to be cognizant that competitors may well react on the basis of decisions made by the business arising out of its marketing research.

- Marketing research needs to be cost-effective, in terms of both money and time. Any marketing research must be up-to-date, otherwise its value is limited; therefore any marketing research programme has to have a definite purpose and deadline.

The majority of marketing research projects are typified by following a clear series of tasks. These are:

1. define the problem
2. determine research design
3. identify data types and sources
4. design data collection forms and questionnaires
5. determine sample plan and size
6. collect the data
7. analyse and interpret the data
8. prepare a research report

Birks, David and Malhotra, Naresh, *Marketing Research: An Applied Approach*. London: Financial Times, Prentice-Hall, 2002.

Markup

Markup is usually expressed as the gross profit achieved as a percentage of the costs. More definitively, it is the percentage added to the cost which is used to obtain the selling price. Markup is often referred to as a **margin**, which should reflect a reasonable profit on each sale once all necessary costs have been incorporated into the equation.

Maslow, Abraham

Abraham Maslow categorized human needs into five groups, which he arranged as a hierarchy (see Figure 18, p. 172). Whilst Maslow's theory has been systematically applied in the field of Human Resource Management, marketing has much to learn from the concept.

Maslow's theory can be directly adapted to marketing, as can be seen in Table 12, p. 173.

Maslow, Abraham H. and Frager, Robert (ed.), *Motivation and Personality*. Harlow: Longman, 1987.

Master budget

A master budget is a consolidated budget into which all other subsidiary budgets are incorporated. The master budget will normally include the budgeted profit and loss account, balance sheet and cash flow state-

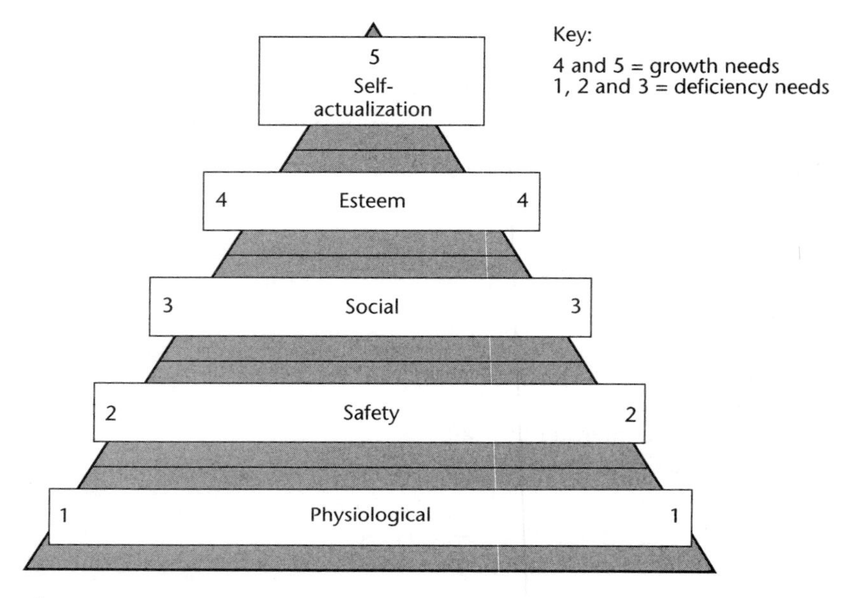

Figure 18 Maslow's human needs hierarchy

ment. The master budget is essential in order for a business to be able to plan and control its activities in the next financial period.

Matrix structure

The use of a matrix organizational structure allows the opportunity for teams to be developed in order that particular tasks can be undertaken. Matrix structures often develop in stages, with the first being the establishment of temporary teams, who, having studied a particular problem and suggested recommendations, might be considered significant enough to be retained on a more permanent basis. These teams will consist of a number of different individuals from the different functions of the organization (see Figure 19, p. 174).

As can be seen in Table 13, p. 175, a matrix structure has some advantages and disadvantages.

Sutherland, Jon and Canwell, Diane, *Organisation Structures and Processes*. London: Pitman Publishing, 1997.

Weiss, Joseph, *Organisational Structure and Processes*. Cheltenham: Nelson Thornes, 1999.

Table 12 Maslow's theory in relation to marketing

Maslow needs category	Product suggestions	Target groups
Physiological	Products which give customers a sense of well-being, such as warming foods in winter.	Grey market, which has concerns over health.
Safety	Support services, including road-side assistance, insurance cover, private health care and extended warrantees.	Safety-based products and services for those with children or valuables to protect.
Social	Products which allow customers to maintain and improve their social lives, such as cheap rate calls in the evening, reduced rate internet connections and membership privileges to clubs allowing customers to bring friends free.	Networking solutions for people moving to new areas, contact with like-minded individuals (clubs and societies etc.) and groups set up for single people or single-parent families.
Esteem	Products which give customers the feeling that they are successful, such as luxury cars, electrical products and jewellery items.	New high-income earners and higher-status groups with a need to show outward signs of conspicuous consumption.
Self-actualization	Higher, further or additional education aimed at self-improvement in the job market.	Higher-educated individuals seeking vocational skills and learning, or adolescents looking for opportunities to conform to perceived ideals in terms of fashion and looks.

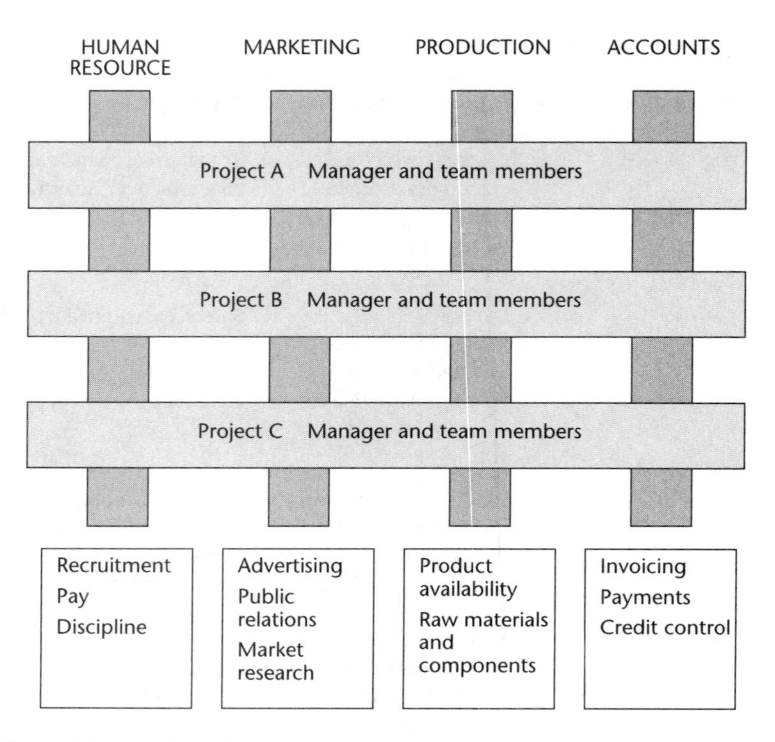

Figure 19 A matrix structure

McGregor, Douglas

McGregor was a management consultant theorist and a social psychologist. In 1954 he became Professor of Management at the Massachusetts Institute of Technology, and later he taught at Harvard where he helped establish the Industrial Relations section. Douglas McGregor's book *The Human Side of Enterprise* was published in 1960, examining the behaviour of individuals at work. He formulated two models, which he called Theory X and Theory Y.

Theory X assumes that the average human has an inherent dislike of work and will do all that is necessary to avoid it. This assumes the following:

- because people dislike work they have to be controlled by management and often threatened in order to work hard;
- most people avoid responsibility, need to be directed by management but seek security within work as a primary concern;

Table 13 Advantages and disadvantages of matrix structures

Advantages	**Disadvantages**
Good use can be made of specialist and functional knowledge from within the organization.	Because there is not a clear line of command and authority, this may affect a manager's ability to understand requirements and make changes.
Enhanced communication can be facilitated between departments, providing a greater level of consistency and efficiency of policies.	There is often a higher level of stress and a feeling of constant competition with added responsibility.
The availability of multiple sources of power allows the establishment of recognized mechanisms to deal with different forms of culture.	Demand on individuals and departments may be inconsistent, resulting in a high demand on some areas and only a limited demand on others.
The structure enables the organization to adapt to environmental changes by moving their main emphasis from a functional one to a project-based one.	There may also be inconsistency between individuals with the ability to flourish and those who are more technically minded. This could cause exclusion for some employees by those who are competitive enough to wish to manage the project teams.

- managers who adhere to the Theory X approach rarely give their subordinates any opportunity to show traits other than those associated with Theory X.

Theory X has given rise to what is often known as tough or hard management, typified by tight control and punishment.

Theory Y, on the other hand, assumes the following:

- most people expend the same amount of energy or effort at work as in other spheres of their lives.
- providing the individuals are committed, or made to be committed, to the aims of the organization in which they work, they will be self-directing.
- **job satisfaction** is the key to involving and engaging the individual and ensuring his or her commitment.
- an average individual, given the opportunity and encouragement, will naturally seek responsibility.

- ensuring commitment and responsibility enables employees to use their imagination, ingenuity and creativity to solve work problems with less direct supervision.

Managements which follow Theory Y are often considered to be soft management systems and aim to create a degree of harmony in the workplace, recognizing that the intellectual potential of their employees is vital to the success of the business. In many cases, it is argued, businesses ignore the Theory Y benefits and under-utilize their employees.

McGregor saw his two theories as being very separate attitudes. He believed that it was difficult to use Theory Y for large-scale operations, particularly those involved in mass production. It was an ideal choice for the management of professionals. For McGregor, Theory Y was essential in helping to encourage participative problem-solving and the development of effective management.

McGregor, Douglas, *The Human Side of Enterprise*. New York: McGraw-Hill Education, 1995.

M-commerce

M-commerce is shorthand for mobile commerce, which is widely believed to be the next generation of **e-commerce**. M-commerce uses hand-held communication devices such as mobile phones and personal digital assistants in order to enable the user to access the internet to buy and sell products and services. The technology is based upon wireless application protocol (WAP) and also uses Bluetooth technology (which uses short-range radio signals to connect electronic devices) in the creation of Smart phones which can provide conventional telephone facilities in addition to **email**, fax and web browsing.

Schneider, Gary P., *Electronic Commerce*. Boston, MA: Course Technology, 2003.

Meetings

See **general meeting**.

Memorandum of association

A memorandum of association is a key constitutional document which details a business's name, objectives and capital. It also notes the date and place of incorporation, as well as the liability of members and the authorized share capital.

Merchant services

Merchant services are **outsourced** pay processing systems which are used for ATM card transactions, as well as credit and debit transactions. They also provide cheque guarantees and internet checks for **e-commerce**. Merchant services allow payments to be made via the internet, electronic cash registers or point of sale terminals. The customer's chosen method of payment is inputted into the vendor's payment system and the merchant service handles the authorization and transfer of funds. The merchant service provides the vendor with monthly billing statements for which the vendor pays a fee or a percentage of sales. Merchant services also provide the vendor with terminals and connection facilities to their services.

Micromarketing

Micromarketing is a dependent form of marketing which relies heavily on accurate **market segmentation**. Micromarketing seeks to target specific and often relatively small groups of customers, through purpose-built promotions to that defined group. Typically the target markets may be defined geographically, demographically, behaviourally or psychographically. In this way micromarketing allows a business to concentrate on fulfilling the specific needs, wants and expectations of target groups without risking the message that they wish to convey to them being lost in a more general marketing campaign.

Micro-payment

Micro-payment is an internet payment facility which has failed to capture the imagination of **e-commerce**. The system is based upon internet users' ability to pay for low-cost services via a virtual wallet which plugs into their web browser. Initially there has been considerable difficulty with the applications used to run this form of technology, since they are not considered secure enough, neither are they efficient or simple to top up. As a result, websites which would have considered micro-payments in order to fund their operations have tended to rely on web advertising as an alternative.

Minority shareholder

Minority shareholders are those shareholders whose combined shareholdings are insufficient to be able to affect resolutions which have been put to a **general meeting**. The term is usually used to describe the differences in position between the majority shareholders who favour a particular resolution and smaller shareholders who are opposed to it. In most countries there are checks and balances in place in order to ensure that minority shareholders are not adversely affected by the wishes of the majority and that decisions carried despite their opposition are not unfair or discriminatory.

Misfeasance

A charge of misfeasance may be brought against directors or other senior officers of a business by a liquidator who feels that they have breached their duties of responsibility towards the business. Misfeasance implies misconduct and suggests that the directors, or others, did not do everything in their power to ensure that the best interests of the **stakeholders** or shareholders were always considered.

Mission statement

In many cases indications of a business's fundamental policy will be contained within a mission statement. A mission statement essentially describes, as succinctly as possible, the organization's business vision. This would include the fundamental values and the essential purpose of the organization. It will also make allusions as to the business's future, or its pursuit for the future, as mission statements tend to be a statement of where a businesses wishes to be rather than a description of where it is at the current time. In this respect, mission statements, although the fundamental ethos may remain the same, are subject to periodic change. A business may choose to incorporate within its mission statement a vision of how it wishes its employees and systems to respond, react and fulfil the needs of its customers or clients. Businesses will, therefore, seek to match these aspirations by instituting employee development programmes and associated training, in order to fulfil the espoused desires and commitments made in the mission statement.

Talbot, Marianne, *Make Your Mission Statement Work: Identify your Organisation's Values and Live Them Everyday*. Oxford: How to Books, 2003.

Mortgage

A mortgage is the transfer of property to a lender on the assumption that the borrower agrees to terms of repayment of the debt, after which time the asset will be transferred to the borrower's ownership. A mortgage is a common form of security for a creditor.

Motivation

Motivation implies the instilling in employees of a drive to take action. In human resource terms this means inducing, or providing an incentive to, employees to perform to the best of their abilities. The subject of motivation has been at the heart of a large number of theories over a number of years, including those of Maslow and Hertzberg. Both theorists recognized that there were a series of actions or circumstances which could be initiated by an employer in order to achieve a degree of motivation. Both recognized, too, that simply providing pay and a degree of security were insufficient in the long term to motivate employees. Motivation needed to be longer lasting and reinforced by concrete rewards and praise. At its most basic, motivation needs to be sustained by employers in order not only to ensure continued high performance and productivity, but also to create a situation where employees have a positive attitude towards work, a commitment to the organization and, above all, a belief that their individual roles are not only valued but of crucial interest to the organization.

Multi-skilling

The term 'multi-skilling' relates to incorporating a higher level of flexibility into the job roles across an organization, usually in those activities requiring unskilled to skilled or technical expertise. This flexibility often crosses boundaries which have historically or traditionally been set, and it requires the willingness of employees if it is to succeed. The newly multi-skilled employees would also have to be prepared to work at their newly acquired skills and follow training or retraining programmes in order to do so. Commonly, trained employees will assist with the retraining of those going through the multi-skilling process.

There are some advantages and disadvantages to multi-skilling, including those shown in Table 14 (see p. 180).

The introduction of multi-skilling can affect employees in more than their work situation and may spill over into their domestic life, particularly if their extended role involves irregular work hours. However, employees could find that their **job satisfaction** is increased because they are no longer so strictly supervised or controlled.

Table 14 Advantages and disadvantages of multi-skilling

Advantages	**Disadvantages**
An organization can introduce new equipment and working methods quickly.	Labour turnover can increase as employees become more skilled.
The employees improve their overall level of skills and knowledge.	The costs of training and retraining programmes can be high.
All of the organization's resources are used to their full potential.	Because individuals can move from one group to another, there could be resultant shortages in particular groups. This can affect the way the group performs in the longer term as there is a constant risk that a member of the group or team will be missing.
The employees can contribute more effectively and to their full potential to meeting the organization's objectives.	Managers tend not to be involved in the multi-skilling process and often remain rigid in their views of the tasks they should perform.
	Employees do not always enjoy job satisfaction, particularly if they are not involved in tasks they were initially trained to do.

NA (national association) (US)

A national association, in US terms, is an overarching body to which various associated charities and non-profit organizations belong. National associations can be likened to an executive committee or forum which is concerned with issues that affect all of its member organizations.

Negotiation

Negotiation is a vital communication skill required by both managers and human resources departments. Negotiation has a great deal to do with the relative power of the negotiators. Negotiations can occur either at an individual level or between employees' representatives, such as between **trade unions** and another group of individuals who represent the business. Equally, negotiation can take place at local, national or even international levels, between employee representatives and representatives of employer groups and/or governments.

French and Raven suggested eight key areas which largely determine the basis of negotiations and how they may be expected to progress. These eight considerations are summarized in Table 15.

French, John R. P. and Raven, Bertram, 'Basis of Social Power', in Dorwin Cartwright (ed.), *Studies in Social Power*. Ann Arbor, MI: University of Michigan, 1959.

Goldberg, Stephen B., Sander, Frank E. A. and Rogers, Nancy H., *Dispute Resolution: Negotiation, Mediation and Other Processes*. New York: Aspen Publishers Inc., 1999.

Table 15 Negotiation requirements

Consideration	**Description**
Positional power	This type of power derives from an individual's position within the organization relative to other individuals. This form of power is particularly in evidence when negotiations occur between managers and their direct employees.

⇒

Table 15 Negotiation requirements (*continued*)

Consideration	Description
Information power	This type of power derives from differences between people in terms of their access to important information. An individual who lacks access or information can be controlled by another individual who has that information. In other words, some individuals find themselves dependent upon those who have already acquired the information, possibly by virtue of their position within the organization.
Control of rewards	Those individuals in managerial or supervisory positions within an organization have the ability to dispense rewards to less senior members of staff, making their subordinates dependent on them.
Coercive power	This type of power is related to the ability of a manager or supervisor to punish less senior employees. Once again, the less senior employees are dependent upon their supervisor or manager.
Alliances and networks	This type of power is derived from both an individual's access to information and his or her relative position within the organization. More senior individuals are members of stronger alliances and networks and can use this to exercise power and authority.
Access to and control of agendas	The setting of the ground rules or topics to be discussed within a negotiation process is obviously a determining factor in the outcome of the negotiations. If an individual can set the agenda or, in other words, determine what will be discussed, then the negotiation process has already been somewhat undermined before it even begins.
Control of meaning and symbols	This is particularly relevant to a jargon-ridden organization, where the use of language can radically affect the negotiation process. Access to these symbols and their meaning can strongly determine the effectiveness of negotiators who are not conversant with the jargon.
Personal power	The adoption of characteristics of an effective role model, or the use of these characteristics by a dominant negotiator, can determine the negotiator's effectiveness.

Net present value (NPV)

Net present value is the difference between the sum of the discounted cash flows which had been expected from an investment and the amount which was originally invested. The net present value can be shown as either a positive or a negative figure.

Netsourcing

For smaller businesses netsourcing is a much more viable alternative to the acquisition of expensive licensed **applications** and the necessary investment in hardware and technical support. Increasingly smaller businesses turn to internet companies which are variously known as either **application service providers (ASP)** or business service providers (BSP). These organizations offer an extensive range of applications and the ability to rent or lease hardware, and have technical staff on hand to support and deal with any problems which may be encountered by their clients. Prime examples of netsourced applications are accountancy software and systems and the more sophisticated human resource management software and applications.

Networking

In the business sense, networking has a number of different associations. Internally it refers to managers and employees of a business forming working relationships with other members of the organization in order to achieve greater understanding and mutual dependence.

Externally, networking can refer to either individuals or organizations collaborating with one another with no real formal guidelines to their relationship.

Non-financial performance indicators (NFPIS)

This is another term for non-financial performance measures.

Non-financial performance measures

As the term implies, non-financial performance measures are derived from and used by operating departments in order to monitor and control their activities, without incorporating accounting information. It is widely believed that these measures give a better indication of performance than standard financial ratios, although they are more prone to distortion as a result of variations in market forces.

Non-profit corporation (US)

A non-profit or not-for-profit corporation is a US-registered type of organization which tends to be, but is not exclusively, similar to a charity in Britain.

Offene handels gesellschaft (Germany)

This is a German form of partnership, which requires at least two partners. The partners have unlimited liability.

Offsite storage

Offsite storage is an increasingly popular choice, for individual users and for businesses, which allows them to store documents electronically on the offsite storage provider's computer systems. In effect, this is a digital form of document warehousing, where customers lease storage space on the provider's computer system, enabling them to send files, retrieve files and have access to files on a 24-hour basis, provided that their computer is linked to the internet. Most of the storage providers incorporate automated backup services, which eliminates the need for the individual clients to back up their own documentation. Businesses are increasingly moving over to this form of document storage as retrieval is easy and fast and the offsite storage providers are gradually incorporating systems which ensure that there are no security lapses, which could mean that unauthorized individuals could gain access to the document storage facility. Some businesses are reluctant to move over to this form of document storage on the basis that they do not wish their documentation to be under the control of a third party, and they do not believe that the internet is, as yet, sufficiently secure.

Ombudsmen

An ombudsman is an independent individual or office which responds to complaints from consumers regarding the service which they are receiving. The ombudsman also initiates proactive investigations, protecting the interests of the consumer. Once the ombudsman has intervened, an attempt is made to determine whether action, under the particular circumstances, is valid. Ombudsmen seek to act as negotiators between the providers and recipients of a particular service and come to a conclusion about satisfactory redress.

Ombudsmen are considered to be mediators or negotiators, acting independently and being an accessible service.

One-click shopping

One-click shopping is a facility that was originally introduced by Amazon. The system enables credit card customers to place orders on-line by simply clicking a single button. This has proved to be a considerable advantage over using a traditional website shopping cart and the requirement to fill out an order form on-line. The system automatically references the relevant stored address, and shipping and billing information. It also consolidates orders placed within specific time periods and generates a confirmation **email** to the customer. Many other internet-based businesses have tried to emulate Amazon's one-click shopping technology, but at present few have been able to reproduce the sophisticated system.

On-line analytical processing (OLAP)

OLAP is a software application which allows the user to selectively choose and view data from any number of points of view. It uses multi-dimensional views to replace standard relational databases, enabling the user to make a faster and more efficient analysis of the multi-dimensional information.

On-line banking

In most banks' view, on-line banking will eventually replace expensive and potentially inefficient branches. The vast majority of banks have an on-line presence of varying sophistication. Within the secure area of the bank's website customers are able to access their account balances, make transfers and pay bills on-line. Clearly there is no facility to be able to pay cash or cheques into the account. These transactions still have to be carried out on a more traditional basis. The advantages to the banks are that customers can access their accounts at any time, and that it reduces the need to store significant amounts of paperwork.

On-line bill payment

On-line bill payment allows customers to send and receive bills electronically via a bank or a secure service provider. Theoretically, these secure payments avoid paperwork, but few businesses have actually configured themselves to be able to receive and send payments electronically. This means that the majority of businesses still operate using a paper-based system, coupled with electronic payments.

On-line brokers

On-line brokers operate in the traditional way in which brokers buy and sell mortgages, loans, financial services, property, products, services and shares. It is believed that in the US the value of on-line brokerage has exceeded $1bn annually. On-line brokers continue to act as an intermediary between the buyer and the seller, and charge a commission for their involvement.

On-line conference calls

On-line conference calls are the natural successor to videoconferencing. They allow various individuals in different geographical locations to see and speak to one another via digital images and audio links in real-time. In effect the on-line conference is a form of chat in web-speak; a facility which allows individuals across the world to talk to one another through a chat room facility. Clearly on-line conference calls are a more sophisticated version of this facility and increasing numbers of telephone companies offer these services.

On-line parts purchasing systems

On-line parts purchasing systems are an increasingly useful component in **business-to-business (b2b)** as they allow manufacturers to purchase components either in a conventional way, by placing an order, or through auctions. Theoretically, the purchasing system allows a business to access the on-line marketplace and find the most appropriate parts at the best possible price. It is believed that in time this form of purchasing system will revolutionize the industrial parts market and public procurement.

On-line profiling

Websites use **cookies** and other personal information in order to create a profile of a user's buying and browsing habits. The website is then able to specifically configure particular pages and increasingly web advertising to suit that individual user's preferences. This means that the messages incorporated on the web pages are far more targeted towards the customer.

On-line transaction processing (OLTP)

On-line transaction processing allows multiple users to access large databases and is fundamental in dealing with **e-commerce** and electronic payments. On-line transaction processing incorporates electronic funds transfer, automated bill payments, reservations and electronic banking.

Operating profit

An operating profit, or indeed an operating loss, is calculated using the total trading activity of a business. The operating profit is calculated by deducting the operating expenses from the trading profit, or adding operating expenses to a trading loss, excluding any extraordinary or exceptional items which may otherwise distort the appreciation of the business. Interest is not deducted at this stage in calculating operating profit.

Operational resource management (ORM)

Operational resource management is a method used by businesses to acquire a better view of the costs of products and services in order to gain better financial control during the maintenance, repair and operation procurement process.

Operations management

Formerly, operations management was known as 'production management' and was applied almost exclusively to the manufacturing sector. For many organizations it is still used as a term in place of 'operations management'. However, the management function related to manufacturing has broadened to incorporate many other aspects related to the supply chain. It has therefore become common to use the term 'operations management' to describe activities related both to manufacturing and increasingly to the service sector. At its heart, operations management deals with the design of products and services, the buying of components or services from suppliers, the processing of those products and services and the selling of the finished goods. Across all of these disparate areas of business, operations management can be seen as an overarching discipline which seeks to quantify and organize the whole process. None the less, there is still a considerable emphasis placed on issues directly related to manufacturing, stock control and, to a lesser extent, the management of the distribution systems. As Figure 20 illustrates, a large manufacturing organization will include aspects of operations management under a wide variety of different, but closely related, managerial disciplines. Primarily, human resources, marketing, administration and finance and, of course, the research and development department of an organization support and are mutually dependent upon the operations division.

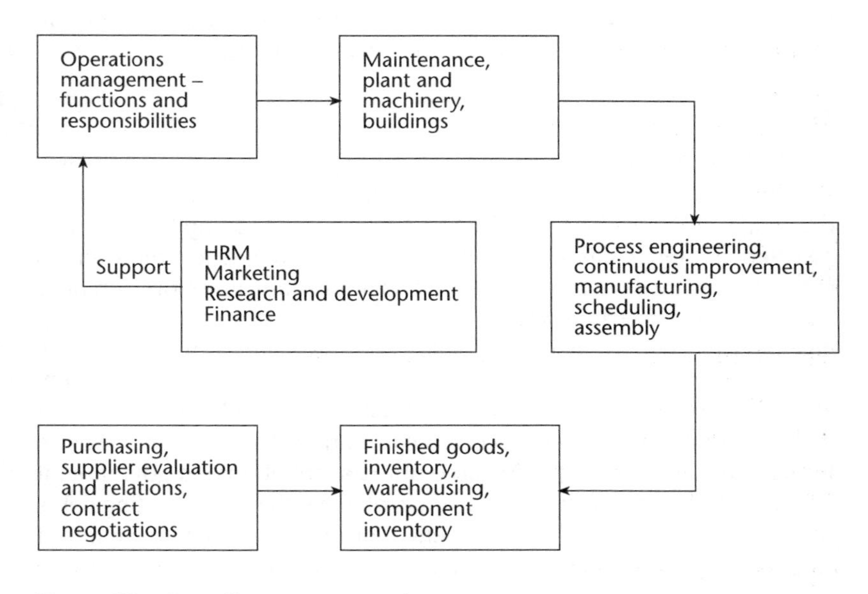

Figure 20 Operations management

Given the wide spread of different job roles and tasks within operations management, it is notoriously difficult to give a perfect definition of what an operations manager would actually do. Certainly they would be responsible for a wide range of different functions, but the functions themselves will often be determined by the nature of the business itself, whether it is a service-based industry or an organization primarily concerned with manufacturing.

Hill, Terry, *Operations Management: Strategic Context and Managerial Analysis*. Basingstoke: Palgrave Macmillan, 2000.

Opportunity cost

Opportunity cost, although strictly speaking an economics term, can be equally applied to marketing and advertising. Each time a business chooses to pursue a particular form of activity it has made that choice after having investigated all of the other options. Given the fact that it is unlikely, even with the largest budgets available, that a business can pursue all forms of activities simultaneously, some options have to be discarded. Opportunity cost argues that the potential benefits which could have been enjoyed by choosing a particular activity have to be considered if they are not chosen and an alternative action is preferred. In other words, opportunity cost examines the real cost of an action in terms of the next best alternative, which has been forgone.

Ordinary share

An ordinary share is a fixed unit of share capital of a business which is a publicly quoted organization whose shares are traded on the stock exchange. Ordinary shares yield a dividend on the capital that was invested in the purchase of the share. These dividends represent a proportion of the profits made by the business. Many investors purchase shares for longer-term rewards, taking the gamble that, whilst providing dividends throughout their ownership period, at some point in the future the shares will be worth considerably more than the price paid for them at the beginning of the investment. Ordinary shareholders are the last investors in the business to receive any return if the business goes into **liquidation**. Holders of **preference shares**, creditors and government agencies, including the Inland Revenue, all have their outstanding debts settled before ordinary shareholders. This makes ordinary shares a higher risk, yet they enjoy the benefits of the business should it prove to be successful.

Organizational culture

There are a number of ways in which an organization's culture can be classified. The main classifications were suggested by a number of researchers, including Harrison, Handy, Deal and Kennedy, and Quinn and McGrath. As years have passed, so these classifications have become more developed, making it impossible to approach them in anything other than broad terms.

In 1972 R. Harrison suggested four main categories of organizational culture – power, role, task and person. Charles Handy reworked Harrison's theory and identified them as described in Table 16.

During the 1980s Terence Deal and Allen Kennedy developed their own set of theories about organizational culture and the way in which it affected how management made decisions and formed strategies. Their conclusions are shown in Table 17.

Table 16 Organizational culture as seen by Handy

Culture	Description
Power	This type of culture is based on trust and good personal communication. There is little need for rigid bureaucratic procedures since power and authority are based on only a few individuals. The power culture is dynamic in that change can take place quickly but is dependent on a small number of key, powerful individuals. This culture tends to be tough on employees because the key focus is the success of the organization, often resulting in high labour turnover.
Role	This type of culture tends to be bureaucratic in nature, thus requiring logical, coordinated and rational processes with heavy emphasis on rules and procedures. Control lies with a small number of employees who have high degrees of authority. They tend to be in stable organizations, operating in a predictable environment with products and services that have a long lifespan. Not considered to be innovative organizations, they can adapt to gradual, minor change, but not to radical ones.
Task	This type of organizational culture relies on employee expertise. The matrix structure tends to prevail in these organizations, with teams of individuals specializing. They need, and tend, to be flexible organizations with individual employees working with **autonomy**, allowing fast reaction to changes in the external environment and having set procedures in place to address this aspect.
Person	This type of culture relies on collective decision making, often associated with partnerships. Compromise is important and individuals will tend to work within their own specialist area, coordinating all aspects and working with autonomy without the need to report to other employees.

Robert E. Quinn and M. E. McGrath also identified four different organizational cultures, as shown in Table 18.

It should be remembered that no one organization fits neatly into any one of the categories mentioned and the majority are too complex to be categorized generally. The classifications should be regarded only as a reference point for comparison of extremes.

Deal, Terrence and Kennedy, Allen, *Corporate Cultures*. New York: Perseus Publishing.
Handy, C. B., *Understanding Organizations*. Harmondsworth: Penguin, 1985.

Table 17 Organizational culture according to Deal and Kennedy

Culture	Description
Macho	These types of organization have to make decisions quickly and adopt a tough attitude towards their employees and managers. There is a high degree of internal competition and the operations tend to be high risk. The majority of these organizations do not form strategies or plan for the long term but are considered short-termist, with a low level of cooperation within the organization itself. There is a high labour turnover resulting in a weak organizational culture.
Work hard/ play hard	This type of culture tends to be associated with sales. The majority of individual employees are sales orientated but the level of risk is low. It is the employees' ability to accumulate sales that is important and the culture tends to encourage team-building and social activities for employees. The organization encourages competition and offers rewards for success, but does not necessarily rate quality as highly as volume.
Company	These types of organization are often in high-risk areas and operate on the basis that decisions take a long time to come to fruition. Decision making takes place at the top of this hierarchical organization and the overall approach can often be old-fashioned. Each new invention or technical breakthrough will pose a threat to the business.
Process	This type of culture operates in a low-risk, slow feedback environment where employees are encouraged to focus on how they do things rather than what they do. They tend to be based on systems and procedures, requiring employees to work in an orderly and detailed fashion, attending meetings and work groups. There will be rigid levels of management in the hierarchical structure, but because the organization operates in a predictable environment, reactions from management are often slow.

Harrison, R., 'How to Describe Your Organization', *Harvard Business Review*, September–October, 1972.

Quinn, R. E. and McGrath, M. R., *The Transformation of Organizational Cultures: A Competing Values Perspective in Organizational Culture*, ed. C. C. Lundberg and J. Martin. London: Sage Publications, 1985.

Schein, Edgar H., *Organizational Culture and Leadership*. San Francisco, CA: Jossey Bass Wiley, 1997.

Table 18 Organizational culture as classified by Quinn and McGrath

Culture	Description
Rational	The rational culture is firmly based on the needs of a market. The organization places emphasis on productivity and efficiency and encourages management to be goal-orientated and decisive. All activities are focused on tangible performance and employees are rewarded on achievement.
Adhocracy	This type of culture is an adaptive, creative and autonomous one where authority is largely based on the abilities and charismatic nature of leaders. These organizations tend to be risk-orientated and emphasis is placed on employees' adherence to the values of the organization itself.
Consensual	These types of organization are often concerned with equality, integrity and fairness and much of the authority is based on informal acceptance of power. Decisions are made by collective agreements or consensus and dominant leaders are not often present. Morale is important, as is cooperation and support between employees in order to reach organizational objectives. Employee loyalty is high.
Hierarchical	This type of culture relies on stability and control through the setting of rigid regulations and procedures. Decisions are made logically on facts alone with the management tending to be cautious and conservative. The employees are strictly controlled, with management expecting obedience.

Organizational development (OD)

Organizational development is a planned process of change. Organizational development is about performance improvement, in which businesses will seek to align more closely to the environment and markets in which they operate in order to achieve their strategies efficiently and effectively. OD can involve developing organizations in terms of culture, values, people, structures, processes and resources.

OD is a complex issue and often specific in terms of process, timing and those involved. There are, however, some overarching processes and elements that can be identified as being common to many OD situations. OD tends to begin with research into the current situation to assess all the issues. This research will inevitably involve the following aspects:

- clarifying the impact obligations which have to be honoured;
- the availability of appropriate resources such as skills, facilities and finances;
- the desires and career aspirations of those who will be affected;
- the proposed plan's overall fit with future business strategy.

Once the research process is completed, the organization should have a better view of how the OD will work in practice. This begins with the planning the change programme, which may involve the design of a new organizational structure, job descriptions and evaluation, salary and benefits provision, physical resources, phasing of the overall project and the management of impacts on existing employees.

Throughout the process, the organization needs to ensure that it conducts communication, development and counselling events to assist the establishment of the new organizational structure. It may also be necessary to reshape or re-profile certain areas of the organization with the intention of improving employee retention and the best use of skills and expertise in order to make the intended developments in efficiency.

Hamlin, Bob, Keep, Jane and Ash, Ken, (eds), *Organizational Change and Development: A Reflective Guide for Managers, Trainers and Developers*. London: Financial Times, Prentice-Hall, 2000.

Mello, Jeffrey, *Strategic Human Resource Management*. Mason, OH: South Western College Publishing, 2001.

Organizational effectiveness

The organizational effectiveness is measured in various ways by different businesses. Essentially, organizational effectiveness is a measure of performance against set standards, such as profitability, efficiency, earnings per employee, or a variety of other means. More generally, organizational effectiveness can be typified as being the business's ability to achieve predetermined outcomes or targets within a given time frame.

Organizational mapping

Organizational mapping seeks to identify the tasks and functions carried out by each individual employee, to act as a means by which under- or over-commitment of individuals can be identified. The process begins with assigning a number to each task which needs to be performed. It also requires the name of the responsible individual and the projected time which is required to perform the task, usually expressed as either hours or weeks. Once this has been carried out, it is possible to total up the projected time for the completion of all necessary tasks for each individual, which will produce either a negative or a positive number. The process should then reveal where key employees are over- or under-committed. Typically, the organizational mapping is displayed as a traditional organizational chart, which details the over- or under-commitment.

Organizational procedures

Organizational procedures are the rules and regulations which govern the ways in which a business operates. Most businesses develop, over a period of years, specific ways of dealing with particular situations and particular tasks. Adopting a series of organizational procedures should ensure that any relevant issues related to a task or situation are covered and dealt with by the relevant employee. Organizational procedures may incorporate specific statements related to a code of practice or a set series of steps which ensure that the task is carried out to the desired standard.

Organizational structure

The organizational structure of a business details the hierarchical levels in the case of a horizontally organized entity. Organizational structure can also be vertical by function or operation and indeed by use of a matrix. Traditionally, organizational structures kept functional areas separate, each having its own hierarchical levels. Increasingly, however, businesses have reduced the number of management layers and re-organized their businesses into operational units. Each operational unit will have access to marketing and production and other specialists in the form of a matrix.

See also **flat structure, functional structures, hierarchical structure, matrix structure.**

O

Outcome measure

An outcome measure can be defined as a means by which an intervention in a certain issue can be assessed. There are two ways of calculating the outcome measure; either the efficacy outcome (where the intervention was successful and produced the intended result) or the adverse outcome measure (where it was not successful).

Output measure

The output measure is an alternative means of describing the capacity of a business over a given period of time.

Outsourcing

The outsourcing of human resources is gradually gaining ground as a primary means by which the functions related to employees are handled by a business. There have been significant changes in policy where a shift has been in progress from providing human resources in-house to using external organizations. In effect, outsourcing is the use of another organization or an agency for some, or all, of the human resource functions.

Outsourcing is not merely restricted to the smaller business; notably, a business which has grown significantly over recent years has a greater tendency to consider outsourcing, largely as it prefers to focus on the operations of the core business, and there is a culture of outsourcing which has enhanced the growth.

In the US, the human resource industry as a whole was worth an estimated $13.9 billion in 1999 and, according to research businesses such as Dataquest, it is expected to have reached $37.7 billion in 2003.

Outsourcing human resources falls into four broad categories:

- Professional Employer Organizations (PEO) take on all of the responsibilities of the human resource administration for a business, including the legal responsibilities, the hiring and termination of employment. Typically, the relationship is cooperative, with the PEO handling human resources and the business itself dealing with all other aspects of operations. Not all PEOs take the full responsibility for human resources, and some merely handle payroll and benefits systems.
- Business Process Outsourcing (BPO), although a general term used to describe outsourcing in the broadest sense, refers to human resources in respect of supporting the human resource functions with technology and software (including data warehousing and other services).
- **Application Service Providers** (ASPs) restrict their relationship with a business to providing either web-based or customized software to help manage human resource functions such as payroll and benefits.
- E-services can be either ASPs or BPOs, whose relationship is again restricted to web-based services such as recruitment, software and data warehousing or other forms of data storage and access provision for human resources.

Incomes Data Services, *Outsourcing HR Administration*. London: Incomes Data Services, 2000.

Vanson, Sally, *The Challenge of Outsourcing Human Resources*. Oxford: Chandos Publishing Oxford, 2001.

Outworker

An outworker is an employee who carries out work for a business in a location other than the business's own premises. Although outworkers are directly employed by the business, they do not carry out their work under supervised or managed conditions, yet their output is assessed by quality control measures.

Overhead

Overheads are costs which are generated by a business that are not directly related to the production process. Many businesses refer to overheads as either **fixed costs** or **indirect costs** as they include costs related to the ownership and maintenance of the property in which the business operates, heating and lighting, and administrative costs.

Overtrading

Overtrading occurs when a business enters into commitments or transactions which are in excess of its available short-term resources. In other words, they have taken on commitments which, under current circumstances, they will find it impossible to complete. Overtrading can occur even when a business is trading profitably and, in most cases, it happens when there are financial strains on the business which are imposed by lengthy production cycles. The net effect of overtrading is to render the business incapable of continuing its operations, as it has over-committed its resources and will find it impossible to meet those commitments.

Pareto Principle

Vilfredo Pareto (1848–1923) was a French-born Italian economist and sociologist, known more widely for his theory on mass and elite interaction as well as his application of mathematics to economic analysis.

The fundamental concept of Pareto Analysis or the Pareto Principle is that a business derives 80% of its income from 20% of its customers (known as the 80:20 rule). In other words, this 20% of loyal customers are the foundations upon which a business can build its profits and its market share. On the reverse, the remaining 80% of its customers only provide the business with 20% of its income. This is largely due to the fact that these customers are irregular purchasers and are far more prone to brand switching.

Marketing aims to ensure that the profitable 20% of customers retain their customer loyalty and that, gradually, significant numbers of the remaining 80% are transformed into loyal customers, thus increasing market share and profitability.

Partnership

In partnerships those involved share the control, responsibility and finances. A partnership can consist of between 2 and 20 people and in essence the partners take on joint or shared responsibility for the running of the business. Both the profits and the liabilities are shared.

In the majority of countries there are two forms of partnership; an ordinary partnership means that the partners have unlimited liability and all profits are shared equally. Another feature of an ordinary partnership is that partners take on equal responsibility for decision making. Limited partnerships, on the other hand, offer limited liability – profits are shared equally, but the responsibility and control of the business lies with the ordinary partners. Limited partners do not necessarily involve themselves with the day-to-day running of the business.

Legally the partnership has to be set up in accordance with the Partnership Act (1890) and it is usual for partners to draw up a **partnership agreement** which legalizes the partnership. This details profits, liabilities and responsibilities.

Partnership agreement

A partnership agreement is generally drawn up either by the partners themselves or by a legal advisor. In essence the partnership agreement incorporates the following features:

- the amount of capital that each partner will invest;
- the profit ratio linked to the amount that was originally invested or will be subsequently invested;
- debt liabilities;
- seniority and control;
- rules regarding the admission of new partners;
- rules on ending the partnership.

In Britain, should disputes arise as a result of there not being a partnership agreement, the guidelines as set out in the Partnership Act (1890) are followed.

Passing off

Passing off occurs when a business adopts a similar name to an existing business, with the purpose of trying to use the other business's reputation in order to attract customers and sales. In effect, they are trying to take advantage of the **goodwill** which has been built up by the original business. In the vast majority of countries, passing off, if proved, is an illegal action, punishable by court action.

Password authentication procedure

A password authentication procedure is a validating process when a user requests network connection. Once a link is established, the user sends the network a password and identification. The server then validates and acknowledges this request. If the password and identification cannot be validated then the server will request that the information be entered once again, or will terminate the connection. A more secure version of this authentication procedure is known as the **challenge-handshake authentication protocol**.

Payback

Payback, or the payback period, is the time required for a project to repay the initial investment which was made by the business. Although the payback period calculations are not very sophisticated, they are often used as a method of investment appraisal. Typically, the formula to work out the payback period is:

$$\frac{\textit{Investment outlay}}{\textit{Contribution per month}} = \textit{Payback period}$$

The payback method is particularly useful for businesses which have somewhat erratic **cash flow** as it helps them to assess how long it will take for an investment in a particular project to repay itself. Unfortunately, the payback method is somewhat short-term in the way it approaches the possible return on investments. Should a project take a considerable amount of time to payback, it becomes increasingly difficult to predict exactly what might happen far into the future. This methodology also ignores profits and focuses on time, which means that this form of investment appraisal needs to be coupled with other assessment methods.

Payment processing

Payment processing refers to the use of third-party processors to assist in dealing with transactions. Typically, this would include banks and other organizations capable of dealing with **electronic payment systems**, including the use of debit and credit cards, ATMs, corporate purchasing and the payment of wages and salaries (**payroll processing**). For the most part, businesses **outsource** these payment systems, particularly as a result of the payment processors offering hardware, software and support services to allow a fully integrated payment-processing transaction system.

Payment systems

Payment systems can include a variety of hardware and software systems aimed at automating payment transactions. These would include payment systems at point of sale, credit card transactions and commercial accounts receivable. Internally, payment systems are also used for **payroll processing**.

P

Kou W. (ed.), *Payment Technologies for E-commerce*. Berlin and Heidelberg: Springer-Verlag, 2003.

Payroll processing

Payroll processing is the business function which deals with employee compensation. As an integral part of payroll processing, the employer needs to maintain records which track employer-paid benefits, deductions, pay and expense details, attendance records and a variety of other payroll-related issues. Payroll processing can be carried out internally using proprietary software programs or, increasingly, the function is **outsourced** to a specialist organization which also provides human resource management and administrative backup.

Performance appraisal/evaluation/review

Performance appraisals are the most common form of performance management, but the concept also incorporates employee feedback, development and compensation. Overwhelmingly, however, the majority of employees are dissatisfied with performance management systems (the Society of Human Resource Management quotes a 90% figure).

Framing an effective performance management system can be fraught with difficulties; however, the following aspects are seen to be integral to the creation of such a scheme:

- A clear definition and measurement of performance is vital.
- Content and measurement should derive from internal and external customers.
- There should be a formal process of investigating and correcting situational influences and constraints on performance.

Above all, accurate and fair performance management needs to assess employees in relation to the factors listed in Table 19.

360-degree appraisal has rapidly become an integral part of performance management. A standard 360-degree appraisal system requires face-to-face feedback sessions, where employees are given an opportunity both to ask their own questions and to listen to feedback.

Table 19 Performance management requirements

Communication, coordination and support	Equipment and environment
Amount and relevance of training received.	Equipment and tools necessary to do the job.
Information, instructions and specifications needed to do the job.	Process for obtaining and retaining raw materials, parts, supplies.
Coordination of work activities.	Dependability of equipment.
Cooperation, communication and relations between co-workers.	Conditions in which job is performed.
Financial resources available and time allowed to produce quantity and quality of work.	

Many businesses have instituted a more sophisticated system in which employees are evaluated by a number of individuals, including senior staff and colleagues. The quality of the data which is collected is high and becomes the primary focus and driving force behind training programmes. In order to ensure that the system works to its best potential, there are six steps which need to be considered. These are summarized in Table 20.

After these six steps, a development plan needs to be agreed in order to identify specific steps and intended outcomes. There also needs to be a genuine commitment by the business to provide resources and other support in order for these outcomes to be achieved.

Table 20 Six requirements for employee evaluation

Steps	**Description**
Open mind	Those undergoing the appraisal need to have commitment, vision and often the courage to face how they are viewed, as well as a willingness to implement any suggestions. As drawbacks are highlighted, an objective and open-minded view needs to be taken towards criticism.
Self-evaluation	A clear and honest listing of current competences is essential. The gaps in competences should be highlighted and prioritized, as this gives a clear message to those providing feedback that the individual is prepared to discuss critical areas of his or her abilities.
Plan of action	There needs to be a clearly established set of performance categories. Normally feedback will be provided by managers and peers, both direct and indirect colleagues. The ideal number should not exceed 6–8 individuals.
Mental preparation	Self-evaluation techniques require an individual not to be defensive and to be prepared to receive feedback. Whatever is said needs to be listened to and accepted.
Action	During the interviews those providing feedback are delivering the information for a positive purpose. Advice, suggestions and assistance should be sought, as well as clarification. The interview should be frank and honest.
Analysis	In essence, the feedback needs to be analysed in terms of strengths and weaknesses that have been identified. The strengths and weaknesses need to be categorized in order to identify areas of improvement or, perhaps, clarification. Specific areas may need specific actions.

Appraisals are, in effect, a way of judging an employee's performance in a given job. The performance appraisal considers more than productivity, but is often used as the basis upon which increases in wages or salaries are considered. Whilst managers and colleagues constantly form and reform opinions of those who work for them or with them, a formal appraisal meeting puts these considerations into a more formal context.

The basic functions of an appraisal system are:

- to determine the short-, medium- and long-term future of the employee;
- to identify possible training needs;
- to motivate the employee;
- to assist management in deciding what levels of pay increases will be accorded to that individual.

Typically, appraisals will take the form of a performance review, a potential review or a rewards review. There are, of course, a number of different ways in which appraisal schemes are organized, which include the ranking method, the 360-degree performance appraisal, rating scales and behaviourally anchored rating scales (BARS).

Appraisals rely on being able to provide positive criticism to individuals, and the setting of realistic standards which require the employee to give maximum effort in order to achieve the set goals. Appraisal systems need to have clearly defined rules and expectations and, above all, the appraiser (the individual delivering the appraisal) and the appraisee (the individual being appraised) need to be speaking the same language. This implies, therefore, that a degree of training for both parties needs to be instituted prior to the running of an appraisal system. This not only sets the pattern and nature of the appraisal, but also allows for the unscheduled reviewing of factors which have been brought up during the appraisal interviews. Clear documentation needs to be drawn up, as well as a log to note performance deficiencies and performance improvements.

DeNisi, A. S. and Kluger, A. N., 'Feedback Effectiveness: Can 360-degree Appraisals be Improved?' *Academy of Management Executive*, 14 (1) (2000), pp. 129–39.

Ghorpade, J., 'Managing Five Paradoxes of 360-degree Feedback', *Academy of Management Executive*, 14 (1) (2000), pp. 140–50.

Maddux, Robert B., *Effective Performance Appraisals*. New York: Crisp Publications, 2000.

Neal, James E. and Neal, James E., Jr, *The #1 Guide to Performance Appraisals: Doing it Right!* Perrysburg, OH: Neal Publications, 2001.

Neal, James E., Jr, *Effective Phrases for Performance Appraisals: A Guide to Successful Evaluations*. Neal Publications, 2003.

Soltani, Ebrahim, Gennard, John, van der Meer, Robert and Williams, Terry, *Content Issues of HR-Related Performance Measurement: A Total Quality Management Approach*. Research paper, University of Strathclyde.

Performance gap

A performance gap is the difference between an objective and the actual results. Most businesses will establish their own key **performance indicators**, which will allow them to focus on the **critical success factors**. The indicators can be used to determine the degree of change and are invariably an established target associated with a particular date. The performance gap is, therefore, the difference between where the business is at that date and where it had hoped or assumed it would be.

See also **gap analysis.**

Performance goal

Central to the concept of performance goals is the setting of specific measurable goals. In achieving all conditions of a measurable goal a business can be confident and comfortable in its achievement. However, if it consistently fails to meet measurable goals, these will need to be adjusted or an analysis needs to take place to find out the reason(s) for the failure. Businesses will often set unrealistically high goals for various reasons, including:

- setting the goals in accordance with an external party's over-optimistic appraisal, which may not take into account the actual abilities of the business;
- insufficient information – the business will often not have a clear, realistic understanding of what it is trying to achieve or the skills and knowledge that are required;
- expecting that the business will always perform well and at its optimum; this is an unrealistic suggestion as many factors can affect performance and it is often better to set goals based on average performance, which could be consistent.

Alternatively, goals can be set too low for the following reasons:

- Fear of failure – a business that lacks self-confidence will not consider it wise to set goals which are risky. It will ignore the fact that failure can be positive as it shows where skills and performance need to be improved.
- Taking the easy option – this is an attractive basis for goal setting as it does not require the business to stretch itself, but the achievement of these goals would probably be worth very little.

Goal-setting needs to be at the correct level and this is a skill which can only be acquired by practice. Unrealistic goals are self-defeating because the business will quickly realize that there is little point in putting serious effort into goals which cannot be reached. Goals should not be set in stone; they need to be continually measured and adjusted.

Performance indicator

Performance indicators are the key measurement of performance in a business and are continually monitored and assessed. They aim to identify particular strengths and weaknesses. Whilst many businesses may adopt a series of key performance indicators (KPIs), measuring efficiency (input versus output), adaptability (reconfiguring time), financial strength (return on equity) and effectiveness (non-defects produced), others divide them into the following key areas:

- Behaviour – relating to the management of staff, including labour turnover, absenteeism, accidents, etc.
- Confidence – examining the relationship between the organization and its broader environment, specifically its **stakeholders**.
- Ethics – considering the standards of behaviour of the organization against set criteria.
- Operation – which considers profitability, product mixes, portfolios, productivity and output.
- Specific issues – such as profit per employee, returns on investment, delivery speed and quality targets.
- Strategy – considering the overall effectiveness of the organization.

Businesses will attempt to identify leading indicators which will help them quickly respond to conditions just as the situation is beginning to have an impact on their operations. They can then make adjustments to their processes before unexpected outcomes affect them.

Performance management

Performance management can be seen as a systematic and data-oriented approach to managing employees, based on positive reinforcement as the primary driver to maximize their performance. Performance management assumes that there is a disparity between what an employee is currently achieving (on the basis that they have to do this work and perform to this standard) and the possibility that they desire to perform better (based on the assumption that they have desires to perform more effectively if given the opportunity and the encouragement). In many respects, the concept behind performance management is a recognition of this potential gap between actual performance and desired performance. This can be illustrated in the graph in Figure 21, which identifies the discretionary effort of an individual. This discretionary effort is applied according to circumstances and is variable. Performance management seeks to identify the gap between 'having to' and 'wanting to' and to push the performance up to the 'want to' level.

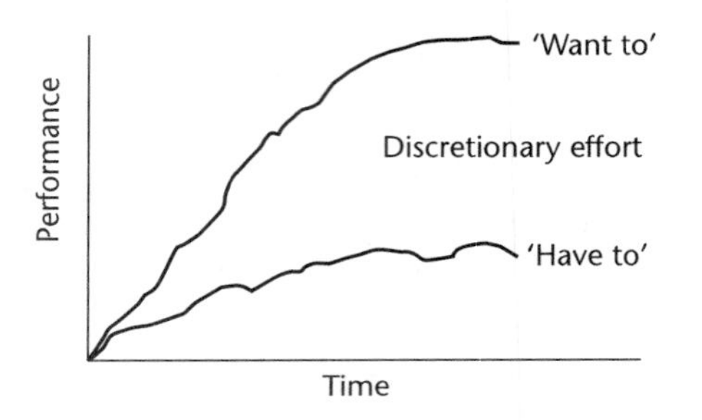

Figure 21 The performance gap

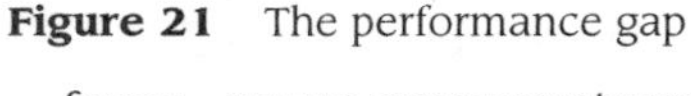

Performance management has been used in its various forms since the mid-1970s and it is believed to be applicable to almost every area of a business. Its primary focus is, of course, employees. The first major step in implementing a performance management system is to move away from negative reinforcement of standards, which seeks to punish individuals for not performing to (often) unspoken levels of performance. Performance management uses positive reinforcement to generate effort beyond what is normally (minimally) exhibited by the employees. In this way, the discretionary effort is encouraged and the organization as a whole can move towards a maximization of performance.

Kotter, John P. and Heskett, James L., *Corporate Culture and Performance*. New York: Free Press, 1992.

Porter, Michael, *The Competitive Advantage: Creating and Sustaining Superior Performance*. New York: Simon & Schuster, 1998.

Performance measurement

Performance measurement is a means by which a business can monitor its key **performance indicators**. Typically, these may include output, cost and asset utilization and other measures. Performance measurement is an important tool in business improvement.

Permission marketing

Permission marketing is also known as request marketing and involves direct marketing approaches to customers who have expressed an interest in receiving further information, news and updates from a particular business. Permission marketing is used in several different areas of marketing and across a wide variety of different industries. Conventional forms of permission marketing relate to the continued contact with customers who have requested brochures or sales literature on a previous occasion, but who may not have yet purchased products or services from the business. Alternatively, they may be lapsed customers who are still on a business's database.

Permission marketing has developed considerably over the last few years alongside the increased intensity of business use of the internet. It is closely associated with concepts such as opt-in **email** or other positive customer-initiated contacts with a business. Permission marketing practitioners distinguish their form of marketing from the more intrusive forms of direct mailing or emailing unsought sales messages to customers. Permission marketing, by its very nature, assumes that the customer has a basic form of interest in what the business is offering and that they welcome the periodic contact with the business.

Godin, Seth, *Permission Marketing: Turning Strangers into Friends and Friends into Customers*. New York: Free Press, 2002.

Personal development plan

Increasingly, individuals have ultimate career ambitions or career goals. With many organizations offering fewer advancement opportunities, individuals are gradually taking ownership of their own careers. In order to achieve this they set themselves time-related career objectives. These detail a list of knowledge and skills which are required, and which form the basis of a training plan. This is the very essence of a personal development plan: the gradual and timely acquisition of knowledge and skills by participation in seminars, workshops, secondments and conferences. Personal development plans do not necessarily have to evolve around traditional qualifications. Increasingly, knowledge and skills are acquired by experience rather than examination.

Personal digital assistants (PDAs)

A personal digital assistant is a hand-held device which offers a variety of functions, including diaries or internet access. PDAs are essentially the modern-day equivalent of a Filofax but these hand-held minicomputers are capable of storing all the data an individual may need during the day, incorporating spreadsheets and word processors. PDAs can use keyboards, computer stylus or touch screen displays and allow the user to transfer information to and from desktops or laptops into the PDA. The great advantage of PDAs is their battery life, weight and size, making them an increasingly viable alternative to laptops.

Personal information management (PIM)

PIM is a software program which enables users to organize the information which they have to deal with on a daily basis to suit their own personal style. It can be loaded onto a standard desktop, laptop or **personal digital assistant**. PIMs are also available on the internet and they are currently being offered free in order to improve their **stickiness**.

Personalization

Personalization is a growing area of sales and marketing, as it seeks to provide individual customers, or groups of customers, with adapted versions of the basic product. Specific changes or amendments can be made to the standard offering – for example, customers can buy a regular model of a vehicle but determine the colour, the trim and the internal colours and layout. Personalization has become possible as businesses adopt a more market-orientated approach and adapt their production systems to produce products and services on demand, rather than stockpiling supplies in the anticipation of sales. Personalization allows marketing to focus on the individuality of the products and the options and choices available to each and every customer.

Kasanoff, Bruce, *Making it Personal: How to Profit from Personalization without Invading Privacy*. Chichester: John Wiley, 2001.

Personnel specification

A personnel specification highlights the main characteristics which will be required from the individual who is to undertake a job role. Dependent on the requirements of the job, these characteristics will include:

- physical attributes;
- current attainments;
- intelligence levels;
- aptitudes;

- interests;
- disposition;
- circumstances.

The personnel specification is used in relation to a **job specification**, from which a **job description** is written.

PEST analysis

See **Five Forces.**

Piecework

Piecework means that employees are not paid for the hours that they work but instead are paid for the number of items produced. A worker should, theoretically, not get less than the minimum wage if paid on a piecework basis.

Many factories pay staff a flat rate per hour plus 'piece' work (so much extra per piece of work), which allows experienced staff the opportunity to increase their wages.

Portal

A portal is, in effect, a gateway onto the internet. From this initial gateway users can access all information, connect to other websites or check their **email**. The most common forms of portal include Yahoo and AOL which are designed to be user-friendly and offer a variety of general information on the portal page. Businesses have developed their own portals, which are designed for employee access to information from the databases, human resources, press releases and on-line newsletters. Some portals are essentially directories or a catalogue of information regarding websites. Increasingly, towns and cities have their own portal, linking to sporting events, cultural activities, classified advertising and weather forecasts, etc.

Portfolio analysis

Product portfolio analysis is probably most closely associated with attempts to assess the market growth rate and a product's relative market share. Product portfolio analysis is a key marketing activity in determining the direction and intensity of marketing strategies.

See also **Boston Growth Matrix.**

Preference share

Preference shares pay a fixed dividend and compared with **ordinary shares** they offer greater security to the investor, as they are repaid in full before ordinary **shareholders** are paid. Unlike ordinary shares, however, preference shares do not normally have voting rights and neither do the shares entitle the owner to a slice of the business's profits, in as much as if profits are up, the fixed dividend remains the same.

Press releases

Press releases, or news releases, are an integral part of **public relations**. They are written and designed in order to provide the media with an easy to translate, newsworthy story regarding the business or its products and services. Press releases are sent to reporters and editors, in the hope that some editorial space will be assigned to the story. Typically, press releases will include quotes that have a personal angle and may be accompanied by relevant photographs or other illustrative material, in order to reduce the amount of legwork that needs to be done to follow up and present the story in the media.

Northmore, David, *How to Get Publicity for Free: How to Write a Press Release, Contact the Media, Gain Radio and Television Interviews and Organise Press Conferences*. London: Bloomsbury, 1993.

Private limited company

A private limited company is a joint stock, privately owned business which raises capital through selling parts of the business in the form of shares. Normally, limited companies were either former **partnerships** or family concerns. Under Britain's Companies Act no more than 50 people can hold shares with a company and they must be 'desirable individuals'. A private limited company needs a board of directors who will control the business and these are usually elected or appointed by the shareholders. This usually means that some form of election process needs to be carried out. In addition to this the business needs to have the following:

- a **memorandum of association**, which details the business's name, address, what they do, liabilities and the amount and division of shares;
- **articles of association** stating who owns the shares, the qualifications and duties of the directors, the division of profits and the methods of audit;

P

- a statement of the nominal capital;
- a list of the directors;
- a list of declarations, which state that the business has put in place the regulations as set out in the Companies Act.

Once this has been completed the business will receive its **certificate of incorporation** and will be able to trade as a limited company. As a private limited company the business must publish its annual accounts and send them to Company's House, where they will be available for inspection. Shareholders have limited liability, so beyond the amount which they originally invested, or have subsequently invested, in the business, they do not stand to lose further.

Privatization

Privatization is the process of selling publicly owned operations to the private sector. This is also known as denationalization. Politically, in Britain, privatization was a major trend during the 1980s and 1990s when the majority of large nationalized industries were sold, including the railways, telecommunications, electricity supply and generation, and the water authorities. It was argued that many of the businesses had become inefficient and bureaucratic and that they were monopolies which exploited consumers. The government used the money received from the sale of these nationalized industries to reduce the tax burden.

Process characterization model (PCM)

This is a model which aims to describe the behaviour and capabilities of a particular process, independent of a particular application. Typically it would attempt to capture numerical data regarding the dynamic behaviour of a process.

Process management

Process management involves the investigation of the activities of a business which contribute towards the total activity of the organization. Typically this would include the **procurement** of materials and equipment, the development of products and services, the production or creation of those products and services, delivery, distribution and customer support. A key aspect of process management is to break down each of the steps and see where improvements need to be implemented. In ensuring this process, a process-orientated model needs to be developed, an example of which can be seen in Figure 22.

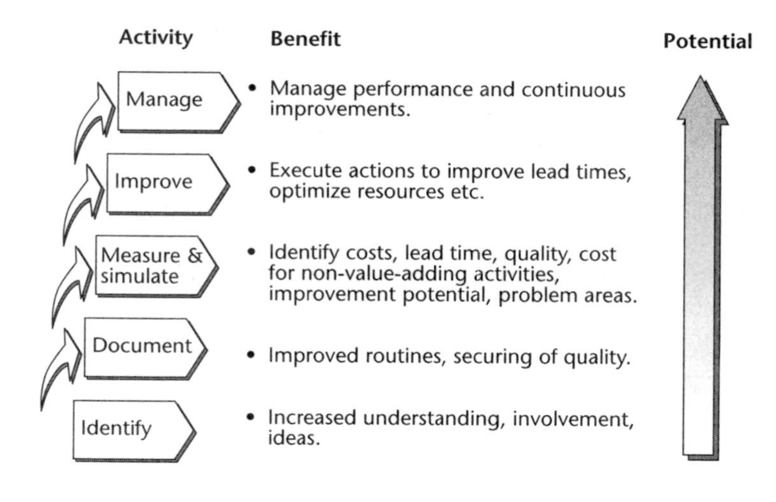

Figure 22 A process management model

Building models such as these requires an intimate knowledge of all of the functions of the business, as a full model would include specific activities, steps in the process, functions of different parts of the organization, and available information and materials. Models can also contain information regarding potential problems and ideas for future improvement.

Process mapping

There are four major steps in process mapping:

1. Process identification – which entails a full appreciation of all of the steps of a process.
2. Information gathering – which seeks to identify objectives, risks and controls within that process.
3. Interviewing and mapping – collating the views of all individuals involved in the process, and then designing the actual process maps.
4. Analysis – the careful analysis of the process map in order to ensure that the process operates efficiently and effectively.

Two of the most important documents which underpin the process mapping are the process profile worksheet and the workflow survey. The process profile worksheet looks at the trigger events, the inputs and the outputs, the risks, key controls and other measures of success. The workflow surveys are carried out by employees working on the process and include a detailed list of all of the tasks carried out. Business process mapping should enable the business to understand what it is trying to achieve and highlight ideas which could streamline those operations.

Jacka, J. Mike and Keller, Paulette J., *Business Process Mapping: Improving Customer Satisfaction*. Chichester: John Wiley, 2002.

Process paradox

The process paradox suggests that a business can decline, or even fail, at the very point when changes in its processes have dramatically improved their efficiency and saved the business time and money, whilst improving quality. The concept, which was suggested by Peter Keen, suggests that this paradoxical situation can occur because the immense benefits are not translated into business value.

Keen, Peter, *The Process Edge: Creating Value Where it Counts*. Watertown, MA: Harvard Business School Publishing, 1997.

Streatfield, Philip J., *The Paradox of Control in Organizations: Complexity and Emergence in Organizations*. London: Routledge, 2001.

Process planning

Process planning involves the development of a set of instructions which describe a sequence of tasks to be performed in order to achieve a particular goal. Typically they will specify the raw materials and components required to produce a product and what tasks are required to transform these into a finished product. Process planning, therefore, specifies, in the most precise terms, how a business manufactures a particular product in line with its technical specifications. Process planning is essential in order to make the link between product design and product manufacturing.

Procurement

Procurement is the purchasing of products and services which fit a clearly defined purpose. In addition to this, procurement involves the selection of quality products and services, which are not necessarily the lowest priced. Sound procurement management requires not only quality but the right products and services, which deliver value for money and, above all, are delivered when promised. Procurement is one of the fundamental functions of a business and, increasingly, it is not simply the buying process but is a move towards forging partnerships with suppliers in order to secure cost-effective and reliable products and services to agreed standards. As such, procurement also incorporates the liaison and negotiation with suppliers, the analysis of bids, the agreeing of contracts, the maintenance of records and the handling of problems. Procurement also incorporates having to remain within budget and the responsibility of spending money wisely on behalf of the business.

Baily, Peter, Farmer, David, Jessop, David and Jones, David, *Purchasing Principles and Management*. London: Financial Times, Prentice-Hall, 1998.

Product life cycle

The product life cycle is a widely accepted model which describes the stages a product or service, or indeed a category, passes through from its introduction to its final removal from the market. The model suggests that the introduction stage, or the launch, of the product, during which the product sells in small numbers and marketing activities are expensive, is superseded, if successful, by 3 other stages (see Figures 23–5). The growth stage is characterized by higher sales, greater profitability, but crucially, more competition. At the maturity stage, providing a product has managed to survive, stable sales and a higher level of profitability are enjoyed. The final stage, known as the decline stage, shows that the product is finally declining in terms of demand and associated profits. Optionally, it is possible to insert a further stage between maturity and decline, denoting a period of the product's life cycle when competition has reached a stage which makes it difficult to sustain the original product. Indeed, it may be the case that the product is already growing stale. This saturation period marks a slight downturn, which can be adjusted by a re-launch or a repackaging of the product, otherwise it will begin its inevitable slip into the decline stage. At the decline stage, the business needs to carefully consider its policy towards the product or service, as it is not merely a question of letting the item fade away over a period of time (perhaps when stocks are finally exhausted). An abandonment policy must be put in place which takes into account the ramifications in terms of its impact on staffing levels, the deployment of human and other resources, as well as its impact on the market, suppliers and distributors.

Rink and Swan (1979) presented product life cycle patterns, which affords an opportunity to consider whether a business is able to influence or manage the shape of the curve (see Figure 26). Specifically, the implicit ideas of the various shapes offer the following opportunities:

P

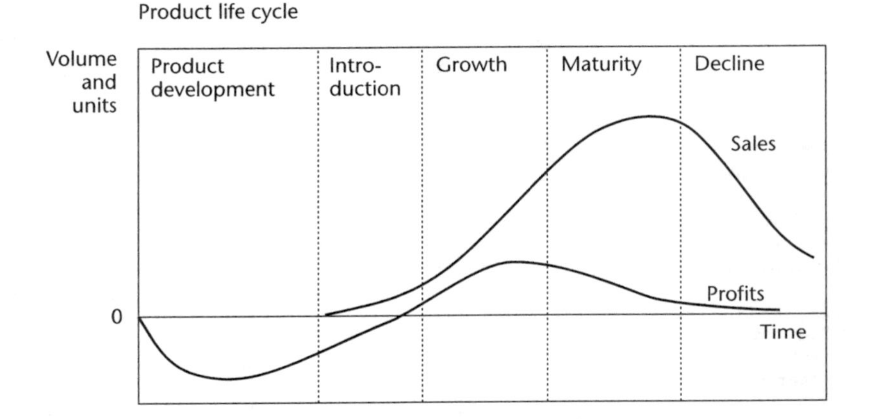

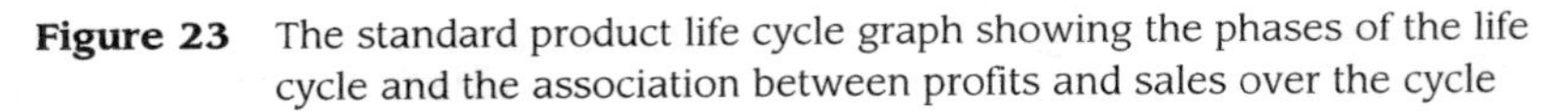
Figure 23 The standard product life cycle graph showing the phases of the life cycle and the association between profits and sales over the cycle

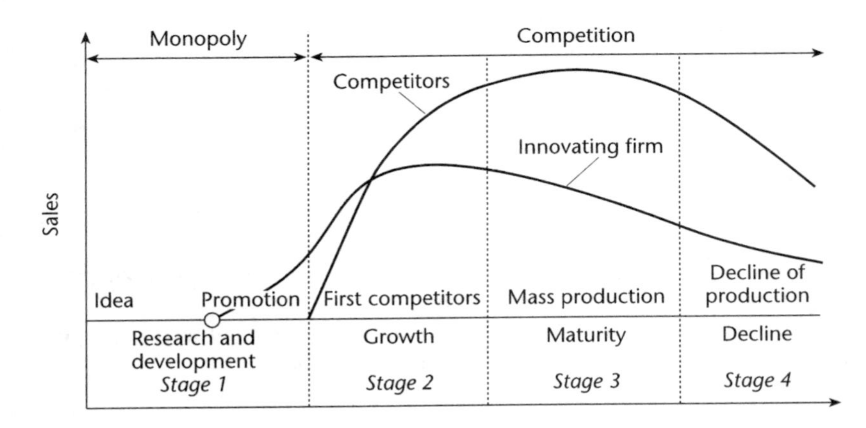

Figure 24 This is a more complex view of the product life cycle, which illustrates the dangers often faced by product innovators in developing new product ideas only to lose the potential of sales as a result of the actions of competitors.

1 The most critical problem for a multi-product business is to determine how its limited resources will be allocated to various products in the most optimum way. In this respect, the product life cycle concept is an ideal basis for optimizing the allocation of the resources.

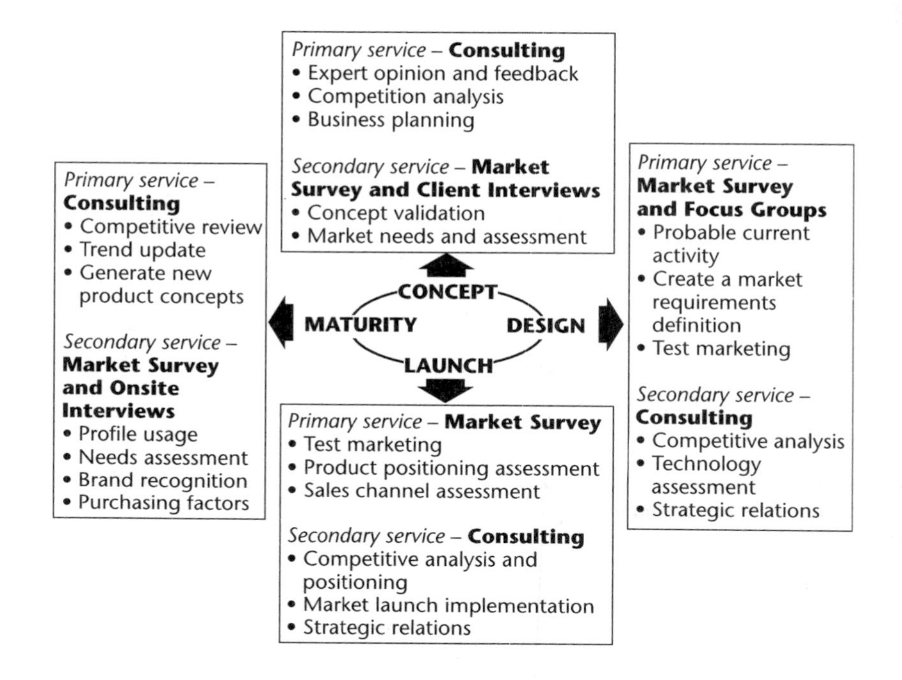

Figure 25 Product life cycle

2 The multi-dimensional approach is useful in conceptualizing the product life cycle of future products.
3 The use of product life cycles is ideal when brought into the equation as far as business planning is concerned.

Onkvisit, Sak and Shaw, John J., *Product Life Cycles and Product Management*. Westport, CT: Greenwood Press, 1989.

Rink, D. and Swan, J., 'Product Life Cycle Research: A Literature Review'. *Journal of Business Research*, vol. 40 (1979), pp. 219–43.

Production scheduling

Production scheduling involves the organization of production in order to meet either actual or forecasted customer demand. Usually a schedule chart is used to show the progress of particular jobs and where they are on the schedule for completion at the assigned times.

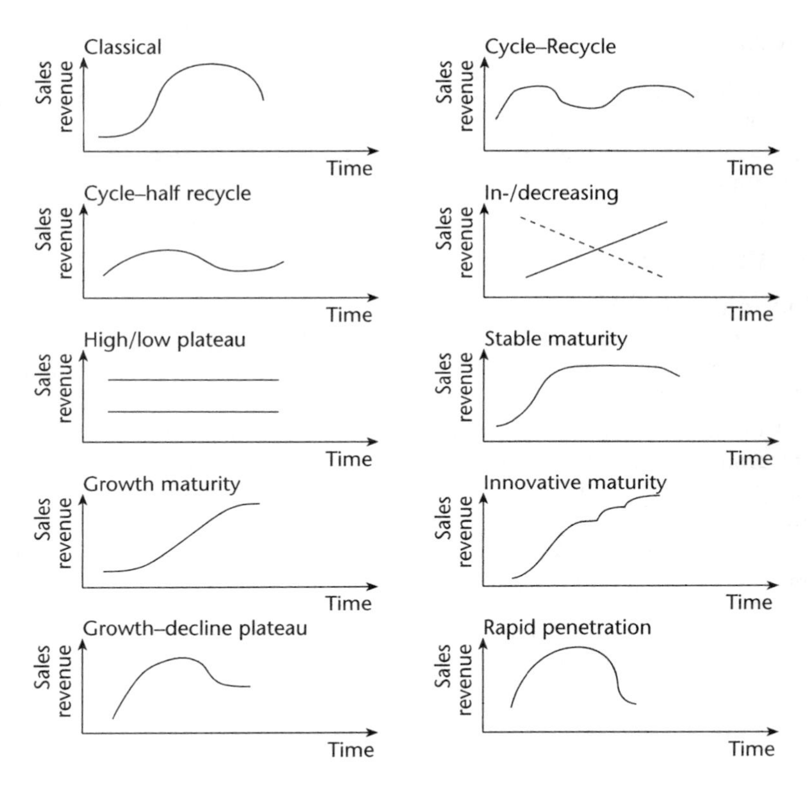

Figure 26 Product life cycle patterns

Source: Rink and Swan (1979).

Productivity

Productivity is a measure of an organization's outputs divided by its inputs. In other words an estimation of the value of products and services produced and offered by the business compared with the costs of employees, capital, materials and other associated costs.

Professional services administration (PSA)

Professional services administration, also known as service process optimization, aims to make the best use of resources, including people, intellectual capital and time. It also considers both outward functions and inward processes. PSA is used to analyse the knowledge gained from each project to improve planning, increase profitability and decrease inefficiencies.

Profit centre

A profit centre is an area of a business to which revenue can be traced. Part of the process in establishing the profitability of a particular part of a business is to compare the revenue derived from that section or department against the costs of running that operation.

Profit sharing

This is a term which is applied to a number of schemes offered by employers which aim to give the employees a stake in the business; many were prompted in the UK by the Finance Acts (1978, 1980 and 1984).

Around 20 per cent of UK business has some form of employee share ownership and the move is seen as being a form of employee participation and industrial democracy. In reality, however, the level of share ownership is low and the employees have little or no real control over the business (mainly as the shares tend to have non-voting rights). The three most common forms of profit sharing are:

- Employee share ownership plans (ESOP), which were brought to the UK from the US and provide a means by which employees can gain equity in the business. A trust is formed and the dividends on the preference shares pay off the loans used to purchase the shares on behalf of the employees. The shares are held in trust, but employees have the right to sell them.
- Profit sharing schemes (PSS) usually take the form of approved profit sharing (APS) schemes, which involve the distribution of shares to employees free of charge. Shares are purchased through a trust, which is financed from the profits of the business. Alternatively, employees can become involved in SAYE (save-as-you-earn), which is when employees sign a savings contract with the option to purchase shares at the end of a contract period at a predetermined price. Both of these methods are popular as they have tax benefits attached to them.
- Profit-related pay (PRP) schemes are present in around 20 per cent of private-sector business and are, essentially, an element in the total employee pay package. Profit-related pay is variable according to the profits made by the business, making a direct link between the activities of the employees, their productivity and the extra pay that they ultimately receive in the form of PRP.

Profit sharing is seen as being an effective means by which a business can encourage individual performance and motivation. Employees have a direct interest in the success of the business and therefore greater commitment and profit-consciousness.

The obvious downside as far as employees are concerned is that they are tying both their jobs and their savings to the success or failure of the business. As far as the business is concerned there is also a worry that increasing staff involvement (particularly in share ownership) may mean that they will make increasing demands on the business to have a greater role in the decision making. Management may be unwilling to concede in the area of strategic decision making which can affect the profitability and employee pay, as they may be considering longer-term issues.

Project accounting (PA)

Project accounting is neither **project management** nor financial accounting. Project accounting takes traditional accounting data and measures variations between estimated and actual costs. It does this on a real-time project-by-project basis, allowing adjustments to be made to correct **variance**. Project accounting has grown out of the need by businesses to analyse their performance at a micro-level in order to become more efficient and competitive.

Project management

Project management involves the planning, organizing, controlling and directing of usually one-off activities. Typically, a team will be assigned to manage a specific project and will use a project evaluation and review technique (PERT) or **critical path analysis** in order to structure the management of the activities related to the project.

Project planning

Project planning is the process which is concerned with organizing the implementation of a project in order to meet its objectives in terms of costs, functionality, quality, reliability and scheduling. A project plan serves five main functions:

- It defines the scope of the project and states the end products that will be delivered, taking into account any assumptions or constraints.
- It details the project activities and how they will be performed.
- It details the inter-dependence between the activities and a schedule of when these activities will be accomplished.

- It identifies the resources required in order to develop the project to meet its end results.
- It describes all the procedures and processes which will be managed during the project in terms of scheduling, cost, **procurement**, risk and quality.

Figure 27 illustrates the inter-relationship between the activities. The core processes are those required to implement the project, whilst the facilitating processes ensure that the project meets the goals and will be managed in a successful manner.

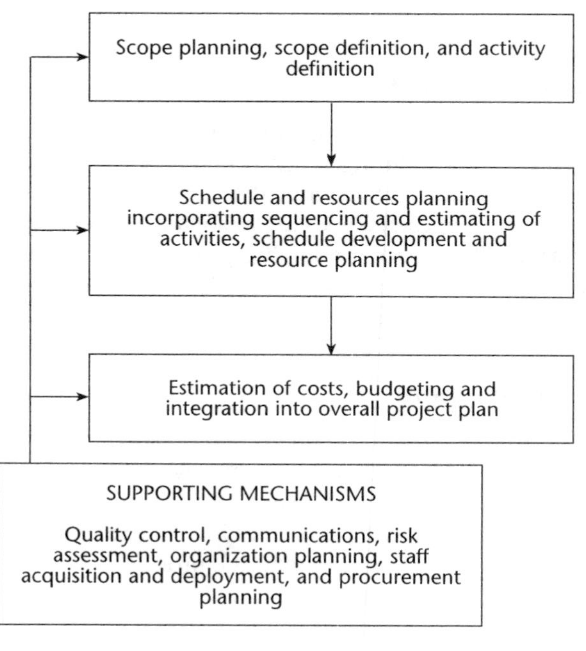

Figure 27 Project planning

Lester, Albert, *Project Planning and Control*. Oxford: Butterworth-Heinemann, 2003.

Project portfolio management (PPM)

A project portfolio is simply a collection of projects. The projects will be at various stages in their progress and some will, at different times, need more attention than others. The art of project portfolio management is to balance the needs of all of the projects throughout their life cycle and ensure that each of them remains consistent with the **project management** process, provides progress reports, and that systems are consistently applied to them across the organization. This will enable the business to better allocate resources, with a clearer understanding of forthcoming requirements.

Lester, Albert, *Project Planning and Control*. Oxford: Butterworth-Heinemann, 2003.

Pty (South Africa, Australia)

A Pty is shorthand for proprietary and is used for a company definition in Australia, South Africa and several other countries. A Pty is the equivalent of the British **private limited company**.

Public key encryption

A public key encryption is a cryptographic system which uses two keys. The public key is widely known and a private or secret key is only known to the recipient of a message. Public key systems are becoming popular for transmitting information via the internet as they are secure and comparatively simple to use. They do, however, require the sender of the message to know the recipient's public key in order to encrypt a message for them.

Public limited company (Plc)

A public limited company is a British form of business which has at least £50,000 of authorized share capital. These businesses, with the Plc suffix, are quoted on the stock exchange and their shares can be publicly traded. The majority of public limited companies were former **private limited companies** who have chosen this route in order to attract greater investment.

Public relations

The basic function of public relations is to establish and maintain a mutual understanding between a business and its publics. Typically, public relations activities will include the preparation of press kits, holding seminars, making charitable donations and sponsorships, fostering community relations, and lobbying.

Broadly, public relations have the following objectives:

- Establish and maintain the prestige and reputation of the business.

- Support the promotion of products and services.
- Deal with arising issues and opportunities.
- Establish and maintain goodwill with customers, employees, government, suppliers and distributors.
- Deal promptly with unfavourable publicity.

In effect, public relations seeks to transfer a negative or null opinion of the business into knowledge or a positive attitude. Public relations can be seen as distinctly different from advertising, as can be seen in Table 21.

Table 21 Public relations and advertising compared

Public relations	Advertising
Informative	Informative and persuasive
Subdued messages	Immediate impact
No repetition	Repetition
Credibility	Less credible
Newsworthy	Not necessary
Low cost	High cost

Davis, A., *Mastering Public Relations*. Basingstoke: Palgrave Macmillan, 2004.
Mazur, Laura and White, Jon, *Strategic Communications Management: Making Public Relations Work*. Reading, MA: Addison-Wesley, 1994.

Purchasing systems

Increasingly, purchasing systems have been converted into automated hardware and software purchasing systems. An increasing amount of purchasing transactions are being carried out through electronic exchange. Traditional purchasing systems required the purchasing department to acquire authorization to place an order and all of the aspects of the transaction were backed up with paperwork, which has now largely been replaced by virtual systems.

Pure play

'Pure play' is a term used to describe a business which is engaged in a single type of business activity, such as retailing. Pure play organizations do not involve themselves in unrelated business that is not directly associated with their core activities. In internet terms a pure play business would be an organization that just sells over the internet and has no high street presence, such as Amazon. Whereas there are many organizations which have both internet and high street presence, these are not pure play organizations.

Quality assurance

Quality assurance represents attempts by a business to ensure that agreed quality standards are met throughout the organization, primarily to ensure **customer satisfaction**. There has been a degree of international agreement about quality, consistency and satisfaction, which are enshrined in the International Standards Organization (ISO) 9000 series of quality systems standards. If businesses meet these standards, it is normally assumed that they have achieved quality assurance.

See also **ISO 9000, ISO 14001**.

Quality circle

A quality circle is a discussion group which meets on a regular basis to identify quality problems, investigate solutions and make recommendations as to the most suitable solution. The members of quality circles are employees and may include individuals with specific skills or expertise, such as engineers, quality inspectors or salespersons. Quality circles were first created in the 1950s in the Toyota motor company. In the 1980s this Japanese form of employee participation and consultation was adopted on a large scale in both Europe and the US. Quality circles aim to use untapped knowledge from their employees, as well as providing them with the opportunity to show their knowledge and talents in using their problem-solving skills.

Quality control

Quality control essentially involves ensuring that a product or service conforms to predetermined specifications. In its most basic form, quality control is addressed in three major areas of the manufacturing process:

- At the input stage – where only the parts, components and partly finished products which conform to the given specifications are used or identified as being suitable for the production process.
- During the production process itself – when parts, components and

other items are converted into finished products, all systems and control procedures need to be in place to continue to check that specifications are conformed to on a consistent basis.

- At the output stage – only products which are seen to conform to the specifications are allowed to exit the system and become available to customers.

The conclusion of this holistic system therefore incorporates input, process and output control. Typically, input control would incorporate an inspection of raw materials, any subcontracted or purchased parts and a periodic review and rating of suppliers. During the process control, inspection is a key issue of **work in progress**, along with swift correction or rectification of problems, usually using control charts. At the output stage, again inspections are crucial, as are performance tests. Customers will provide a genuine assessment of the products being used as they were designed to be used. Therefore, interaction with customers and a swift response to any problems they encounter are essential, the findings of which will then be passed down for action at the input and process stages.

Wild, Ray, *Essentials of Production and Operations Management: Text and Cases*. London: Thomson Learning, 1995.

Quality of service (QOS)

Quality of service is an internet or computer-related concept which has various applications. These include the standard of networks, communication protocols, operating systems and the degree of quality of the service received from an **internet service provider**.

The term 'quality of service' can be equally applied to traditional functions of a business and how the customers perceive the service they receive from that business.

Real-time marketing

Real-time marketing is the process of providing on-line customers with product or service information and making immediate recommendations to them in response to their inputs. This is a form of **interactive marketing** and **personalization** of the sales effort.

McKenna, Regis, *Real Time: Preparing for the Age of the Never Satisfied Customer*. Boston, MA: Harvard Business School Press, 1997.

Real-time pricing

In increasingly competitive markets, suppliers have recognized the need to be able to adjust their prices and immediately inform their customers of these price fluctuations. Real-time pricing requires the business's **inventory** and financial systems to be accessible by both customers and salespersons (with appropriate authorization), so that they can obtain current price information, as well as details of availability and other relevant information.

Receiver

A receiver is an individual or a business appointed by the creditors of a business which has entered a state of bankruptcy. The receiver's primary function is either to sell the business as a **going concern** and to raise as much capital as possible to pay off the creditors, or should the receiver fail to raise enough capital, then to place the business into **liquidation**.

Referrers

Referrers consist of information which is sent by a web-browser to advertising networks, providing an on-line profile of a user. This enables the advertisers to target their messages more precisely.

Registrar of companies

The Registrar of Companies is a British-based organization which holds a record of all joint stock companies, including the **memorandum of association**. They also keep the annual reports and accounts of larger businesses. In Britain the Registrar of Companies operates from Companies House.

Relationship marketing

Relationship marketing attempts to develop a long-term relationship with customers on the premise that it is far cheaper to retain existing customers than it is to attract new ones. There are a number of factors involved in relationship marketing, which tend to frame the exact nature of how it works within a given organization. These are:

- a primary focus on customer attention;
- an orientation towards product benefits rather than product features;
- an emphasis on commitment and contact with customers;
- the adoption of a total quality approach;
- the development of ongoing relationships with customers;
- the deployment of employees at various levels to maintain contact;
- the cultivation of key customers;
- the emphasis on trust, honesty and promise keeping.

Egan, John, *Relationship Marketing.* London: Financial Times, Prentice-Hall, 2001.

Payne, Adrian, Christopher, Martin, Peck, Helen and Clark, Moira, *Relationship Marketing for Competitive Advantage: Winning and Keeping Customers.* Oxford: Butterworth-Heinemann, 1998.

Relocation

In certain instances it may be unavoidable that employees are asked to continue to work for the same organization, but in an alternative location. There may be many reasons why relocation has been considered and approved by the business. Typically, the closure or merging of branches or offices within an organization, or location changes as a result of an acquisition, may entail the redeployment of staff to alternative premises. Under most circumstances the employer, at the first instance, will offer relocation to most, if not all, employees, assuming of course that this will not mean duplication or over-manning at the new location. It is certainly the case that specific employees will be approached and offered a relocation package as they continue to be considered vital to the long-term prospects of the business.

Relocation programmes and associated assistance becomes a considerable task for human resources personnel, in as much as they may have to be simultaneously dealing with employees who have been offered, and have accepted, relocation packages and others who have not been offered this assistance, or have chosen not to accept it.

Remote sales force applications

Remote sales force applications, or sales force automation, has become an essential link between a business and sales employees operating in remote locations. These applications allow information and transactions to be relayed back and forth between the sales force and the business itself. The sales force is able to gain access to current pricing, stock levels and other information and send back to the business orders, customer information and requests for further details. Usually the remote access is available via internet connection or, increasingly, **personal digital assistants** or WAP enabled telephones.

Report format

Reports issued or received by an organization can be either informal or formal, but both contain common elements, although not necessarily in the same format. Report writing plays a vital role in an organization's achievement of meeting its goals. The key decision-makers will often commission specialists to research and process information or, alternatively, this task may be carried out internally via the Research and Development department. Reports may be commissioned for any of the following:

- the identification of problems associated with equipment;
- to obtain up-to-date information on sales;
- to receive progress on certain projects;
- to ensure **health and safety** legislation is being adhered to;
- to identify production process problems;
- to investigate particular processes;
- to identify **market research** data;
- to forecast potential sales;
- to identify the need to change policies.

A report may contain research which has been carried out for a specific purpose; it may be the findings and recommendations of work that has been carried out for a specific purpose; or it may be an account of something which has taken place and been reported on.

A formal report will contain the following headings:

- title page;
- terms of reference – which will state the purpose of the research;
- procedure – which will state how the information has been gathered, for example by interview, visits, observation or examination;
- findings – which will state what has been discovered as a result of the research;
- conclusion – which will be a general statement that would conclude and sum up the findings;
- recommendations – which would be made by the report writer on the basis of the findings and conclusions;
- appendices – which will be used to include more extensive information than could be included in a footnote.

The report headings can be broken down to make smaller, individual sections by the use of a series of numbers and sub-numbers, for example: 3, 3.1, 3.2, 3.3.

A short informal report tends to be used for less complex data and may be commissioned by a line manager for research by a member of their staff. The format would include:

- an introduction;
- the basic information;
- the findings;
- the conclusions;
- any actions required.

Papers and briefs take the form of additional information provided to assist decision-makers within an organization. They will contain essential background information on a particular subject, usually written by an individual with particular interest or experience in the area concerned. A discussion document also offers advice on appropriate or alternative decisions that could be taken.

Request for comments (RFC)

Simply, this is an invitation to suppliers or internal parties within an organization to state their opinion on a particular issue.

Request for information (RFI)

This is a request for suppliers to give information regarding products or services that the organization has an interest in learning more about.

Request for proposal (RFP)

The term 'request for proposal' is an invitation to service providers to quote on how they would carry out a particular project and to outline a preliminary budget. It would include technical specifications and time and cost details.

Request for quote (RFQ)

This is an invitation to suppliers to bid on the supply of products or services which match the business's specific criteria in terms of quality or specification and delivery timescale.

Responsibility centre

A responsibility centre is a part of an organization in which the manager is accountable for specified activities. Types of responsibility centres could include **cost centres** (where the manager is responsible for costs), revenue centres (where the manager is responsible for revenues) or a **profit centre** (where the manager is responsible for revenue and expenses).

Restructuring

Simply a mention of the word 'restructuring' brings enormous dread and connotations to both an organization and its employees. Restructuring is recognition of the fact that as the organization is currently structured there are severe deficiencies in its operations. Inevitably, for employees and human resources departments, any restructuring exercise will involve an enormous degree of upheaval. Restructuring tends to occur either when a business is teetering on the brink of disaster, or as a pre-requisite demanded by a financial institution as a priority before funds will be released to the organization.

For human resources, restructuring can mean not only dealing with a potentially large percentage of the employees as casualties of the process, but also that those that remain may have their jobs entirely redesigned or re-aligned to match the new structure, which aims to be more efficient and productive.

Return on capital employed (ROCE)

This is an accounting ratio which expresses the profit of an organization in a given financial year as a percentage of the capital employed. It is one of the most useful ratios which illustrates organizational performance. Typically the formula is:

$$\frac{\textit{Operating profit}}{\textit{Capital employed}} \times 100 = \textit{return on capital}$$

Profit is usually taken as profit before interest and tax, and capital employed refers to the fixed assets plus the circulating capital, less the current liabilities.

Friedlob, George T. and Plewa, Franklin J., *Essentials of Corporate Performance Measurement*. New York: John Wiley, 2002.

Return on investment (ROI)

This is the US equivalent of **return on capital employed (ROCE)**. Whilst management may use this formula, assessing profit before tax and interest as a percentage of total assets, shareholders are more interested in the calculation of profit after interest, and comparing this with the assets less the liabilities.

Friedlob, George T. and Plewa, Franklin J., *Essentials of Corporate Performance Measurement*. New York: John Wiley, 2002.

Routers

Routers can be either hardware or software which sends data packets from one network to another. The router checks to see if the main network server is free. If not, it finds the most efficient route through the networks to the recipient. Routers also check errors and determine the **quality of service** along each of the networks.

Sale and leaseback

Sale and leaseback is a transaction in which the owner of an asset sells it to a third party and then immediately purchases back the right to use that asset under a **lease**. The capital released by this process is used to enable the leasing organization to either expand, or survive during a difficult trading period. The key to successful sale and leaseback is to ensure that the profits which are generated by the sale are in excess of the lease payments.

Satisficing

The concept of satisficing involves the acceptance of the satisfactory, rather than the optimum. Given the fact that most strategies are based on compromise, particularly when considering objectives, it is often prudent for a business to identify the acceptable, rather than just the ideal. Equally, achievements such as complete efficiency are unlikely, therefore the satisfactory is a good compromise.

Scalability

Scalability is a computer-network or internet-related term which refers to the ability to add or subtract from a system without having adverse performance-based problems.

In the two diagrams in Figure 28, scalability is linear, meaning that there is a constant performance decrease relative to the load increases.

When considering linear scalability relative to resources, it means that with a constant load, performance would improve at a constant rate, assuming additional resources.

In essence, scalability is the ability of hardware, software and applications to adapt to increased demand but to continue to function. It can also refer to websites which can be scaled up once they have attracted a large number of users, usually at little additional cost.

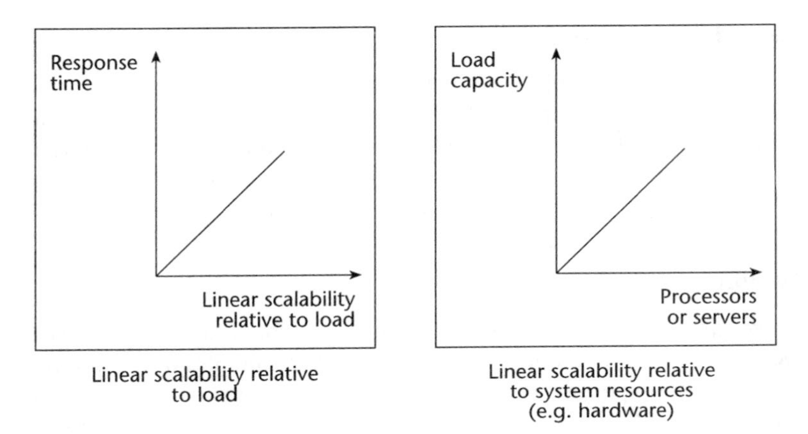

Figure 28 Linear scalability

Search engine

A search engine is a website or a **portal** which allows internet users to input key words or search criteria in order to locate other websites on various topics.

Secure electronic transaction (SET)

Secure electronic transactions are one of the latest developments in privacy and protection for credit card transactions over the internet. The system is increasingly being used by many major **e-commerce** businesses as it utilizes **digital signatures**, ensuring that the transaction is secure and confidential for both the customer, the merchant and the bank. The buyer does not have to input a credit card number because that information is already verified by the digital signature. It is believed that provided the complex software can be built into all browsers, it will assist in the elimination of **cyberfraud**.

Secure multipurpose internet mail extension (s/mime)

This has become an industry-standard code which defines exactly how **email** messages are sent in code and then decoded at their destination. It utilizes an **encryption** system which offers a higher level of security. The messages can also include encryption information and a **digital certificate**.

Security software

These are systems which are installed on an individual computer or a network to protect it from attack. The most common form of security software deals with viruses. However, **firewalls** are increasingly the security software of choice as they provide a series of layers between a business's computer system and potential attacks.

Servers

These are computers or **work stations** which handle processing requests from other computers. They store data and files and contain the main processing power of a network. Typical servers include file or mail servers or web servers. The servers on **local area networks** can control access to the internet, store files centrally, provide access to network resources and otherwise allocate resources to various work stations.

Shared services

Shared services are an organizational model where support services are separated from the main area of business activity and usually have their own management system. Removing support services from the core activities of the business enables the main operations of the organization to concentrate on delivering better customer value, efficiency and profitability. Typically, shared services would include the finance and accounting processes, purchasing and human resources.

Shareholder

A shareholder is the owner of shares in a **limited company**. In the US, shareholders are known as stockholders.

Rappaport, Alfred, *Creating Shareholder Value: The New Standard for Business Performance*. New York: Simon & Schuster, 1998.

Shopping bots

Shopping bots enable internet users to experience a form of shopping such as they would encounter in a mall or a high street. In effect they are websites where a number of vendors are selling their products and services. The users can navigate around the websites, 'visiting' each of the vendors and choosing the products and services they require. A simple mouse-click selects the item and the user can then continue shopping. The total of the shopping trip is given and the user then makes a single payment which may include shipping.

Shopping bots allow users to search for the best possible price.

Shopping cart software

Shopping cart software is essentially an order-processing program which gathers information about the user who is browsing a website. It then suggests potential purchases to that user. It also allows the user to select a series of purchases, which it tallies, and then adds the shipping charges, if applicable. The user can then make a single payment for all of the products or services.

Increasingly, shopping cart software also incorporates a 'wish list' which it will store on behalf of the user, detailing products and services that may well be purchased by that user at some point in the future.

Short message service (SMS)

This is essentially a text messaging system which allows messages of up to 160 characters to be sent from one mobile phone to another. It was introduced into Europe in 1991 and the industry standard is known as Global System for Mobile (GSM). In effect, SMS replaced paging as the SMS centre receives, stores and forwards messages to telephones over the wireless network. SMSs can be from a website to a digital telephone, and digital telephones can accept SMSs even if a voice call is in process.

Simple mail transfer protocol (SMTP)

Simple mail transfer protocol, TCP/IP (transmission control protocol/ internet protocol), is the way in which **email** messages are sent between servers on the internet.

See also **TCP/IP**.

Smartcard

A smartcard is essentially a credit card-sized device with an embedded microchip which can store programmable data. The most common forms of smartcard are telephone cards, although increasingly smart-cards are being used for electronic cash, parking and public transport. The theory is that smartcards will eventually replace cash and will be able to be recharged once the value of the card has been depleted.

Guthery, Scott and Jergensen, Tim, *Smartcard Developer's Kit*. London: Pearson Education, 1998.

Société à responsabilité limitée (France)

This is a suffix, often reduced to the acronym SARL, which is the French equivalent of a British or American **private limited company**. It has between 1 and 40 partners, with a minimum share capital of €12,400, and the shares have a minimum nominal value of €25. The transfer of shares is restricted and the SARL needs to be notified of any share transfers.

Société anonyme (France)

This French form of business is broadly the equivalent of a corporation or a joint stock company in British or American law. SAs have at least two **shareholders** and share capital of €31,000, of which a quarter must be paid up. The nominal value of each of the shares must be at least €1.25. The SA is administered by a board of at least three directors and there must be at least one **general meeting** held annually.

Société civile (France)

This is a French form of business which is equivalent to a **partnership** with full liability.

Société en nom collectif (France)

This is the French equivalent of a general or ordinary **partnership**.

Société en participation (France)

This is the French equivalent of a silent partnership.

Sole proprietor (US)

This is the American equivalent of the **sole trader**.

Sole trader

Effectively this is the simplest form of self-employment, but if the business fails then the owner is responsible for all of the debts. The finance to run the business usually comes from the owner but all profits go to the owner. Since the sole trader is self-employed, all profits on the business are taxable. Sole traders can start trading straight away without any specific legal requirements, but if the individual trades under another name the sole trader must display his or her own name and address alongside the trading name. Table 22 summarizes the advantages and disadvantages of sole trading and also indicates the setting up procedures.

Table 22 Advantages and disadvantages of being a sole trader

Sole trader	Summary
Advantages	It is quick and easy to start. Record keeping is simple, although proper accounting records must be compiled. The sole trader keeps all the profits of the business after tax has been deducted. There are few legal formalities or regulations.
Disadvantages	The sole trader is liable for all the money owed by the business. The sole trader's personal possessions and property are at risk if the business fails. The responsibility for completion of work lies solely with the owner. Managing to take time off work could prove problematic. Holidays and sickness are unpaid.
Setting up	There are no legal restrictions regarding the setting up of a business as a sole trader.
Business name	The owner can use his or her own name when setting up the business, but they do need to display their name and address on the premises and on their stationery.
Registration	Sole traders must register as self-employed with the Inland Revenue within the first three months of full trading, as well as informing the local tax office that they have commenced trading.

Span of control

The span of control is the number of subordinates for whom a manager has direct responsibility. The ideal number frequently quoted is between five and nine individuals under the control of one manager. Beyond this it becomes increasingly difficult to react or respond to their specific needs. Span of control, therefore, implies that additional levels of hierarchy need to be inserted, both above and below each manager, in order to reduce the span of control to a manageable level.

See also **Fayol**.

Spin-off

This is the sale of a subsidiary or division by an organization in order for it to become a separate entity. It is sometimes known as **spin-out**.

Spin-out

A spin-out occurs when a business sells a proportion of a non-core activity to a third party whilst still retaining a degree of control over that new entity. It is distinguished from **spin-offs** as it is widely believed that these involve areas of activity which the main business is not necessarily interested in pursuing. Spin-outs are partially sold off in order for them to flourish separately and remain unaffected by the main activities of the business which created them.

Stakeholder

A stakeholder is an individual or a group that is either affected by, or has a vested interest in, a particular business. Stakeholders can include customers, managers, employees, suppliers and the community, as well as the organization itself. Each business apportions a degree of importance to each stakeholder and will attempt to understand what its stakeholders require of it. Businesses will take these views into account when making decisions.

Rahman, Sandra Sutherland, Andriof, Jorg, Waddock, Sandra and Husted, Bryan, *Unfolding Stakeholder Thinking: Relationships, Communication, Reporting and Performance*. Sheffield: Greenleaf Publishing, 2003.

Standardization

The term 'standardization' refers to an organization's efforts to ensure that all their workers are performing their tasks or activities in a consistent manner. An organization striving for standardization would do so to assist in ensuring consistent levels of safety, productivity and quality. The term 'standardization' may also refer to an organization's desire to standardize the parts and components which it uses.

Startup

'Startup' is a term used to describe a new business which requires both talent and capital. It is at this point that the new business is seeking venture capital in order to ensure its successful launch.

Stickiness

'Stickiness' is an internet-marketing term which describes the effectiveness of a website in being able to retain the interest of a user. Stickiness is measured specifically by the length of time an individual user spends browsing the website.

Stock option scheme

A stock option scheme is the American equivalent of a share option scheme, which applies to situations where a business will offer shares in the business as a reward or part-payment to employees. It may also apply to situations where a business seeks to raise additional capital by offering more shares, in which case existing **shareholders**, in order to keep their proportion of ownership equal to what it had been before the new issues, are offered a number of shares commensurate with the quantity of shares they currently own.

Strategic architecture

Strategic architecture is a disciplined and organized process of building up a picture of the overall networks and contacts involved within a business. It may also incorporate networks and contacts outside the business which are vital to its continued operations. Each of the resources is examined, as well as the inflows and outflows, with a view to understanding how these dependencies operate. The inter-dependencies can then be visualized on a single map illustrating the business's strategic architecture.

Strategic business unit (SBU)

A strategic business unit is a part of an organization at which strategy needs to be developed. Each strategic business unit will have the responsibility for determining its own strategies. The concept revolves around the fact that many large multinationals are simply too big to focus upon key issues, and therefore SBUs are developed to focus the attention on specific projects and issues. In other words, large divisions can be split up into strategic business units which can separately plan, and these will have a manager who has the authority and control needed to directly impact upon the profits and the development of that unit.

Segev, Eli, *Business Unit Strategy*. New York: John Wiley, 2000.

Strategic fit

Strategic fit involves the matching of strategy and organizational structure. It is widely accepted that there are five main stages in developing a strong strategic fit:

- A description of the business need and its contribution to the organization's overall business strategy.
- What are the objectives of the project in question?
- Why is the action required now?
- What are the key benefits which will be realised?
- What are the **critical success factors** and how will they be measured?

Strategic plan

A strategic plan is an overarching series of activities which aim to implement and develop a new concept, deal with a problem, or establish the foundation of the business's objectives in the coming period. As the illustration in Figure 29 shows, there is a close relationship between the implementation and the strategic development process.

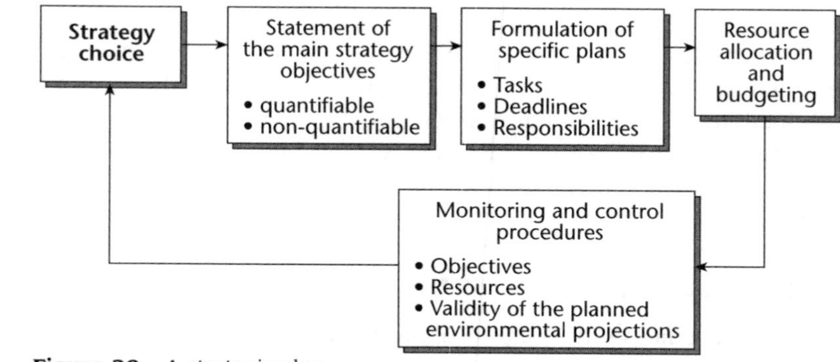

Figure 29 A strategic plan

Strategic planning should, as the diagram illustrates, be a continual process, with the monitoring and control procedures providing the information for the development of the strategic plan and future strategic plans.

Subculture

As an organization establishes **autonomous** or semi-autonomous groups, variations or radically different cultures will develop in these parts of the organization. Providing these subcultures do not actively work against the core values and norms of the organization, they may prove a positive benefit, particularly if the nature of the work carried out by those in the subcultures requires a radically different approach. Physical separation, in the form of remote geographical location, may be one reason why subcultures may develop. However, in other organizations it may simply be as a result of the members of the subculture undergoing training and development which differentiates them from the rest of the organization. Individuals in different departments or divisions of the organization will naturally have a number of shared values, which will lead to the development of a subculture which does differ from the norm. The larger the organization, the more likely there is to be a profusion of subcultures in various parts of the business.

Superfine market segmentation

This is the targeting of quite small audience segments. It is also known as micro-segmentation. Increasingly databases allow businesses to specifically target individuals who have particular characteristics. In the US, for example, cable technology has allowed advertisers to broadcast advertisements to single city blocks.

Supply chain

The supply chain is simply a generic description of the processes and organizations involved in converting and conveying raw materials to the end-user. The supply chain may involve organizations which extract raw materials, and others which carry out a basic form of process upon these raw materials, which are then passed on to a manufacturer who will turn them into usable parts. Parts are then converted into components, which in turn are assembled or processed into a form of finished goods. These finished goods may then pass through the hands of distributors and retailers, before reaching the end-user. Supply chains may involve several suppliers, several more manufacturers and a related distribution system. In other words, the supply chain incorporates all the costs, time, transportation and packaging that may be associated with the various stages of the process of conversion. Increasingly, supply chains take into account the return journey which many finished products undergo after having spent a considerable time with the end-user. Therefore a reverse supply chain is often in operation alongside the standard supply chain. This reverse system incorporates replacement parts and their flow, as well as the disposal and recycling of parts, components or whole products.

Supply chain management

The supply chain management approach involves the integrated managing and control of the flow of information, materials and services from the suppliers of the raw materials, through to the factories, warehouses and retailers to the end customers. The benefits to an organization involved in supply chain management should be lower inventory costs, higher quality and higher customer service levels. These benefits will only be gained, however, if all those involved in the supply chain are conforming to the standards set.

Christopher, Martin, *Logistics and Supply Chain Management*. London: Financial Times, Prentice-Hall, 1998.

Support vendors

Support vendors are essentially **outsourced** business services who increasingly provide specialist assistance to a business in order for the business to concentrate on its core activities. Support vendors are external to the organization and have their own employees. They can provide a wide range of support services to the organization, such as managing the mail, dealing with warehousing and shipping or providing technical support. This is particularly useful to businesses who do not have the skills, finance or inclination to develop their own support services and it is especially useful for businesses which operate with low profit margins.

SWOT analysis

SWOT analysis is a very useful technique in looking at the overall future of an organization, as well as considering the launch of a new marketing activity. SWOT analysis covers the following aspects, of which the first two considerations look at the internal workings of the organization.

- Strengths – what is the organization or business good at? What are its key advantages over the competition in terms of its products and services as well as its facilities, customer service and the expertise of its employees?
- Weaknesses – what is the organization not good at? Where does the business fall down in terms of the ways it does things? Are the products and services good enough? Is the marketing good enough?
- Opportunities – what is happening OUTSIDE the organization that offers some opportunities to the organization? Has the transport system in the area been improved? Has a major competitor closed down?
- Threats – what is happening OUTSIDE the organization that could threaten it? Are there more competitors?

Figure 30 is a common SWOT analysis grid which helps to place all of the considerations in the right place. The marketing function would need to consider all of these strengths, weaknesses, opportunities and threats before making any major decisions.

Strengths	Weaknesses
Opportunities	Threats

SWOT analysis

Figure 30 A SWOT analysis grid

Dealtry, Richard, *Dynamic SWOT Analysis – The Developer's Guide*. Birmingham: Dynamic SWOT Associates, 1994.

S

Symbiosis

Business symbiosis implies a total partnership with another business entity, particularly service providers and **consultancy** work. Symbiosis aims to create a resonance across all parts of the organization through mutual understanding and dependence. Manufacturers, for example, would seek to establish a business symbiosis with organizations which use their products, and collectively deliver a total product offering which not only seeks to address the needs of the end-user of the product, but also enables the two businesses to enjoy efficiency, profitability and the nurturing of innovation. Manufacturers of mobile phones, for example, would seek to work in a state of symbiosis with network operators, collectively playing their part in developing and delivering a network infrastructure.

True business symbiosis must yield benefits for both of the partners. They will collectively evolve and begin to recognize potential opportunities. True symbiosis is rather more than exchange, as the collaboration should create a new set of values. In essence, the alliances are not formal but rely upon interpersonal connections and internal infrastructures that enhance learning in both organizations.

Synergy

Synergies are the benefits which can result from combining different aspects of an organization, rather than allowing them to act separately. In other words, organizations will seek to group complementary activities in situations where there is a strong possibility of collaboration. This means that a mutual benefit can be enjoyed, particularly when common work or activity form the basis of the alliance.

Synergies can also be enjoyed between organizations where complementary skills or production processes, or indeed knowledge of a specific market, can be brought together in order to achieve far more than the two organizations could possibly have hoped for individually. Synergies can either bring about short-term project-based alliances between businesses, or may well prove to be the foundation of a longer-term relationship.

'Business synergy' is a term often applied to **franchise** operations, in as much as when individuals purchase a franchise they become part of a larger 'family'. All of the members of the family work together and the most effective ideas are shared.

Systems integrator (SI)

The term 'systems integrator' can be applied either to a business or to a collection of hardware or software. Increasingly, businesses are seeking to combine and ensure compatibility with their existing software applications. A systems integrator, as a business, seeks to provide the infrastructure platform which enables organizations to bring together the various aspects of their business into a fully integrated system. This has been particularly important for businesses involved in **e-commerce**, which require a series of applications which are fully compatible and work together to provide software solutions.

There are also software packages which seek to link the various software applications used by a business, very much to the same end.

Tangible asset

Tangible assets are items which have a physical substance and may well be used as part of the production or supply of products and services. In accounting terms, tangible assets also include **leases** or company **shares**. They are, in effect, the fixed assets of the organization and can be differentiated from intangible assets such as **goodwill**, trademarks or patents, which do not have a physical substance but are still valuable concepts and assets.

TCP/IP

Transmission control protocol/internet protocols are the two primary protocols in internet communication and are used to connect hosts on the internet. The TCP/IP is the protocol which establishes a connection between two hosts so that message exchange is possible. TCP/IP has become the standard data-transmission protocol for the internet and networks must have their own protocols which support TCP/IP.

Tender

The term 'tender' has in fact two distinct meanings. The most common, however, relates to a closed bidding process to obtain a contract for a specific project for another organization. Usually, under the terms of the tender outlines, the potential bidders are required to establish the fact that they can provide the service, product or construction work at the standards which have been laid down by the organization offering the tender. The bids must be submitted by a particular day and are sealed. The organization receiving the tender applications will then check the bids for the work and, provided the quality and specification standards are correct, then they will inevitably choose the bidder who has offered their services at the lowest price.

'Tender' also has an application in respect of the purchase of treasury bills at a fixed price on the stock exchange. These treasury bills are also referred to as government securities.

Time and attendance (T and A)

'Time and attendance' is a generic term used to describe the process of tracking the hours and attendance patterns of employees. In the past, mechanical time clocks punched in the arrival and departure times of employees. But increasingly, software systems, coupled with the use of swipe cards, carry out this function, and at various points around the building employees can also be required to use this swipe card to positively locate them on the premises.

The tracking of employees has become a high-tech industry and it is now possible to track employees' attendance hours without administrative work or manual calculations. Some time and attendance systems even work on a proximity basis and a chip on the name tag of the employee communicates with the proximity system automatically.

Time and attendance systems now incorporate not only Smart access control, but also fingerprint access and visitor monitoring systems.

Top–down planning

Top–down planning is a feature of many businesses with a formal **hierarchical structure**. The philosophy of these organizations is to ensure that decision making, and consequent instructions or orders, emanate from the higher levels of the hierarchy and are filtered down through the layers of the organization, being translated into a series of tasks by the levels of management. Top–down planning does not necessarily take into account the realities of the organization and may assume that plans framed by the senior management can be fully implemented further down the structure.

Top–down planning does not seek to incorporate the ideas or positions of the subordinate managers or those carrying out the tasks. It also means that these organizations do not tend to involve their staff in the decision-making process, unlike **bottom–up planning**, which is a more consultative leadership style, promoting employee participation.

Tort

Tort is, in UK legal terms, a civil injury which is actionable in court and may result in damages being awarded. The law of torts aims to protect individuals against infringements of their rights. The individual who brings the action is known as the plaintiff and will have to establish, on the balance of probabilities, that his or her rights have been infringed. In other words the burden of proof lies with them. If it is proved that their rights have been infringed, then the other party, known as the defendant, will be required to pay compensation.

A tort is a civil wrong other than a claim for breach of contract. The modern interpretations of the law of tort aim to compensate for harm suffered as a result of the conduct of others. Traditionally, money is paid in compensation although, in some cases, restraining orders or injunctions are taken out on the defendant in order to ensure that the tort is not repeated.

Cooke, John, *Law of Tort*. London: Longman, 2003.
Mullis, Alastair and Oliphant, Ken, *Torts*. Basingstoke: Palgrave Macmillan, 2003.

Total quality control (TQC)

Total quality control, as the term implies, is a process by which the manufacturer embeds and instils in the entire organization a comprehensive **quality control** programme. TQC is applied to all areas and all levels of the organization, making quality a responsibility of every employee in every task, activity or function.

See also **total quality management (TQM)**.

Total quality management (TQM)

The concept of total quality management (TQM) has been stimulated by the need for conformity by organizations with regard to quality levels. This need has been brought about in essence by an increased demand by customers and suppliers for higher-quality products, parts and components. The fundamental principle behind total quality management is that the management of quality is addressed at all levels of an organization, from the top to the bottom. Improvements are made on a continuous basis by applying the theories and approaches of management theorists in an attempt to improve quality and decrease organizational costs. The emphasis, primarily on quality, is also very much on people and their involvement, particularly with regard to suppliers and customers. The fundamental principles of TQM are summarized in Table 23.

Bank, J., *The Essence of Total Quality Management*. New York: Prentice-Hall, 1999.
Oakland, J. S., *Total Quality Management*. Oxford: Butterworth-Heinemann, 1993.

Total time taken (TTT)

Total time taken is equivalent to the total number of labour hours which have been used to produce the output throughout a product's life to date. By calculating the total number of production hours and dividing

Table 23 Total quality management

TQM principle	**Description**
Committed and effective leaders	A commitment to and a belief in the principles of TQM by those key decision-makers at the top of the organizational structure is essential. They have to portray this commitment to the lower levels of management in an effective style of leadership by providing resources to make changes happen.
Planning	It is imperative that all changes are planned effectively, particularly as the TQM approach may be fundamentally different from the approach currently adopted by an organization. All planned changes must be integrated throughout the whole organization with cooperation throughout all levels and functions. With quality, or improved quality, as the key dimension, a longer-term strategy will be adopted throughout the whole of the organization's functions, from new product design through to getting the product to the end-user.
Monitoring	A continuous monitoring system will be put into place so that the process of continuous improvement can be supported and developed. Problem identification and the implementations of solutions will be sought.
Training	Without education and training, employees and management will lack expertise and awareness of quality issues. It will be difficult to implement changes in organizational behaviour unless there is a comprehensive and effective educational scheme which not only seeks to provide the initial information and understanding of techniques, but constantly updates those techniques in order to reinforce understanding. Without this investment, short-term TQM benefits will be difficult to achieve, as will the long-term impact of TQM through conventional measurements, such as increased efficiency and general growth.
Teamwork	The development of empowered cooperative teams is an essential prerequisite of TQM. Under the system teams are encouraged to take the initiative and often given responsibilities which would have formerly been management roles. Without involvement and empowerment, TQM is almost impossible to implement as it requires both the participation and the commitment of individuals throughout the whole organization.

⇒

Table 23 Total quality management (*continued*)

TQM principle	Description
Evaluation and feedback	It is imperative that individuals within the organization see the fruits of their labour. TQM implies that there should be an integral system which not only provides positive feedback but also gives rewards for achievement. The evaluation and feedback of TQM will invariably involve the measurement of achievement in both internal and external targets, notably through **benchmarking**.
Long-term change	As TQM becomes embedded and very much a fact of life in the ways in which employees think and processes are carried out, there is a permanent change to the way in which attitudes, working practices and overall behaviour are approached.

this by the units produced, an average production time can be calculated. Equally, by using time series analysis it is possible to calculate the gradual changes in the number of labour hours associated with each unit of production in order to assess whether the production, compared with hours expended, has changed. This can form the basis of **learning curve** calculations.

Trade unions

Trade unions protect the interests of their members in areas relating to wages and salaries, working conditions, job security and welfare benefits. They negotiate with the management of organizations on behalf of members of the trade union who work for the business. The national committee of the trade union is an elected group of permanent employees who implement the policies of the members. Regional and district committees are formed around the country, with branches in the larger towns, to one of which each union member is attached. Trade union representatives negotiate with the management of an organization during the documenting and implementation of collective agreements, collective bargaining and dispute resolution. They would also be entitled to attend disciplinary and grievance interviews, as well as being involved in discussions regarding dismissal.

Trait theory

Trait theory takes the view that the personality of individuals consists of a series of broad dispositions, otherwise known as 'traits'. It is these traits that lead to characteristic responses, and individuals can be described according to the ways in which they behave, such as 'dominant', 'assertive', 'friendly' or 'outgoing'. It is widely accepted that there are five basic factors which determine the personality of an individual:

1. Emotional stability – whether the individual is calm, anxious, secure, insecure, self-satisfied or self-pitying.
2. Extroversion – whether the individual is sociable, retiring, sober, fun-loving, affectionate or reserved
3. Openness – whether the individual is practical, imaginative, prefers routine or variety, and whether they conform or are independently minded.
4. Agreeableness – whether the individual is ruthless or caring, trusting or suspicious, helpful or uncooperative.
5. Conscientiousness – whether the individual is organized or disorganized, careful or careless, impulsive or disciplined

By considering these five factors it is also possible to ascertain whether particular individuals are more inclined towards collectivism (sharing the values of the group and subordinating their own personal goals) or individualism (in which they place their personal goals above the group goals).

Trait theory is not universally accepted as a means by which to understand personality and many critics believe that trait theory does not actually predict real behaviour. When it is coupled with situationism, suggesting that personality can change according to the situation, there is a much clearer and more applicable set of measures.

Coupling trait and situational variables can assist in understanding personality. It also assists in predicting behaviour. It is certainly clear that traits are sometimes more influential than situations, but in many cases, when the situation and the trait are taken together, it is possible to be much more accurate in predicting exactly how someone will behave in a similar situation.

Transfer pricing

Transfer pricing is a form of internal pricing policy which requires a particular part of a business, or group of businesses, to ensure that they still meet their profit targets, even when supplying products and services to another business, or division, under common ownership.

Feinschreiber, Robert, *Transfer Pricing Handbook: Transfer Pricing International: A Country-by-Country Guide*. Chichester: John Wiley, 2000.

Transformational change

Transformational change is a root-and-branch change process which seeks to fundamentally improve the way in which a business may operate. It requires considerable planning, coupled with an overarching strategy and commitment across the entire organization. There are some seven steps which are associated with transformational change:

- *Defining the change strategy* – which assesses the need and readiness for change, the best change configuration and how the process of change will be controlled.
- *Management commitment* – this entails developing a sense of ownership amongst the management, and working towards a strategic vision for the change, as well as identifying how that vision relates to each manager.
- *Creation of the change strategy* – creating a change strategy that will be meaningful to all employees and defining the way in which the vision can be communicated to all **stakeholders**.
- *Building employee commitment* – the creation of the means by which the change can be 'sold' to the employees and the identification and management of resistance to that change.
- *Development of a new culture* – incorporating the development of new values for employees and new behaviours which are aligned to the vision, including a regular review of the support required.
- *Reconfiguration of the organization* – redesigning roles, competences and structure, and the identification of appropriate individuals who will assume those roles.
- *Managing performance* – the creation of a new working environment with relevant **performance measurement** and the alignment of business performance to individual objectives.

Anderson, D. and Anderson, L. S. A., (eds), *Beyond Change Management: Advanced Strategies for Today's Transformational Leaders*. New York: Jossey-Bass Wiley, 2001.

Transitional change

Transitional change seeks to achieve a known desired state that is different from the existing one. Its foundation is based on the work of

Kurt Lewin, who believed that the change process consisted of three stages. First, the organization needs to accept the need to change and make positive steps towards that change. The organization then moves to the new position and 'refreezes' itself in a new equilibrium position.

See also **freezing/unfreezing**.

Amado, Gilles and Ambrose, Anthony, *The Transitional Approach to Change*. London: Karnac Books, 2001.
Lewin, Kurt, *Field Theory in Social Science*. Chicago, IL: University of Chicago Press, 1951.

Transmission control protocol (TCP)

Transmission control protocol allows servers on the internet to establish connections and exchange data streams. It seeks to deliver data packets in the same order in which they were sent.

Travel and expense (T and E)

'Travel and expense' is a generic term which is used to describe the management of travel expenses and other related expenditure. Increasingly, businesses seek to adopt a flexible and cost-effective response to the **procurement** of travel. In effect, money spent by employees represents a purchase and all such expenses need to be monitored by the organization. In the majority of cases these purchases are dispersed in their very nature, with any number of employees making purchases on behalf of the organization at any given time. It then falls to management and finance staff to check, collate and record the receipts. It is therefore difficult for businesses to enforce any travel and expense policy across the business as many of the expenses are either *ad hoc* or discretionary. Businesses are turning increasingly to smarter travel and expense systems, which include software that is capable of data capture and retrieval, which can be either loaded onto computers at the place of work, **outsourced** to a third party, or undertaken through secure servers via the internet.

Treasury management

Treasury management is the provision of management reporting and **performance measurement**, which aims to support decision making, assess performance and monitor compliance. Treasury management takes a key role in managing the liquidity of a business, examining its funding and financial risk taking. Treasury management has come into sharp focus as many businesses are under considerable pressure to optimize their **shareholder** value. Treasury management assists a business in examining financial risks which it may face. Treasury management is, in effect, a form of structured risk management which incorporates the examination of liquidity, funding, bank relationships and the control of all systems related to finance.

Collier, Paul A., Cooke, Terry E. and Glynn, John J., *Financial and Treasury Management*. Oxford: Butterworth-Heinemann, 1988.

Turnover

Turnover is the aggregated total of sales of an organization over a given period of time. It is the total revenue for all products and services, less any trade discounts or tax based on the revenue.

Many companies use turnover to determine other measures, such as how quickly some assets are turned over. In other words, stock turnover is obtained by dividing the total sales figures by the number of units sold.

A turnover ratio is an accounting ratio which effectively shows the number of times an item of capital has been replaced within a given financial period.

Unique selling point (USP)

'Unique selling point', or 'unique selling proposition', is a marketing term which is used to identify a specific product or service benefit that is only available through that product or service. It is not a feature which can be clearly associated with any of the competitors' products or services. In effect, this unique feature allows the business to create a unique selling proposition. In other words, this single feature becomes the focus of the advertising message and any other associated marketing or selling activities.

At its very core, the unique selling proposition, assuming it has a meaningful significance to the target market, is the basis for brand differentiation.

Forte, Alessandro, *Dare to be Different: How to Create Business Advantage through Innovation and Unique Selling Proposition*. Weston: Forte Financial Group, 2002.

Unity of command

Unity of command was originally suggested by **Henri Fayol** as one of his primary principles of management. Fayol suggested that employees should only receive instructions from a single superior. If this principle was undermined then it would bring about violations in authority, and discipline would be jeopardized. Ultimately, Fayol argued, the stability and order of the organization would be threatened.

Many subsequent theorists have disagreed with Fayol and, given the fact that he was writing in the late 1940s, he could not have anticipated the changes in **organizational structure** and the way in which work is carried out. None the less, he proposed that any form of dual command would lead to uncertainty and hesitation and, ultimately, conflict between management.

Fayol, Henri, *General and Industrial Management*. London: Pitman, 1967.

Utilization

Utilization involves the creation of ratios to compare output with design capacity. In other words, utilization looks at the resource productivity and attempts to apply a measurement. Since productivity is normally seen as being the difference between inputs and outputs, utilization seeks to improve this ratio as far as is practicable. In essence, the higher the utilization, the higher the **value added**.

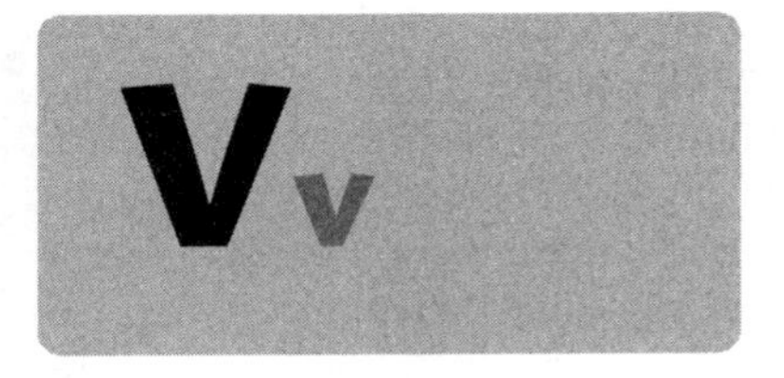

Value added

Value added, or added value, is an increase in the market value of a product, part or component which excludes the cost of materials and services used. In other words, this is a cost-plus-profit concept, defining value added as either the difference between the cost of producing a product and the price obtained for it (the selling price), or an additional benefit offered to a purchaser in order to convince them to buy. Added value is the key concept in both the internal and the external accounting systems of an organization and is a useful means of identifying the relative efficiency of a business. It should be noted that the value-added concept looks at the internal input costs in such a way that they are not confused with the external output costs, which may be beyond the control of the organization.

The value of the goods or services supplied may depend on a number of different variables. Obviously, if the organization is processing raw materials into finished products and is responsible for all stages of the production process, then it has a relatively high degree of control over the level of added value involved. Organizations which buy in components or part-finished products do not have this depth and length of control. They purchase products which have had value added to them already. The supplier will have gone through a similar set of calculations prior to selling the components or part-finished products on to the organization, which in turn will continue their processing. In the final analysis, the level of value added to the goods or services supplied is directly related to the price the customer is willing to pay. An organization may decide to add value which would raise the price beyond that which the average customer is willing to accept. In such a case, the supplier would have either to accept that it cannot receive the price which it expected, or to drastically reduce the costs, that have contributed to the end-user price.

The most common definition of value added is profit. Before the profit is realized, however, it is necessary to be able to cover the directly applied or overhead costs of the organization. If the organization is able to cover the various costs, then it has gone a considerable distance towards being able to break even. It is only when added value exceeds the **breakeven point** that the organization moves into real profit. It is, perhaps, this part of the value-added concept that is most important. Profit means a number of things to an organization; for example, additional investment potential, expansion, reorganization or acquisition. The nature of value added has a tendency to push up the end-user price from the moment the raw materials are extracted. In stages, some more dramatic than others, added value will be heaped upon the product. Each layer of the supply chain will demand its rightful profit in handling the product or service. Consequently, if an organization is not involved in the total extraction, processing and sale of a product or service, then it may not be able to curb unnecessary levels of added value elsewhere in the trading cycle.

Value chain

The term 'value chain' was coined by Michael Porter in 1985 and is used to describe the activities of an organization and how they are linked to the maintenance of a competitive position within the market. The value chain can be used to describe activities both within and external to the organization, relating them to the competitive strength of the organization. The analysis itself values each activity which adds to the organization's products or services. In other words, it considers the organization's employees, its available funds, as well as machinery and equipment. The supposition is that the ways in which these resources are deployed determine whether the organization is able to produce products and services at a price which customers are prepared to pay. By successfully organizing the resources, the business may be able to achieve a degree of competitive advantage.

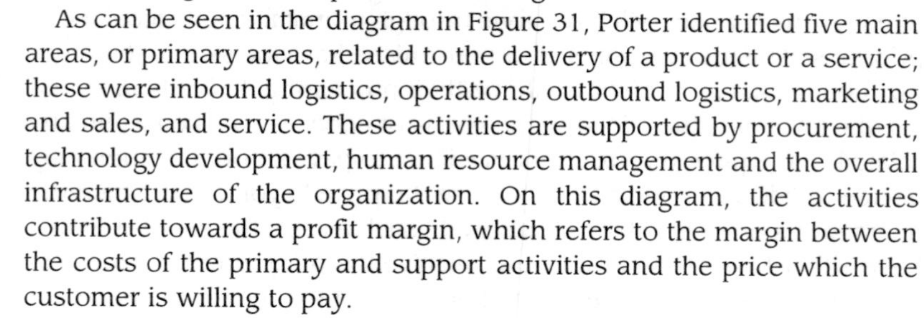

As can be seen in the diagram in Figure 31, Porter identified five main areas, or primary areas, related to the delivery of a product or a service; these were inbound logistics, operations, outbound logistics, marketing and sales, and service. These activities are supported by procurement, technology development, human resource management and the overall infrastructure of the organization. On this diagram, the activities contribute towards a profit margin, which refers to the margin between the costs of the primary and support activities and the price which the customer is willing to pay.

In the majority of industrial sectors, however, the organization's value chain is simply part of a larger structure, which incorporates the supplier's value chain, the channel's value chain and the customers' value chains. The position of the organization can be seen in the diagram in Figure 32.

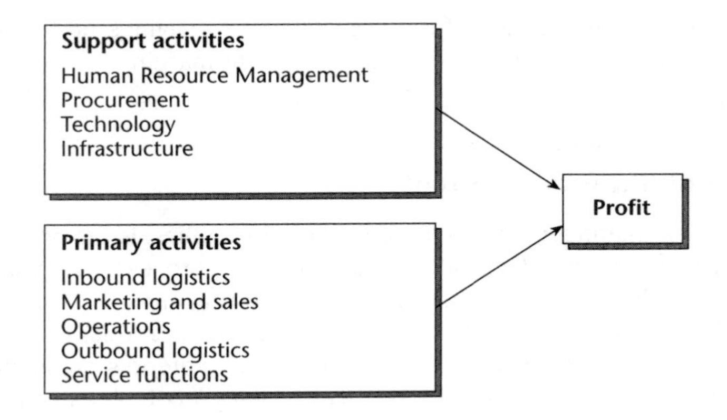

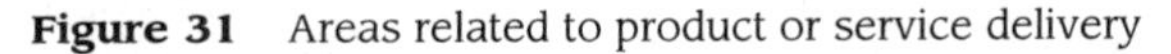

Figure 31 Areas related to product or service delivery

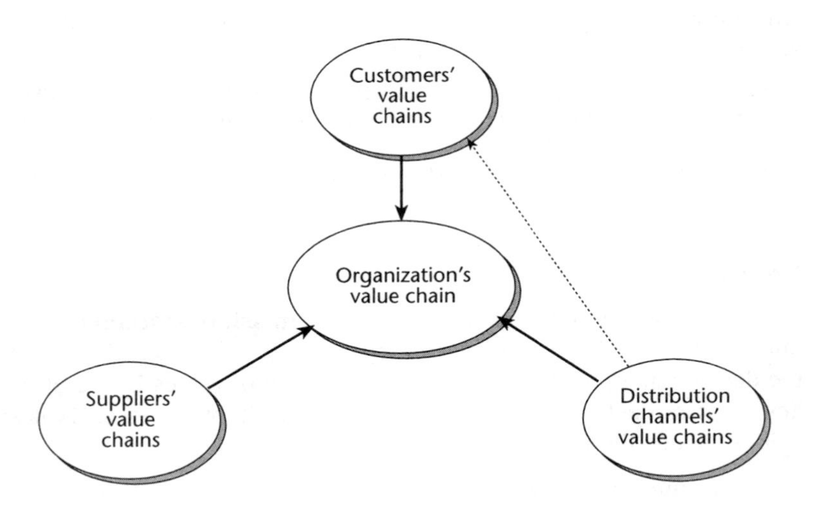

Figure 32 Position of the organization within the value chain

This more holistic impression of the overall system implies that the progress of raw materials, components and products across the entire value chain requires consideration of the other elements' requirements in the form of a profit margin. In other words, depending upon the relative strength of these elements within the value chain, margins can be squeezed or enlarged. Internally, at least, an organization can seek to improve its margins by adopting tactics such as **just-in-time (JIT)**, whilst not passing on any of the associated cost savings up the value chain, but retaining these as an additional profit margin.

Porter, Michael E., *Competitive Advantage*. London: Free Press, 1985.

Value chain management

Value chain management, as the **value chain** implies, is the process of adding value at each step of the manufacturing process. The value of raw materials over the course of the manufacturing process, which ends with the production and ultimate sale of a finished product to an end-user, has transformed the value of those raw materials significantly. Managing this value chain involves dealing with a complex network of various interactions. Value chain management, therefore, aims to optimize this network so that costs associated with the process are minimized and the maximum value to the end-user is achieved.

A subset of value chain management is **supply chain management**, which primarily focuses on the activities associated with raw materials and the manufacturing operation itself.

Heskett, James L., Sasser, W. Earl Jr and Schlesinger, Leonard A., *The Service Profit Chain: How Leading Companies Link Profit and Growth to Loyalty, Satisfaction and Value*. New York: Simon & Schuster, 1997.
Hines, Peter, *Value Stream Management: Strategy and Excellence in the Supply Chain*. London: Financial Times, Prentice-Hall, 2000.

Values

Values are beliefs, perhaps enshrined in a **mission statement** or a philosophy which has meaning to a business. It is widely believed that the development, adoption and implementation of values is one of the key success factors in high-growth, high-profit businesses. Typical values include the following:

- **continuous improvement**;
- customer delight;
- people development;
- innovation;
- society commitment;
- maximum utilization.

Variable costs

Variable costs are expenditure which varies directly with changes in output. In other words they are inextricably linked to the level of activity. Variable costs would include raw materials, components, labour and energy, which would vary according to the degree of production.

Variance

Variance is used in standard costing and budgetary control and is used to describe the difference between budgeted costs or income, and the actual costs or income that were achieved or incurred. Should the variance be better than what had been predicted or budgeted, then it is considered to be a favourable variance. Conversely, if the variance is worse than had been predicted, it is known as an adverse variance.

Vendor-managed inventory (VMI)

In a VMI programme the sellers maintain the **inventory** of stock they own on the buyer's premises. The buyer is billed for the stock as it is consumed. This form of relationship is at variance with the normal procedure where buyers are billed for products when the items are shipped by the seller. The purpose of VMI is to not only minimize the buyer's investment in stock, but also to drastically improve the replenishment of stock. In this way the sellers hope to improve the consumption of their stock on the buyer's premises. It requires a managed system by which consumed items are accounted for and subsequently billed, as well as replenished.

www.bbriefings.com/purchasingbriefing/contents/gifpmm_oct2001

Venture capitalist (VC)

A venture capitalist is an individual who invests money in a **startup** company. Many venture capitalist organizations are run as part of investment banks. The venture capitalist provides the funding for fledgling businesses which lack the financial muscle to put their ideas into the marketplace. The venture capitalists often retain a controlling share in the business and, should the business prove to be successful, then their initial investment is hugely rewarded by future returns.

Gompers, Paul and Lerner, Josh, *The Venture Capital Cycle*. Cambridge: MIT Press, 2002.

Vertical hub

The term 'vertical hub' has two distinct meanings, both of which are related to internet operations. A vertical hub can be an on-line **busi-**

ness-to-business (b2b) marketplace which aims to serve a vertical or industry-based market, providing content and a facility for businesses to forge relationships. Typically these forms of vertical hubs host **procurement** supplemented by market- or industry-specific website content.

The alternative meaning of 'vertical hub' is something known as a vertical **portal**, which is a website that acts as an entry point to other websites which all share a common interest, subject or theme.

Vertical integration

Vertical integration is the degree to which a particular business owns its upstream suppliers or downstream buyers. Vertical integration can be further defined as either forward integration, which implies the ownership of downstream businesses, or backward integration, with refers to the ownership of upstream businesses, as can be seen in Figure 33.

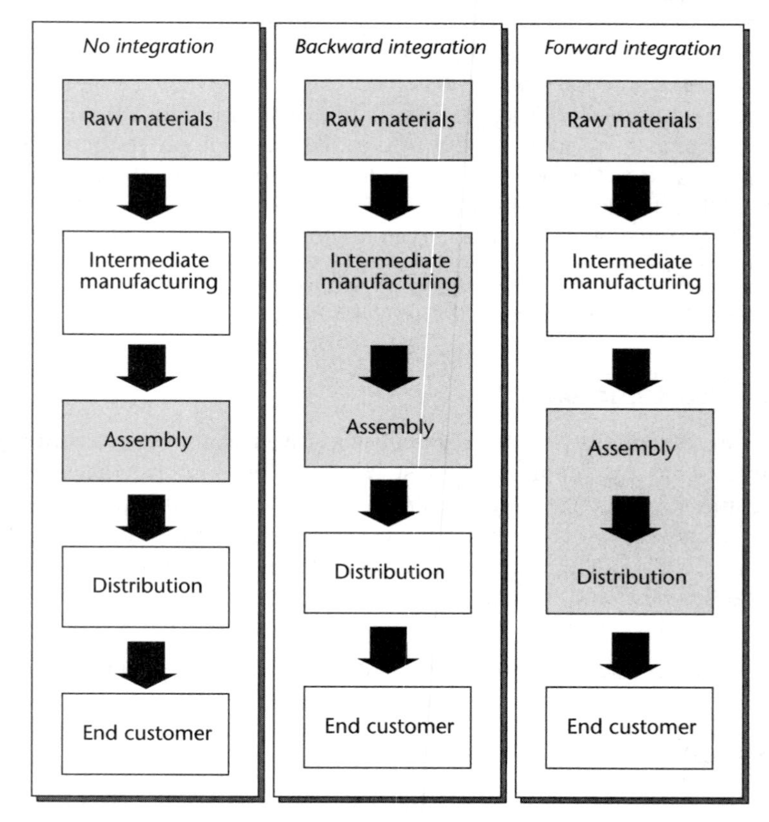

Figure 33 Backward and forward integration

Vertical integration offers a number of advantages, which include the following:

- improvement in supply chain coordination;
- reduction in transportation costs, particularly if the businesses are geographically close;
- an increased control over inputs;
- the capture of profit margins at various levels of the chain;
- increased entry barriers to potential competitors;
- access to distribution channels which would otherwise be difficult;
- investment in assets which independent distribution channel partners would be reluctant to invest in under normal circumstances.

Dubois, Anna, *Organizing Industrial Activities Across Firm Boundaries*. London: Routledge, 1998.

Viral marketing

Viral marketing has something of a bad reputation as in itself it is a form of organic marketing. Viral marketing owes much to more traditional network marketing as it relies on individuals being encouraged to pass on marketing messages to others. Viral marketing is increasingly being used on the internet, where millions of **email marketing** messages are distributed each day.

The concept works very much like a virus, hence the term, as it begins with a selected group of individuals who are emailed with a marketing message, offering them some form of incentive to transmit the message to other known email accounts. The growth is exponential and from this initial handful of individuals, millions of marketing messages can be distributed throughout the internet in a matter of days. In many respects, aside from the fact that there are incentives for people to pass the message on, this is a form of word-of-mouth communication. Effective viral marketing strategies tend to have the following characteristics:

- most offer free or discounted products or services;
- the simplicity of email allows each recipient to bulk email the message on to other users;
- the exponential growth is achieved not by the originator of the email, but by its recipients;
- common motivators and behaviours are exploited (e.g. easy money);
- it utilizes existing communication networks;
- above all, it takes advantage of others' resources and not the originator's resources.

Goldsmith, Russell, *Viral Marketing: Get your Audience to Do your Marketing For You*. New York: Prentice-Hall, 2002.
Perry, Richard and Whittaker, Andrew, *Viral Marketing in a Week*. London: Hodder and Stoughton Education, 2002.

Virtual CEO

A virtual CEO is an individual who tends to be associated with **startup** businesses in the technology field. These individuals assist the businesses in bringing their concept to fruition, but once the business is up and running they step aside and remain in the background, perhaps operating as a **consultant**. The virtual CEO operates, to all intents and purposes, alongside the business's full-time executives, but is not necessarily working at the business on a daily basis, as they may be involved in **incubating** several different businesses at the same time.

Virtual private network (VPN)

A virtual private network is a private computer network which uses the standard public telecommunications infrastructure to transmit its own data. This is achieved by the **encryption** of data, as well as the sending and receiving of addresses before transmission. When the data arrives at its designated destination it is decrypted, thus ensuring both security and privacy.

Virtual private networks, when they are fully developed, should allow a business to send its information over the internet and thus reduce costs in having to **lease** its own lines for its wide area **intranet** (WAN). At present, experimentation is under way with a new set of communication tools called 'point-to-point tunnelling protocol', which would effectively create virtual private networks on the internet which cannot be compromised by unauthorized individuals.

Brown, Steven, *Implementing Virtual Private Networks*. New York: Osborne McGraw-Hill, 1999.

Virtual supply networks (VSNs)

Virtual supply networks are typified by **vertical hubs**, which provide either internet- or extranet-based **procurement** marketplaces. They provide a point of contact between manufacturers, suppliers and service organizations, allowing automated interactions. In effect they are digital or **electronic marketplaces** where electronic exchange takes place.

Vroom, Victor

Vroom, together with Lawler and Porter, put forward his theory to suggest that the relationship between people's behaviour at work and their goals was not as simple as was first imagined. Vroom realized that an employee's performance was based on his or her personality, skills, knowledge, experience and abilities. This being the case, it was apparent that some employees would be more suited to their job role than others and that some would understand instruction more readily than others. The theory proposed that:

- each individual has a different set of goals;
- they will only try to achieve their goals if they think they have a chance to attain them;
- the value of the goal, in personal terms, affects motivation and behaviour.

Vroom's expectancy theory is one of the most popular motivation theories. It basically depends upon the following three factors:

- *Valence* – this is the depth of want that the employee feels for either extrinsic rewards (money, promotion, time off, benefits) or intrinsic rewards (satisfaction). Management needs to discover what the employees want by offering a variety of rewards so they can select something they would value.
- *Expectancy* – everyone has different expectations and different levels of confidence about what they are capable of doing. Even if employees have fulfilled their valence wants, but are asked to do something that they feel unable to do, then they will not be sufficiently motivated to do it. Despite the fact that there may be a promise of an additional desired reward, an employee who is not motivated will not fulfil. Management would need to discover the employees' resource, training or additional supervision needs in order to improve their opportunity to succeed and remove their chances of failure.
- *Instrumentality* – this is all centred around employees' expectations about whether they will get what they want, even if it has been promised them by an employer. Managers should ensure that promises of rewards are fulfilled and ensure the employees are aware of what relevant rewards are linked to improved performance.

Using Vroom's theory, a business could identify the characteristics of the job that would allow the employee some of the following to encourage motivation:

- self-development opportunities;
- satisfaction opportunities;
- recognition opportunities;
- a degree of independence in deciding how tasks should be handled;
- a varied range of tasks;
- a variety of surroundings;
- opportunity for interaction with others;
- challenging and varied, but clearly stated, goals with an indication as to the expected performance.

Vroom, Victor H., *Work and Motivation*. New York: Jossey-Bass Wiley, 1994.

www.mba.yale.edu/framesets/faculty.asp?/faculty/professors/vroom.htm

Web marketplaces

Web marketplaces are, to all intents and purposes, **electronic marketplaces** in which products and services can be bought and sold. Web marketplaces are global in their scope and can operate regardless of different time zones. Theoretically the use of these web marketplaces should enable a business to find products and services of the correct specification, acceptable cost and value and thus eliminate any inefficiency in their **procurement** processes. Again, theoretically, these savings can be shared, with the proposition that prices can be driven down across the whole of the supply chain and ultimately the end-user would benefit from these forms of transaction.

Web presentations

Web presentations are live and interactive meetings, connecting various individuals in remote locations via the internet. There are an increasing number of hosts who provide a series of different presentation tools, including chat functions, voting, and **application** sharing. New developments have also begun to incorporate live video streaming with real-time audio so that web presentations can provide an experience similar to all the participants being in a room together and contributing to a presentation.

Web promotion

Web promotion aims to increase traffic to a particular website. Key to web promotion are strategies aimed at ensuring that **search engines** select the website on the first page of a search result. This is achieved by using a combination of meta tags, keywords, titles, as well as banner and link exchanges. It may also include participation in news groups and ensuring that the website is on directory listings.

Inan, Hurol, *Measuring the Success of your Website: A Custom-centric Approach to Website Management*. French Forest, NSW: Pearson Education Australia, 2002.

Weber, Max

Max Weber (1864–1920) based his conclusions on bureaucracy on his studies of such disparate organizations as the Catholic Church, the Prussian army and the empire of the Egyptians. He concluded that employees frequently suffer from inequity in most areas of work from selection to promotion. His key points can be summarized in Table 24.

Table 24 Weber's key points on bureaucracy

Principle of bureaucracy	Description
Division of labour	The workforce is split into specialized areas according to expertise.
Chain of command	There is a pyramid-shaped organizational structure which defines the hierarchy and the authority of the organization.
Rules and regulations	There are formalized rules that govern the running of the organization which assists the organization in dealing with the potential disruption caused by changes in management.
Impersonality	Management is detached from the workforce to ensure that sentimentality or familiarity does not impede decision-making.
Selection and promotion	Selection of employees and their subsequent opportunities for advancement in the organization is strictly governed by their utility as far as the organization is concerned. Friendship plays no part in the advancement and is usually based on seniority and expressed achievements.
Documentation	There is a meticulous system of document creation, completion and storage to chart all activities for the purposes of monitoring and evaluation of those activities.
Centralization	All decision-making is made from the upper strata of the organization where individuals reside who have seniority and clearly recognizable achievements over a period of time.

Max Weber's homepage: www.faculty.rsu.edu/~felwell/Theorists/Weber/Whome.htm

Whistle blowing

Whistle blowing has become an increasing trend in business and involves an individual, more often than not an employee, who reports to a third party information regarding misconduct within their employer's organization. Whistle blowing does not necessarily have to involve external organizations, as many larger businesses have recognized that there needs to be a mechanism by which a senior individual within the organization can be made available for whistle blowers to report genuine concerns about suspected misconduct. Procedures are in place in many organizations to protect whistle blowers and particularly there is legislation to protect them against reprisals from their employer. Provided the whistle blower reports genuine and non-malicious concerns, then punitive action taken against the employee is deemed illegal.

Winding up

'Winding up' is an alternative term used to describe the **liquidation** of a business. Under the terms of the British 1986 Insolvency Act, a court could place a winding up order on a business, compelling it to go into liquidation.

Wireless application protocol (WAP)

Wireless application protocol is the latest development in intelligent messaging for digital mobile phones, especially as it allows the user to access internet content in a special text format on WAP-enabled GSM (global system for mobile communication) mobile phones. These protocols were established in 1997, allowing hand-held mobiles to access web pages and other forms of data from the internet. The protocols are now accepted and used by over 100 different handset manufacturers, as well as software houses and internet and communication businesses.

Work centre

A work centre is a specific location along a manufacturing process. At the work centre a series of tasks are performed upon each product or batch of products before they are moved along to the next work centre on the production line.

Work in process/progress (WIP)

WIP refers to an organization's entire **inventory** which is currently being processed or has been assigned to a process within the organization. This would include items in the inventory which have been allocated for particular jobs, ready to begin the manufacturing process, or items which are currently a part of a product being processed but which is not yet complete. The work in process inventory is a total count of all the items which fall into this category.

Work measurement

Work measurement is concerned with the determination of the time that it should take to complete a specific job. The fundamentals behind this measurement are the **job design** (which determines the content of a job) together with a methods analysis (which determines how a job is to be performed).

Work measurement, or job time, is invaluable for manpower planning, the estimation of labour costs, scheduling of work, budgeting and the design and parameters of incentive systems. The process of work measurement involves the inclusion of time for probable (average) delays. A standard time is calculated for an average (experienced) employee to complete the task while working at a rate that is sustainable over a period of time (the shift or per hour, etc.) The measurement also takes into account that standard methods will be used to complete the job, with standard tools and equipment. The measurement does assume that the materials and components will be available to the employee and that the working conditions are suitable to carry out the work.

Traditionally, work measurement employs either stopwatch time study, historical times (based on averages over a period of time), predetermined data (perhaps derived from supplier information or ideal times which have been worked into the schedule) or **work sampling** (which involves estimating a mean from a series of observations).

Work sampling

Work sampling involves the observer making a series of random observations of an employee or work taking place on a machine over a period of time. The observer notes the nature of the work taking place and counts the number of times that the observed work took place (using different categories of work type) as well as noting non-work periods.

Work sampling is used in ratio-delay study and the analysis of non-repetitive jobs. Essentially, the process is typified in the following manner:

Work sampling aims to provide a value, ($\hat{p}$), which allows the estimation of the true proportion, p, within an allowable error, e.

In other words, the estimation can be characterized as

$$\hat{p} \pm e$$

There is a normal range of variability in larger samples and, therefore, the estimations can be shown as a normal distribution curve showing the confidence interval (see Figure 34).

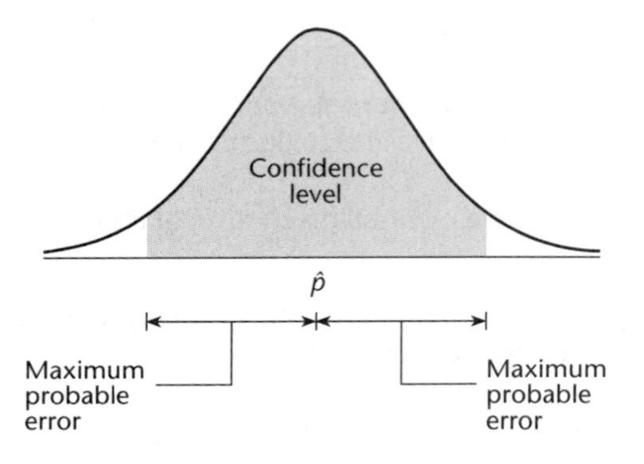

Figure 34 Confidence distribution

The degree of the maximum probable error is a function of both the sample size and the desired level of confidence. However, in larger samples, the maximum error e (as a percentage) is calculated using the following formula:

$$e = z \sqrt{\frac{\hat{p}(1 - \hat{p})}{n}}$$

where Z is the number of standard deviations required to achieve the desired level of confidence; $\hat{p}$ is the sample mean; and n is the sample size.

In solving the formula for n, it is possible to determine the appropriate size of the sample (using the confidence level as well as the amount of allowable error decided by the management). This formula is:

$$n = \left(\frac{z}{e}\right)^2 \hat{p}(1 - \hat{p})$$

W

In cases where there is no sample estimate, a preliminary estimate may be made by using $\hat{p} = 0.5$.

The process of work sampling is therefore typified as following these steps:

1. An identification of the employee or employees and the machine or machines which will be studied.
2. Notification of those involved as to the purpose of the study so that bias associated with observation is not a factor (i.e. the Hawthorne Effect).
3. A calculation of the initial estimate of the sample size p, or the use of $\hat{p} = 0.5$.
4. The framing of the random observation schedule.
5. A recompiling of the sample size during the observations (a double check mechanism).
6. A calculation of the estimated proportion of time spent on the specified activity.

Work sampling can be differentiated from time study as illustrated in Table 25, by examining the advantages and disadvantages.

Table 25 Work sampling compared with time study

Advantages	**Disadvantages**
Observations taken over a period of time.	Less focus on the elements of a job.
Less disruption to work.	Workers tend to alter their work patterns when observed.
Employees feel less observed.	No benchmark as employees' work methods have not previously been recorded.
Less costly.	Random schedules of observations may not be carried out.
Less time involved.	Not suited to short, repetitive tasks.
Lower skills requirements of the analyst.	More time needed to satisfy random requirement for observation.
Studies can take place in concentrated batches.	
No timing required.	
Ideal for non-repetitive tasks.	

Work station

A work station is a single employee area where the individual carries out his or her job using specialized equipment.

Worker directors

Worker directors are often employees who are elected by **works councils** to represent employees on the board of a business. Although there is a growing requirement, under European Employment Strategy and EU Directives related to European Works Councils, for businesses to have employee representation on boards, there has been considerable opposition for a number of different reasons. Most notably, worker directors are reluctant to make decisions without referring back to their peer groups, thus slowing down the decision-making process. Businesses are also very apprehensive on the question of confidentiality, particularly when worker directors have access to information which could have a negative impact with those that placed them on the board in the first place. **Trade unions** have also, in the past, been suspicious of worker directors, feeling that their presence simply confuses the issue as the unions may end up having to fight one of their own members in the role of a member of the board.

Workflow

Workflow simply describes the sequence of operations related to an organization's activities. Workflow identifies how products, services or tasks proceed through the organization; who is involved; and how long the individual stages of the operation need in order to fulfil their part of the whole process.

Workforce agility

Workforce agility is a measure of the flexibility of the employees, allowing them to be deployed in different roles or on different shifts, or indeed involved in different activities within the organization. The workforce agility can be measured in a number of different ways, as can be seen in Table 26.

Hopp, W. J. and Van Oyen, M. P., 'Agile Workforce Evaluation: A Framework for Cross-Training and Coordination', *Proceedings of the 2001 NSF Design and Manufacturing Grantees Conference*. Tampa, FL, 2001.

W

Table 26 Workforce agility

Agility purpose and measure	Explanation
Efficiency	With improved efficiency the organization should be able to meet deadlines, reduce cycle times and achieve a lower level of **work in progress**.
Flexibility	Costs associated with the payment for overtime and the loss of **productivity** as a result of employee turnover or absenteeism can be reduced by multi-skilled employees. These individuals will be able to take on the work of absent employees. In addition, flexibility also offers opportunities to rapidly adapt the production environment.
Quality	A higher-quality workforce means that employees will be able to notice and take remedial action when there are problems. With improved quality of the workforce comes improved quality of the manufacturing process, as well as the prospect of employees being more prepared to suggest methods which would further enhance or improve the processes themselves.
Culture	Workforce agility should bring improvements in **job satisfaction** and **motivation**, particularly if the working environment is constantly upgraded and improved.

Workforce analytics

Workforce analytics essentially comprises two different components. The first component involves a comparison between the internal representation of the employer's workforce and a similarly designated group of individuals from the external labour pool which the employer could use as a recruitment source. The external labour pool must have the necessary occupational qualifications and eligibility and be in the general recruitment area. The external labour pool is also called the 'external representation rate' or 'availability estimate'.

The second component of workforce analytics examines the hiring and promotion of employees and termination of employment, together with an analysis of whether particular group members are concentrated in particular occupation groups. Some occupational groups will be under-represented in terms of particular demographic criteria.

The next stage is to compare the general state of promotions and terminations with those of designated groups to assess whether there are any major differences. This assists the employer in ascertaining whether the designated groups' under-representation in a particular occupational group is as a result of the hiring or promotion process and whether there is a disproportionately high rate of termination.

The purpose of workforce analytics is to enable employers to undertake a review of their employment systems, specifically focusing on under-representation. The under-representation can occur when the internal representation is less than the external representation in a particular occupational group. In this way the employer is able to determine the severity of the shortfalls or gaps and attempt to draw up a plan to eliminate them.

Working capital

Working capital is a measure of the capital which is employed by a business in its day-to-day trading operations. It is calculated by subtracting the business's current liabilities, such as trade creditors, from its current assets, which would include stock, debtors and cash. Ideally the working capital should be sufficient for the business to be able to pay its immediate debts, otherwise it will struggle to continue its operations, which may well indicate that the business needs to reappraise the relationship between its assets and its liabilities.

Working conditions

Working conditions are a primary concern of both management and human resources departments in the sense that employees' working environments can often determine their performance, and their productivity. Poor working conditions, which may include both physical aspects, such as cramped conditions, inadequate equipment or furniture and lack of facilities, are coupled with aspects which may cause unnecessary stresses and strains to the employees. The management of working conditions has increasingly become a vital aspect of human resources as many of the issues have relatively simple solutions. Yet until human resources departments began to appreciate the negative impacts of poor working conditions, little was done to address these issues.

Works council

Although works councils are not legally required in organizations of a certain size in the UK until 2005, they are required by legislation in many other European countries.

The involvement of employees within works councils varies very much, dependent on the nature of the organization, its size and its location internationally. However, the scope of their discussion and decision making can range from recruitment procedures through to the council's legal right to delay complex issues such as merger or take-over discussions.

The introduction of works councils has freed management from a number of issues, including the need to gain acceptance, or go through sometimes lengthy negotiation talks, with **trade union** representatives on issues relating to working conditions. Works councils have the power to execute decisions on issues such as overtime and promotion and have proved a positive step in encouraging management to accept ideas and suggestions from employees. This allows change to be introduced within an organization more easily and the works council members are also able to brief management regarding any issues that may be occurring which could result in some form of conflict within the organization.

There are some disadvantages, however, in that the decision-making process can be slower, the running of works councils can be costly and if not compiled from like-minded individuals, meetings can become hostile and eliminate some of the negotiation elements required.

Workteam

Many organizations have gradually come to the realization that teams represent a proven means by which productivity and performance can be assured. Various industry surveys, particularly in the manufacturing sector, seem to suggest that over two-thirds of all organizations actively encourage teams. The actual nature of the team is of prime importance and their creation is of particular relevance to human resources. Essentially there are three different types of team, all of which have a degree of authority, **autonomy** or **empowerment**.

Empowered teams are usually given the authority to plan and implement improvements. Self-directed teams are virtually autonomous and are mainly responsible for supervisory issues. Cross-functional teams are more complex as they involve various individuals from different departments who are working towards a common end.

Training needs to be provided to teams both before and during their creation in order to assist the members in establishing their relationships with one another and understanding their new responsibilities. It is also essential that teams are given clear instructions and, above all, support from management in order to carry out their tasks. Once a team has been established and a degree of authority delegated to them, management and human resources departments need to step back and allow the team to develop and learn how their new working practices will operate.

The team itself, management and human resources personnel retain the responsibility of monitoring and motivating the teams and their members. This requires effective communication skills and a feedback system which enables teams to request additional assistance should it be required.

Purser, Ronald and Cabana, Steven, *The Self-Managing Organization: Transforming Teamwork Through Participative Design*. New York: Simon & Schuster, 1999.

Written down value

The written down value is the value of an asset which takes into account the result of its reduction in value as it has been used. Typically, for tax purposes, a written down value allowance of 25 per cent is available in the year of purchase. This is deducted from the initial cost to establish the new written down value. In the following year the written down value is reduced by another 25 per cent of the purchase price. In essence the written down value shows the accumulated depreciation of an asset.

Yugen kaisha

This is the Japanese equivalent of a **limited liability company**.

Zero-based budgeting (ZBB)

Zero-based budgeting, or zero budgeting, is used to prepare and justify all budget expenditure from a zero base. It is designed to prevent budgets from gradually increasing year-on-year. The technique sets the budget at zero and the manager responsible for that budget has to justify each and every item of expenditure. Zero-based budgeting allows businesses to identify areas of their work which do not require high budgets, thereby allowing them to place investment in areas of the business which need finance. It is also a means by which a business can reduce the overall base costs of the business.

Zero budgeting does require considerable management time in identifying and adjusting the budgeting levels, but leaves more devious managers able to justify higher budgets than others.

Pyhrr, Peter A., *Zero-base Budgeting: A Practical Management Tool for Evaluating Expenses*. New York: John Wiley, 1978.

Zero defects

For the most part, it was considered that the concept of zero defects was a goal that could not be achieved; in many respects it was also considered to be unnecessary. It was always thought that at some point in the production a defect would inevitably creep into the system and that, provided the product reached the customer in a fit state and defects were minimized, then this would be sufficient.

Both Crosby and Shingo have been credited with developing the concept of zero defects. Shingo certainly developed the concept of *poka yoke* as a way of achieving zero defects. Reducing process variability is a second way to achieve zero defects. The achievement of zero defects became a specific goal during the 1980s, particularly amongst manufacturers producing complex products.

Shingo, Shigeo, *Shingo Production Management Systems*. Shelton, CT: Productivity Press, 1992.

Numbers

4 Cs

See **competitive intelligence**.

5 Forces

See **Five Forces (SLEPT/PEST/STEEPLE)**.

7 Forces

See **Five Forces (SLEPT/PEST/STEEPLE)**.

360-degree appraisal

See **performance appraisal/evaluation/review**.

Index

Note: Page numbers in **bold** indicate **definitions**. References are to the UK, except where otherwise specified